BARBARA
BUSH

MODERN FIRST LADIES

Lewis L. Gould, Editor

BARBARA BUSH

PRESIDENTIAL MATRIARCH

MYRA G. GUTIN

UNIVERSITY PRESS OF KANSAS

© 2008 by the University Press of Kansas

All photographs are courtesy of George Bush Presidential Library,
College Station, Texas.

Published by the University Press of Kansas (Lawrence, Kansas 66045),
which was organized by the Kansas Board of Regents and is operated
and funded by Emporia State University, Fort Hays State University,
Kansas State University, Pittsburg State University, the University
of Kansas, and Wichita State University

Library of Congress Cataloging-in-Publication Data

Gutin, Myra G.

Barbara Bush : presidential matriarch / Myra G. Gutin.

p. cm. — (Modern first ladies)

Includes bibliographical references and index.

ISBN 978-0-7006-1583-4 (cloth : alk. paper)

1. Bush, Barbara, 1925–

2. Presidents' spouses—United States—Biography.

3. Literacy programs—United States—History.

4. Reading—United States—History.

I. Title.

E883.B87G87 2008

973.928092—dc22   2008003945

British Library Cataloguing-in-Publication Data is available.

Printed in the United States of America

10 9 8 7 6 5 4 3 2 1

The paper used in this publication is recycled and contains 50 percent
postconsumer waste. It is acid free and meets the minimum requirements of
the American National Standard for Permanence of Paper for Printed Library
Materials Z39.48–1992.

This book is dedicated to
David Gutin
and
Laura, Sarah, and Andrew Gutin
who were there
and to
Lillian and Stanley Greenberg
who should have been

CONTENTS

EDITOR'S FOREWORD

Barbara Pierce Bush occupies a special position among first ladies. Not since Abigail Adams has a first lady been both the wife of one president and the mother of another chief executive. Beyond these family circumstances, Barbara Bush deserves attention for her performance in the White House from 1989 to 1993. Following the controversial Nancy Reagan and preceding the equally contentious Hillary Rodham Clinton, Bush established an enviable record for personal popularity as a first lady. The public took to her accessible style and self-deprecating approach. Even when her husband's presidency encountered difficult periods, Barbara Bush's poll ratings remained high. Only toward the end of George H. W. Bush's administration did his wife meet criticism for her views on abortion.

Myra Gutin's book shows how carefully managed and executed Barbara Bush's success as first lady was. Gutin uses the records of Bush's many speeches, the only primary materials on her tenure in the White House now available, to show how the public image emerged. Barbara Bush was no White House innovator. Her speeches broke little new ground. Even in her main campaign for literacy, Bush emphasized exhortation and education over programmatic goals. Yet within these self-imposed limits, Barbara Bush was more of an activist than the public realized.

The narrative that Myra Gutin has fashioned also illuminates the intricate dynamics within Barbara Bush's family. Her interaction with her politically ambitious husband and her maternal effect on her oldest son are developed with great skill. Gutin's work contributes to the historical literature on a complex and important presidential family even as it illuminates the record of a first lady whose popularity still endures.

Lewis L. Gould

PREFACE

Barbara Bush had been first lady for seven months when she spoke at a convocation at Smith College in September 1989. She took the opportunity to discuss the potential impact of her White House project, literacy. She quoted former first lady Lady Bird Johnson, who had said, "It would be sad to pass up such a bully pulpit. It's a fleeting chance to do something for your country that makes your heart sing, and if your project is useful, and people notice it, and that reflects well on your husband, Heavens, that's one of your biggest roles in life." Mrs. Bush continued, "Well that's exactly what literacy has been for me. I never could have guessed that I would end up with such a chance to be useful, and such an enormous return on a relatively modest effort."[1]

Barbara Bush remains one of the most admired women in the world and a perennial selection to the Gallup Most Admired Woman poll. In 2006, she still ranked in the top ten among the poll's vote getters. Americans hold Barbara Bush in high regard as the matriarch of an accomplished, powerful, and diverse family. She is seen as America's grandmother, walking a dog and shepherding numerous grandchildren around the family compound in Kennebunkport, Maine. As first lady of the United States, she endorsed a successful literacy program that flourishes even though she has been gone from the White House for many years. With Abigail Adams, she shares the distinction of being only one of two women in American history to have been the wife of one American president and the mother of another. This is the public Barbara Bush, the wearer of faux pearls, the woman known for her distinctive white hair, the woman whose image the television program *Saturday Night Live* caricatured.

As with most public figures, there is much more to this complex person. Barbara Bush is also the tough, down-to-earth, sharp-tongued doyenne of a prominent political family that has had its share of sorrows and setbacks. She has surmounted the death of a child, depression, and a sometimes insensitive spouse. Self-deprecating humor and sarcasm have become both her trademark and her method of survival. She does not suffer fools and brooks no dissent; she can be combative and will go into full battle mode if her husband or children become the object of criticism. Savvy and smart, Barbara Bush presented a glossy family portrait of a large, loving, and supportive group, the ostensibly ideal American family. Behind the facade is a less sunny reality.

From 1989 to 1993, Barbara Bush presided over the White House as first lady. She shared certain characteristics with many first ladies: loyalty to spouse, a commonsense approach to life in the crosshairs of the media, a tendency to roll with the punches. Other qualities were unique to Barbara Bush: great bonhomie, significant patience, the ability to forgive but not forget. She has carefully crafted and nurtured her public image during her years on the international stage. Many people will say that they liked Barbara Bush, she seemed like a real person; at the same time, one felt that he or she should sit up straighter in her presence.

Sheila Weidenfeld, who served as press secretary to first lady Betty Ford, argues that all first ladies furnish a window on the White House, a way in which the public can assess the first family.[2] Few will forget a photo of the Clintons walking to their helicopter after revelations surfaced of Monica Lewinsky's relationship with the president. Mrs. Clinton and her husband are at opposite ends of the photo, looking straight ahead. The only thing between them is their daughter, Chelsea, and dog, Buddy. The estrangement could not have been clearer. Another enduing image is a teary-eyed Gerald Ford announcing to the press that his wife, Betty, had undergone a radical mastectomy for breast cancer. His sadness and concern made evident that the couple were devoted to each other. These enduring images help us to "see through the window" and come away with opinions about the nomalcy and humanity of the president and his family. As a country, we have always responded to the small and seemingly insignificant details of everyday life as proof that the leader of the free world and his spouse are a lot like us. A widely circulated photo of the Bushes showed their grandchildren and adult children visiting with the former first lady and president in the bedroom of their Kennebunkport home. The children are seated on sofas and chairs as the grandchildren play on and around the bed. Barbara Bush looks happy and perfectly at ease; George Bush looks startled by the early morning love-in. Barbara Bush's window afforded a glimpse of a family whose behavior occasionally contradicted what the spin doctors presented.

Numerous questions arise in examining Barbara Bush: As first lady, what topics and issues did she discuss with the president? Why did she choose literacy as an ongoing concern? Did she have an impact on any public policy decisions or legislation? Did she decide on the part she would play in George Bush's political life, or was she obliged to play certain roles? Perhaps most interesting is Barbara Bush's consistent denial that she had any effect on presidential decision making and that she wanted to separate herself from issues that were within her husband's purview. In fact, she was involved in both areas.

There is a sharp division between the public Barbara Bush and the private Barbara Bush. The public image, the good-natured grandmother and helpmate, has been buffed to a sheen. It was easy for the country to accept that nice, seemingly apolitical first lady after tumultuous times with her predecessor, Nancy Reagan. The private Barbara Bush, calculating, tough, never forgetting a slight— that was the woman that George H. W. Bush really needed. She was her husband's political watchdog and was a capable politician; she had a better ear and she was much more attuned to nuance. She is neither fully saint nor sinner, to be sure, but she has lived her life in service to George H. W. Bush and the rest of her family. Her husband wanted to be president of the United States; she was bound and determined that he would have the prize. For years, she has rhapsodized about being the luckiest woman in the world and living the most wonderful life with the best husband and best children. She submerged her own desires and concerns in exchange for living that "wonderful life" that she describes in her memoirs.

Mrs. Bush cannot be easily dismissed or pigeonholed. She grasped the "bully pulpit," and as a result of her advocacy, her name is forever linked to literacy and good works. She used her first lady celebrity to imprint her image on the national conscience. She is multifaceted, complete with truths and contradictions. Biographies by Donnie Radcliffe and Pamela Kilian have hinted at these contradictions, which are also evident in Mrs. Bush's autobiography. It is these nuances and a plethora of unanswered questions that make Barbara Bush such an intriguing subject.

ACKNOWLEDGMENTS

Some years ago, Hillary Rodham Clinton wrote that it takes a village to raise a child. There have been times during the almost eight years that it took to complete this book when I thought it was going to take my whole universe to finish this project. How very fortunate I have been to have the help of scores of people.

Barbara Bush, the subject of this book, was both gracious and helpful. Not only did she permit a personal interview, she also made access available to members of her White House staff. She allowed me the freedom to pursue my research and reach my own conclusions.

Mrs. Bush had, and continues to have, a first-rate staff. I owe debts of gratitude to former staff members Julie Cooke, Director of Projects; Anna Perez, Press Secretary; and Susan Porter Rose, Chief of Staff. A special thank-you is extended to the wonderful Jean Becker, former Deputy Press Secretary, who currently serves the Bush family as Chief of Staff. Jean responded to queries, arranged interviews, and provided encouragement—her aid was invaluable to completing this book. Another special thank-you is extended to Catherine Fenton, former Deputy Social Secretary, who provided detailed information and personal perspectives about the social side of the Bush White House.

Benita Somerfield, Executive Director of the Barbara Bush Foundation for Family Literacy, answered scores of questions about Mrs. Bush's involvement in literacy and the work of the foundation. Marie M. Adair, Executive Director of the New Jersey Association for Supervision and Curriculum Development, aided me immeasurably in understanding the history and evolution of the field of literacy. Almost thirty years ago, as I was beginning my research into first ladies, I spoke with former United Press International Chief White House Correspondent Helen Thomas. I find that the things she told me then still shape my views regarding the Office of the First Lady and the way in which the media cover the first lady's activities.

There are no words to thank Lewis L. Gould, the editor of the Modern First Ladies series for the University Press of Kansas. Lew read every word of every chapter—numerous times—and never failed to be encouraging. He has been both a valued mentor and a friend for more than twenty years. Sincere thanks, too, are extended to Fred Woodward, Executive Director of the University Press of Kansas and his staff, especially Larisa Martin and Susan Schott. John Robert Greene read an early draft of the manuscript and suggested numerous changes. His rigor and commitment to solid scholarship are greatly appreciated.

The archivists at the George Bush Library in College Station, Texas, were wonderful to work with. They accommodated requests, made helpful suggestions about sources, and always had ideas that strengthened the manuscript. A million thanks to former archivist Bill Harris and current archivist Laura Schneider, and a very special thank-you to archivist Mary Finch for helping me with everything visual.

Rider University provided a research leave and two summer fellowships and reimbursements to help me complete my work. The university has been supportive of my projects, and I am grateful for its continued commitment to scholarship.

On a personal note, the many people in my universe—and you know who you are—made this book a reality. They kept me smiling and motivated, listened, provided free food and lodging and light moments. Thank you to Leslie Baer-Bobella, Marcia Gurian, Carol Kanter, Marilyn Kapel, Jean Kauffmann, Ellen Kolodner, Leesa Tobin and Joanne Tortoriello. We discussed this project continually over the years, and they were always upbeat and made useful suggestions. I can never repay their kindness.

Even though this book is dedicated to him, I must acknowledge the contributions of my husband, David Gutin. Years ago, Barbara Bush said that one reason she married George Bush was that he made her laugh—I understand the wisdom of that comment, which applies to David too. Not only does he make me laugh, he keeps me grounded, and I have been blessed to have his unqualified support, wise counsel, and boundless enthusiasm. This book, and many other projects over the course of my career, simply would not have been accomplished without him.

The past eight years have been both challenging and exciting. I extend my most heartfelt thanks to everyone who was involved in *Barbara Bush: Presidential Matriarch.*

BARBARA BUSH

CHAPTER 1

"NO MAN, WOMAN, OR CHILD EVER HAD A BETTER LIFE"

Barbara Pierce was born in New York City to Marvin Pierce and Pauline Robinson Pierce on 8 June 1925. Barbara was the second daughter and third of the four children in the family. The Pierce family moved to the posh suburb of Rye, New York, in Westchester County, where their children grew up in comfort and affluence. The family claimed an impressive social lineage: Barbara's great-great-great uncle was President Franklin Pierce (1853–1857), and her mother was the daughter of Ohio Supreme Court justice James Robinson. At the time of Barbara's birth, Marvin Pierce was serving as assistant to the president of the McCall's Publishing Company. He rose to become president of the company and chairman of the board in 1945. Though the Pierces were not rich, Marvin was earning $22,500 a year during the 1930s, a considerable amount for the time.[1] His success provided his offspring with access to private schools, servants, and the trappings of luxury.

Beneath the surface, however, was a more complex reality. Barbara remembered that her family had to pinch pennies during the Depression. Her mother was a free spender whose debts often strained the family's resources. Pauline Pierce, cultured, formal, and somewhat distant, was known as "a woman of many 'enthusiasms,' none of which, Barbara felt, included her."[2] She doted on her beautiful, elder daughter, Martha, whose photo had once adorned the cover of *Vogue.* For Barbara, who would struggle with her weight all her life, her mother had sarcastic jests. Barbara, she said, weighed a hundred pounds at birth.[3] To her daughters at mealtime, Pauline would say, "Eat up Martha—not you Barbara."[4] The callousness of these comments are reminiscent of the snubs and slights endured by a young Eleanor Roosevelt, whose mother regularly referred to her as "Granny" because of her serious demeanor.[5] Both women seemed insensitive to the fact that these maternal slurs hurt their daughters.

One of Barbara's friends characterized Pauline Pierce as a little mean to her younger daughter. Perhaps in retaliation, Barbara developed a caustic tongue, even though she was otherwise witty and articulate.[6] Her childhood friend June Biedler recalled that Barbara could freeze out other children or saddle them with the kind of nickname that hurt.[7] Barbara's relationship with her mother was always somewhat uneasy and challenging. In her memoirs, Mrs. Bush wrote that she came to understand her mother better many years later: "I certainly didn't appreciate all the pressures she must have felt until I became a mother. She taught me a great deal. . . . Probably her most important lesson was an inadvertent one: You can like what you do, or you can dislike it. I have chosen to like it."[8] Barbara also believed that her mother did not appreciate her own life: "My mother often talked about 'when her ship would come in.' She had a husband who worshipped the ground she walked on, four loving children and a world of friends. Her ship had come in—she just didn't know it. That is so sad."[9]

Barbara's relationship with her father was the polar opposite of that with her mother. Strong bonds between father and daughter were forged early. As a child, Barbara walked her father to the train when he left for New York City each day. The two communicated on a level that she and her mother never attained. There was no criticism or denigration of Barbara. When she was young, her father took Barbara on trips to visit the McCall's plant in Dayton, Ohio. Marvin Pierce was a steadying, sober influence in his daughter's life. In her memoirs, she characterized him as the "fairest man I knew, until I met George Bush."[10] Marvin Pierce had been born and grown up in Sharpsville, Pennsylvania. A gifted athlete, he attended Miami University in Oxford, Ohio, where he earned nine varsity letters and graduated Phi Beta Kappa. While at the university he met and fell in love with Pauline Robinson, who was studying to be a teacher. They were married in 1918. Their four children, Martha, James, Barbara, and Scott were born between 1920 and 1930.

Barbara writes that she enjoyed a carefree childhood.[11] She attended the Milton School, a public school, through sixth grade, then was enrolled in the private and exclusive Rye Country Day School. Three years later, at the age of sixteen, she followed in her sister's footsteps and attended Ashley Hall, an expensive boarding school in Charleston, South Carolina. Pauline Pierce, who was concerned with appearances, hoped that Ashley Hall would "turn Barbara into a marriageable young woman, as it had done for her elder sister Martha."[12]

Founded in 1909, Ashley Hall, whose motto is "Possunt Quae Volunt" (Girls who have the will have the ability), was an independent college preparatory school for girls that demanded adherence to a strict set of rules.[13] One of Barbara's classmates recalled that "being bad meant taking off your hat and gloves when you got out of sight of the school."[14] At the time she attended, Barbara had slimmed down; she was tall, with reddish brown hair. She began smoking, perhaps in an effort to maintain control over her weight. Happy and popular at Ashley Hall, she was a member of the student council, the swim club, and the drama club. She planned to attend college but had little knowledge of the world around her and was isolated from current events. Although the United States stood on the brink of global conflict in 1941, Barbara remembered that "war seemed very far away."[15] Most American girls of her age probably had a similar worldview at the time. However, the real world and war would soon influence Barbara's life.

During Christmas break in 1941, her junior year at Ashley Hall, Barbara attended a dance at the Round Hill Country Club in Greenwich, Connecticut. George Herbert Walker "Poppy" Bush, a senior at Phillips Academy Andover, spotted Barbara across the room and asked a friend for an introduction.[16] Barbara was immediately drawn to young Bush and later recalled that her future husband was so attractive and charismatic that when he was in the room, she had difficulty breathing. Bush was equally enamored of Barbara, and the young people spent part of the evening becoming acquainted. When she returned from the dance, Barbara told her mother that she had met a nice, cute boy named Poppy Bush. Before Barbara awoke the next morning, her mother had learned that Poppy came from a good family and that the Pierces and Bushes belonged to some of the same clubs.[17] Pauline Pierce was pleased, but her inquiries irritated her younger daughter, increasing the tension between the two, and "really burned me up," recalled Barbara.[18] George Bush told his mother "that he had met 'the niftiest girl at the dance' the most terrific person."[19] Years later, Barbara's son Marvin commented, "It seems that my Dad was zonked over the head by this outgoing, charming woman . . . and just like everything else he's done in his life, he decided that she was the one he was going to marry and so he did."[20]

George Bush was the scion of an affluent and socially prominent family. Born in Milton, Massachusetts, on 12 June 1924, he was the son of Prescott and Dorothy Walker Bush. The second of five children, George Bush had been raised with his father's discipline and his mother's sense of fun and athletic competitiveness. His situation was the opposite of Barbara's, with her distant mother and warm father. Barbara and George saw each other the next evening at another dance, and George asked Barbara for a date; they went out together a few nights later.

After Christmas vacation, Barbara returned to school with stories about Poppy Bush. The couple began an ardent and voluminous correspondence. Sometimes, "Barbi" and her Ashley Hall friends "would get together and write love letters to Poppy Bush as a prank," but her friends observed that Barbara was in love with her new beau.[21] Bush asked Barbara to his senior prom.

The Pierce and Bush families had inculcated similar values in their progeny. Family and loyalty were to be prized above all else. A certain stoicism was expected. Both Barbara and George had been taught to grin and bear it; if they had problems, they had to resolve them. George Bush was told he should not claim more than his fair share of attention. A 1987 *Newsweek* story explained, "Talking about yourself was frowned upon in the Bush family. If a Bush child burst into the house to say he'd hit a home run that day, George's mother would reply, 'How did the *team* do, dear?'"[22] Calling attention to oneself was frowned upon; the focus was on the group rather than the individual. The *Newsweek* story points out an important difference between the Pierce and Bush children noted by author Kati Marton. Marvin Pierce taught his children to be aggressive, whereas the Bush children were taught to be competitive but not aggressive.[23] There is a world of difference between the two child-rearing philosophies, and they were apparent in Barbara and George.

A reporter observed that Barbara "was born and raised in a world where manners mattered, and [not just about] which fork to use, but really be interested in other people, what they say and what they think and that's the essence of personal diplomacy."[24] The similarity in upbringing and the ability to practice personal diplomacy would serve both Barbara and George well in their public lives. Their families made both young people aware that they had enjoyed many of life's advantages, and there was pressure to succeed and give back to the community.

The Japanese attack on Pearl Harbor had occurred a few weeks before Barbara and George met. The onset of World War II quickly overshadowed the relationship. Continuing a family tradition, George had applied to and been accepted at Yale University, the alma mater of his father, brother, and uncles. However, he decided to defer his admission and enlist in the U.S. Navy. Shortly after graduation from Phillips Academy, he left for preflight training at Chapel Hill, North Carolina.

Barbara and George continued their correspondence as he began his training. Unfortunately, their letters have been lost. However, George's letters to his parents have survived.[25] Writing to his mother in the fall of 1942, Bush seemed distracted; perhaps he was preoccupied with his training, or the young woman from Rye was in his thoughts. He commented that he was not interested in other girls: "There's a cadet dance Saturday night. I might drop in but I don't know. I just don't seem to care about that stuff now anymore."[26] Shortly after this letter, Barbara came for a short visit. Bush wrote, "I met Barbara at the Inn at 12. She took a cab over from Raleigh. She looked too cute for words—really beautiful. We had a sandwich in town then walked. . . . She was so swell to come way over here."[27]

Bush's flight training took him from Chapel Hill to bases in Minnesota, Texas, Florida, North Carolina, Virginia, and Massachusetts. As he flew around the country, Barbara was never far from his thoughts. Unable to come home for Christmas in 1942, George wrote his parents from Minneapolis, "Barbara is sending me soon what I asked for; namely a decent picture of her."[28]

Barbara knew that flight training was difficult, tiring, and fraught with danger. She learned, as did George's parents, about his thoughts as an aspiring aviator who saw men crash and die even in training: "The flying is going along OK. All of a sudden the enormity of our job has struck me—ie., if we want to do it at all well."[29] Yet there was also a playful side to her flying suitor. Shortly after sharing his apprehensions, George sent Barbara a pet that caused a commotion: "I sent Barbara an alligator; he ate Mrs. Pierce's frog in her pool and finally beat an escape into the woods. If you would like a 'gator' at home—give me the word and he's as good as yours."[30] The "gift" seemed out of character for Bush, who tended to be a sober, responsible young man. Most of his correspondence does not descend to the levity of the "alligator letter"; instead, he commented about the gravity of war, the difficulty of learning how to fly, the spartan living conditions, and, most of all, his affection for Barbara.

Bush prevailed on his mother to write to the Pierces asking permission to have Barbara spend an upcoming leave with him at the Bush summer home in Kennebunkport, Maine. The Pierces granted that permission. Bush wrote to his mother: "I called Barbara up last night. Gosh Mum she is so swell to me. She was just as cute as she could be. . . . What a gal. She is still coming up to Maine with us, thank heavens. Smith starts the 12th or so luckily."[31]

The young couple spent seventeen days together in Maine getting to know each other better. Barbara recalled that she was scared to death to meet the extended Bush family. She characterized them as "overwhelming," and their teasing was "enormous."[32] She was not singled out; they would tease anyone. Prescott "Pres" Bush Jr., George's older brother, took an active part in the teasing. Barbara recalled that the Bushes had a horse in Kennebunkport named Barsil that they used to pull a wagon. Pres would tease Barbara and call her Barsil, the name from which she eventually got her nickname, "Bar."[33] The only person who did not take part in the teasing was George's mother, Dorothy, who separated herself from this Bush family activity, quickly earning Barbara's affection.[34] Everyone liked the outgoing, athletic Dorothy; George's father was another matter.

Everyone was afraid of him; his grandchildren were told to refer to him as "Senator." He became gentler as he got older.[35]

Barbara and George hiked, played tennis, and went on picnics. At the conclusion of the visit, they became secretly engaged and decided to announce their intentions at Christmas. Barbara recalled telephoning her family and telling them that she and George were engaged. Her family's response was, "Oh really." The secret engagement, according to George Bush, was a secret "to the extent that the German and Japanese high commands weren't aware of it."[36]

In spite of their youth (Barbara was eighteen, George was nineteen), neither family opposed the marriage. Some authors have speculated that Pauline Pierce and Prescott Bush, both snobbish, felt that their children could have done better in their choice of spouse, but no serious objections surfaced at the time.[37] The Bush family liked Barbara a great deal, and the Pierces approved their daughter's choice. It was obvious to all that the young couple were in love, and the marriage made sense in other ways. One author underscored the importance of social class and wrote that in the words of George Bush's mother, the couple were "sensible and well suited to each other."[38] They might have been well suited in other ways. One writer observes that the two young people "chose their mirror images: two tall, athletic adolescents from large affluent families who loved dogs, picnics, boats and the sea more than ideas and books."[39]

Even though the Pierces had given tacit approval to the engagement when Barbara and George announced their intentions during the summer of 1943, official confirmation from Marvin and Pauline did not come until November of that year. After receiving a letter from Barbara's father, George wrote to his mother, "I certainly was glad to get Mr. Pierce's letter. It was just a short one saying that he and Mrs. Pierce both heartily approve of our engagement."[40] The formal announcement of Barbara and George's engagement appeared in the *New York Times* on 12 December 1943.[41] They set a wedding date for 19 December 1944.

Perhaps the young couple were "well suited to each other" and came from the same social class, but they were in love; there was no question about George Bush's commitment to his fiancée. Shortly after their engagement he wrote to Barbara, "I love you precious, with all my heart and to know that you love me means my life. How often I have thought of the immeasurable joy that will be ours some day. How lucky our children will be to have a mother like you."[42] Barbara admired and learned a great deal from George's mother, Dorothy. Her future mother-in-law was much more pleasant and easier to deal with than Pauline Pierce. When George Bush's ship, the USS *San Jacinto* was commissioned, Barbara and Dorothy traveled to attend the ceremony in Philadelphia. Barbara was apprehensive and said, "I was scared to death of George's mother, not because she was scary, but because she was so perfect."[43] She had no cause for concern; they got along famously. Nancy Bush recalled her mother's comment about her future daughter-in-law: "That girl could talk to absolutely anybody."[44] A reporter who covered the Bushes had another perspective and wrote, "Her mother-in-law was easy to understand, and consistent in her benignly malicious (or were they maliciously benign?) ways. Barbara absorbed the lesson of how 'to smile and laugh innocently while eviscerating someone.'"[45] One of the factors that contributed to Barbara Bush becoming a formidable woman was her admiration for and emulation of Dorothy Bush.

Barbara began her freshman year at Smith College. Her grades were far from stellar, and she was not serious about academic pursuits. She was more interested in sports (she was captain of the freshman soccer team), and she enjoyed having a good time. Her roommate Margaret Barrett commented, "She was different from the rest of us in that her destiny was already fixed. Her whole life was bound up in [George]."[46]

Barbara attended a summer session and returned to Smith for her sophomore year, but she dropped out shortly after the start of the semester. A classmate recalled that she was both bored in a history of American economics class and preoccupied with her upcoming wedding.[47] Years later she said that she regretted leaving college, but at the time she was convinced of the wisdom of her decision.[48]

While Barbara slogged through classes, George was thinking of his soon-to-be wife. On 26 September 1943, he commented to his mother, "Barbara's letters have been coming regularly and along with yours make for the highlights of every day—and that is no lie. . . . I miss her awfully Mum, and sometimes I find myself wondering how I'm going to stand it. I guess I've got it bad—and that isn't good at times like these. I wish we were each three years older."[49] Perhaps to keep Barbara closer, Bush had "Barbara" painted on the side of his plane.

In February 1944, Bush was commissioned an ensign in the U.S. Navy and assigned to the USS *San Jacinto*. He was the youngest pilot in the navy. The war was raging in Europe and the South Pacific, and George would ship out after a brief leave. He wrote to his mother, "How I am looking forward to this leave—it will be my last for such a long time, I'm afraid. I just wish Bar could stay right with us, but it is her vacation and I guess she should be home and needless to say the distance between Greenwich and Rye won't cramp my style."[50]

Bush was in the Pacific by May 1944, flying the Avenger, a TBF or Torpedo bomber. In June, Bush and his crew were involved in action against enemy fighter planes when "the Barbara" was hit. Bush and the crew had to bail out of their plane. Everyone survived, and the group was picked up within minutes by another vessel that was in the vicinity. Bush and his squadron continued to fly sorties over the next few months. On 2 September 1944, while trying to bomb the radio tower on Chi Chi Jima, one of the Bonin Islands, Bush's plane was hit. He continued on course, released his bombs, and scored damaging hits.[51] Smoke engulfed the plane, and Bush yelled back to his two crewmen and told them to bail out. He received no response. Believing that they were gone, he too, bailed out. For three hours after being shot down, Bush clung to his life raft before being picked up by the USS *Finback*, a "lifeguard" submarine patrolling for men in Bush's situation. His crewmen were killed in the incident.[52]

The Bushes had been told that their son was missing in action; they sought to keep the news from Barbara. She was already worried because she had not received a letter from George in a long time. She was relieved and thankful when Dorothy Bush called to inform her that George was alive and well after his harrowing experience.

From the *Finback*, Bush wrote his parents an anguished letter. He was bereft over the deaths of his crewmen and felt responsible for their fate. In the letter, he revealed that Barbara had been on his mind as he prayed for rescue: "It's a funny thing how much I thought of Bar during the whole experience. What I wouldn't give to be with her right now. Just to see that lovely face and those beautiful eyes."[53] He had much to be thankful for that Thanksgiving. He wrote, "This year Thanksgiving has more significance for me than ever; for heaven knows I have more to be thankful for than ever before . . . my loving happy family and my own precious Bar and the happiness that will soon be ours; and then too my own life which has been guarded and protected during these last few months."[54] George and Barbara had missed their original wedding day, but they happily rescheduled the ceremony for early January.

Just prior to his daughter's wedding, Marvin Pierce took Barbara to lunch to discuss the importance of marriage and the commitment it required. He told her that the primary cause of divorce was money. Pauline Pierce, he said, had difficulty keeping her spending under control. He advised financial sobriety. In addition, he told Barbara that the three most important things that a parent could pass on to a child were "the best education, a good example and all the love in the world."[55] Her actions as a wife and mother in the years to come confirm that Barbara took her father's warning and message to heart.

George Bush arrived in Rye on Christmas Eve. He later wrote that there were "tears, laughs, hugs, joy, the love and warmth of family in a holiday setting."[56] One historian writes that Bush's homecoming was surreal for Barbara, who had believed until a few days before that she might never see Bush again."[57] On 6 January 1945, a cold day when snow turned to ice, making travel difficult, Barbara Pierce, age nineteen, accompanied by eight attendants, and George H. W. Bush, age twenty, were married at the First Presbyterian Church in Rye.[58] Excited and happy on her wedding day, Barbara wore a gown of ivory satin, embroidered with seed pearls. Her veil of heirloom princess and rosepoint lace belonged to Dorothy Bush. Despite rationing, the wedding and reception for more than 250 guests was lavish.[59] One of her Ashley Hall classmates later offered a sardonic assessment: "It was a real storybook romance. They married and went off to New Haven, and she worked her tail off for the rest of her life."[60]

After a honeymoon in Sea Island, Georgia, Bush rejoined his squadron to train for the final assault on Japan. He moved from Florida, to Michigan, to Maine, to Virginia. Barbara joined him whenever possible. She lived in constant dread that the squadron would be called up to take part in the Japanese action. Joy and relief replaced fear when President Truman announced a cessation of hostilities with Japan on 14 August 1945. Because he had flown fifty-eight combat missions, Bush had accumulated enough points to be released from active duty in September 1945. His meritorious service earned him the Distinguished Flying Cross and promotion to lieutenant senior grade.

There was just enough time for the Bushes to move to New Haven, Connecticut, so that George could begin his long-delayed education at Yale University. With thousands of men and women returning from war service, Bush was able to take advantage of a special accelerated program at Yale that would allow him to graduate in less than three years. His education costs were covered by the GI Bill.[61] Money was tight, and they were sharing their kitchen with two other couples in their Whitney Street apartment, but the time in New Haven was a happy one for Barbara and George.[62] To bolster their finances, Barbara worked at the Yale Coop, the campus store, until the birth of their first child, George Walker Bush, on 6 July 1946.

George Bush was a success at Yale, academically, athletically, extracurricularly, and socially. He majored in economics and was inducted into Phi Beta Kappa. He was on the soccer team, but his love was baseball, and he captained the squad in his senior year. Barbara served as the official scorer for many of her husband's games. Prior to graduation, Bush was "tapped" for the secretive and exclusive Skull and Bones. His Skull and Bones connections would serve Bush many times during his business and political careers.[63]

Barbara Bush had always assumed that she and her husband would settle down in New England, not far from their families.[64] However, George Bush, who seemed destined for Wall Street and a place in his father's investment firm, Brown Brothers, Harriman and Company, had been tempted by the potential for growth in the gas and oil business in Texas. His concern for his family's financial future and indecision about a career direction are reflected in a letter Bush wrote to his friend FitzGerald (Gerry) Bemiss in June 1948. He tells his friend that he has a chance to work for Neil Mallon's Dresser Industries in Texas, a company that made equipment for the oil and gas industries. Bush wrote, "Texas would be new and exciting . . . hard on Bar perhaps—and heavens knows many girls would bitch like blazes about such a proposed move. Bar's different though. . . . She lives quite frankly for Georgie and myself. She is

wholly unselfish, beautifully tolerant of my weaknesses and idio-
syncrasies, and ready to faithfully follow any course I choose."[65]
Even for 1948, Bush's comments seem chauvinistic. He proposed
to uproot his wife and son and move thousands of miles from family and everything familiar. His cavalier assessment, "She lives quite
frankly for Georgie and myself . . . and [is] ready to faithfully follow
any course I chose," seems insensitive. First lady Lady Bird Johnson
once explained, "This was your husband, this was your life." Perhaps
Barbara Bush was living Mrs. Johnson's observation. This was the
first of many "uprootings" that she endured. She was somewhat less
than thrilled to leave the East for West Texas, but there is no proof
that she strenuously opposed the move. Bush's statement was confirmation that being his spouse would never be easy.

Perhaps another factor was responsible for the willingness to
move so far from their East Coast universe. Mrs. Bush told former
Reagan and Bush speechwriter Peggy Noonan, "George's mother
was a formidable and strong woman, so was my mother, and we
wanted to get out from under the parental gaze, be on our own!"[66]
Though the Texas summers were unbearably hot, neither Bush was
anxious or lonely. Moving to Texas was an adventure.

In the fall of 1948, Bush headed south to Odessa, Texas, and took
a job as an equipment clerk with Mallon's International Derrick and
Equipment Company (Ideco). Barbara and young Georgie soon followed. Her family, convinced that she was going to an uncivilized
area, sent her packages filled with nice things that they were certain
could not be bought in Texas. In fact, life in West Texas in 1948 was
harsh, and the weather was prone to extremes. George W. Bush recalled giant sandstorms; once "it rained and frogs came out everywhere, like the biblical plague, covering the fields and front
porches."[67] Barbara and George H. W. Bush were forced to grow up
quickly in their new environment.

After a year in Odessa, Bush was promoted to a drilling bit sales-
man, and the family moved to California. The nomadic life continued as they lived in Huntington Park, Bakersfield, Whittier, Ventura,
and Compton, California. Barbara Bush once estimated that the
family had moved twenty-eight times."[68] The frequent relocations
cultivated self-reliance in Barbara.

In September 1949, while the Bushes were living in California, Pauline Pierce was killed in a freak accident when her husband swerved his car to avoid spilling a cup of hot coffee that his wife had placed on the front seat. Marvin Pierce lost control of the car, which plunged a hundred feet down an embankment and slammed into a tree and a stone wall. He sustained a concussion, a fractured nose, four broken ribs, and facial contusions; Pauline Pierce died instantly of a fractured skull.[69]

Concern for his daughter's health prompted Pierce to persuade Barbara, seven months pregnant with her second child, not to fly east for her mother's funeral. Mrs. Bush regretted her decision not to attend her mother's funeral or spend time with her father during his convalescence. She later characterized this time as lonely and miserable.[70] "Doro" Bush Koch, the youngest of the Bush children, writes that her mother always wished she had gone home: "Mom recalled, 'My Dad was in the hospital when the funeral service was held. My mother and I loved each other, but I was not her favorite.'"[71] Two months later, in December 1949, Pauline Robinson ("Robin") Bush, named in memory of her maternal grandmother, was born.

George Bush was transferred to Midland, Texas, in 1950, and the family became involved in their new town. George and Barbara helped to start the YMCA, established three banks, and worked for the cancer crusade, United Way, and Community Chest. George coached Little League, and both Bushes taught Sunday school.[72] The Bush family grew with the birth of John Ellis ("Jeb") Bush in 1953.

Another tragedy would have a profound effect on Barbara and George's life. Barbara recalled that one morning, three-year-old Robin woke up and said, "I don't know what to do this morning. I may just go out and lie on the grass and watch cars go by, or I might just stay in bed."[73] The statement raised a red flag for Barbara, who was not used to such behavior from her active young daughter. After some tests with the local pediatrician, George and Barbara were summoned to the doctor's office to hear the news that all parents dread: Robin had leukemia. Both were shocked to learn that the disease was fatal. In a 1996 interview George Bush recalled, "The doctor said this child has leukemia and we didn't know what the hell the doctor was talking about back in those days, and I said 'what does that mean?' and she said, 'well it means that it's not likely she can live many more weeks longer.'" More than forty years after their loss, the memory brought tears to Bush's eyes.[74] Barbara's reaction was similar to her husband's, and she had difficulty believing that what the doctor said was true.

The pediatrician urged the couple to take Robin home and let her live out the remaining weeks of her life. John Walker, Bush's uncle and a doctor on the staff of Memorial Sloan-Kettering Hospital in New York, agreed that Robin was going to die, but he prevailed on Barbara and George to bring her to New York for treatment that might extend her life.[75] They were on a plane to New York the next day. Robin received state-of-the-art drug therapies, even returning to Midland for a brief visit, but she died in October 1954.

Barbara had decreed that there would be no tears around Robin. Those who could not control their emotions were asked to step outside her room. One of those who had a terrible time was George Bush. Barbara wrote that George could hardly stand to watch Robin undergo medical procedures.[76] However, it was Barbara who sat by Robin's bedside every day for months and watched her daughter suffer through treatment. During Robin's illness, twenty-eight-year-old Barbara's hair turned gray.[77] When Robin died, the roles were reversed, and it was George who was a source of strength and encouragement for Barbara. Her stoicism had come at a high price. She wrote, "For one who allowed no tears before her death, I fell apart, and time after time during the next six months, George would put me together again."[78] George refused to let Barbara withdraw and helped her to grieve and share their loss. Doro Bush Koch writes that her parents dealt with their profound grief by turning to each other: "They reminded themselves to count their blessings, and at the very top of the list was faith, family and friends."[79] Koch continues, "My mother says that Robin's death instilled in both her and Dad a compassion that has stayed ever since. There is a sad part of my mom and dad that those of us who have never lost a child could never understand."[80]

Georgie and Jebby had been left in Texas with family friends. Georgie was seven years old and had no idea of the severity of Robin's illness. When Barbara and George returned from New York, they had the excruciating experience of telling their son about his sister's death. Barbara wrote, "He asked a lot of questions and couldn't understand why we hadn't told him when we had known for such a long time."[81] George W. Bush later recalled, "Forty-six years later those minutes remain the starkest memory of my childhood, a sharp pain in the midst of an otherwise happy blur."[82]

Returning to life without Robin was difficult, and many nights Barbara cried herself to sleep. Things finally turned around as the result of an overheard conversation: "One day I was in our bedroom when I heard Georgie talking to a neighbor child who wanted him to come over and play. Georgie said he wanted to, but he couldn't leave his mother. She needed him." That, writes Mrs. Bush, started her on her way back to normal life: "I realized I was too much of a burden for a seven year old boy to carry."[83] George W. Bush commented on the effect of his sister's death: "The death of a child can really wreck a family, but it certainly didn't in our case. It made Mother and Dad stronger as a couple."[84] Barbara Bush emerged from this terrible period as a more compassionate and stronger person. It took her time to move on and perhaps she had not finished grieving when she heard her son's comment. Years later, she would confront depression, the roots of which might well have resided in the passing of Robin Bush.

The births of Neil Mallon in 1955, Marvin Pierce in 1956, and Dorothy ("Doro") Walker in 1959 lifted the Bushes' spirits. Her large, active, boisterous family kept Barbara busy throughout the 1950s and 1960s. George Bush was away a great deal, building his business. It fell to Barbara to perform the multitudinous tasks of maintaining their home and raising their children. While generally content with the children, Barbara acknowledged that she was "dormant" during this era. There were times when she was lonely and thought she would scream if the children did not say something intelligent. She was lonely, jealous, and more than a little resentful of her husband traveling all over the country. An astute businessman, Bush enjoyed the success that had been his goal in moving to Texas. By his late thirties, George H. W. Bush was a millionaire.

A prototypical fifties wife and mother, Barbara Bush was supermom. Hers was the house where the neighborhood kids congregated. She was the family disciplinarian, the bad cop to George

Bush's good cop. Well organized and focused, she drove car pools, went to an infinite number of Little League games, and took the children to their doctor appointments. Although she did not raise her five children single-handedly, she assumed a majority of the responsibility for their upbringing. She smoked packs of cigarettes. During the vice presidential years, an interviewer was extolling her virtues as a mother when Mrs. Bush stopped her and said that at times, she just barely kept her head above water. It was all she could do to keep the five children clothed and clean. She admitted to being tired a great deal of the time: "I tried my best, but I don't think I did very well."[85]

One particular area in which she did not excel was cooking. In 2001, President George W. Bush was answering questions at a town meeting when a young girl asked if the president's family had eaten meals together when he was growing up. Bush commented, "I did eat with my family, so long as my mother wasn't cooking."[86] Reportedly, Mrs. Bush was not amused at having her son tell the world that she was "a lousy cook . . . a few months later he got his comeuppance, because he choked on a pretzel. I knew it was a heaven-sent message he should stop knocking his mother's cooking."[87]

Barbara was solicitous of George H. W. Bush and catered to his needs. Her husband was always on the go, his pace frenetic. His constant need for people must have exasperated her. A former adviser recalled that Bush would tell his wife they would be having fifty people over for a meal. He'd say, "We'll serve them so and so . . . and then not worry about how the food is going to be purchased . . . and who's going to cook it. He'd say, 'Well, I've got to go golfing. Or play tennis.'" Perhaps the masses of guests and family who peppered the Bushes' life were a substitute for intimacy. For Barbara, whose middle name was sacrifice, it seemed a steep price to pay for the privilege of being Mrs. George Bush.[88]

In 1959, the Bushes moved to Houston. Three years later, local Texas Republicans asked Bush to run for chairman of the Harris County Republican Party. Bush's entrance into politics was not a great surprise; his father, Prescott, had served as the moderator of the Greenwich, Connecticut, Town Meeting, and in 1952, Prescott Bush had been elected to the U.S. Senate. Still, Barbara said that there had not been any discussion of a career in politics when she married George Bush: "No," she said, "he was not into politics and we never thought about it that way really."[89] Bush's decision to enter politics was similar to his decision to move to Texas; it was unexpected, and once again, he surprised his wife.

Barbara entered into the race with enthusiasm. The campaign for Harris County chairman was rough and dirty as the Bushes met the voters in all of Harris County's 189 precincts. George Bush discovered that his wife was a major asset to the campaign. She enjoyed politics, and her warmth and extroverted personality played well with voters. She was adept at small talk and rarely forgot a name. Yet, unfair or untrue statements about her husband provoked immediate and caustic responses. Mrs. Bush had to learn to control herself, to hold back. Years later she commented that she had probably lost her husband hundreds of votes, though this seems unlikely.[90] She was outspoken, but she was also honest, not the optimum mix for the wife of an aspiring politician. During the campaign, Barbara herself became an issue: she was rumored to be a Cape Cod heiress whose father published a Communist magazine. Mrs. Bush told an interviewer that when she read the comment about her lofty financial status, she called her father and asked if she was indeed an heiress. Marvin Pierce's company published *Redbook,* a well-known magazine aimed at women, and *Bluebook,* the periodical of the right-wing John Birch Society.[91] In spite of what the voters might have thought of his wife, Bush was elected chairman of the Harris County Republican Party.

Bush seemed a sure bet to win the Texas Senate seat held by liberal Democrat Ralph Yarborough until the assassination of John F. Kennedy. With Lyndon Johnson heading the national ticket, the election of 1964 unfolded as a landslide victory for the Democrats, and Bush lost his Senate race to Yarborough.[92] The loss did nothing to dampen George's enthusiasm for elective office, but Barbara took the defeat hard. Even though this was her first experience with elective politics, she was as involved as her husband. A reporter commented, "Barbara Bush took it [the loss] as almost a personal shortcoming. 'I hadn't done a good enough job selling my husband and myself.'"[93]

Bush ran for and was elected to the U.S. House of Representatives in 1966; he was reelected in 1968. Barbara met the voters and campaigned for her husband at numerous events. His oil connections earned him a seat on the powerful Ways and Means Committee, and he witnessed a great deal of the debate on Vietnam, but Bush became best known for his strong advocacy of family planning and birth control. Both he and Barbara had been committed to family planning for years, but in Congress, Bush's advocacy earned him the nickname "Rubbers."[94] The Bushes' long association with this issue would allow Barbara to bob and weave when confronted with questions about her stand on abortion during George Bush's presidential campaigns.

In 1970, with the encouragement of President Richard Nixon, Bush made another try for the Senate and lost to Democrat Lloyd Bentsen. Bush's consolation prize for losing the Senate election was to serve as U.S. ambassador to the United Nations (1971–1973). At the time of George's appointment to the United Nations, Barbara had not yet traveled outside the United States; she would not leave American soil until she and her husband were assigned to China. Ensconced in a luxury apartment in the Waldorf Towers near the United Nations, she enjoyed mingling with the foreign diplomatic community. She was comfortable, and the social life must have been reminiscent of both Rye and Greenwich. Mrs. Bush told a reporter, "I'd pay to have this job."[95]

She enjoyed her husband's next post quite a bit less. In the wake of Spiro Agnew's resignation as Richard Nixon's vice president in 1973, the Republican Party needed someone with a spotless reputation to take the helm of the organization. It had been rumored in the press that George Bush was likely to be asked to chair the Republican National Committee (RNC). Mrs. Bush was strongly opposed. She wrote that she had urged her husband to decline the job if it was offered: "I just felt it would be a terrible experience. Party politics are dog-eat-dog, and I knew he would have to travel a great deal." Bush ignored his wife's advice and, ever the good soldier, took the job.[96]

Bush remained as chairman of the RNC until the resignation of Richard Nixon in 1974. After Gerald Ford became president, he offered Bush virtually any job in the new administration; Bush asked for China. Barbara Bush was speechless but, after a while, very excited about her husband's new assignment, chief of the U.S. Liaison Office to the People's Republic of China. Much like Lou Hoover, a first lady who lived there at the beginning of the twentieth century, Mrs. Bush adored China. The Bushes traveled as much as possible, usually by bicycle, studied Chinese, and immersed themselves in the country's art, history, and culture. In addition, Mrs. Bush wrote a column about her experiences in China for Texas weekly newspapers. The children were away at boarding school in the United States, and for the first time since the beginning of her marriage, Barbara Bush had her husband to herself. She reveled in his undivided attention.[97]

The respite was brief. In November 1975, George Bush was asked to leave China and take over the embattled Central Intelligence Agency (CIA). He was shocked by the offer but, ever the party loyalist, cabled Secretary of State Henry Kissinger that he would serve. Barbara explained her husband's decision to return to the United States as "his willingness to do his duty."[98] As always, George Bush was insensitive to the impact that the new assignment would have on his wife. He did acknowledge to a friend that Barbara had "shed a few tears . . . but now she sees that in spite of the ugliness around the CIA, there's a job to be done."[99]

The CIA was unpopular in 1975 and came under fire for abusing its power. A week after he returned from China, Bush's congressional confirmation hearings began. He was so dispirited about his new position that Barbara contacted friends and asked them to keep her husband company during the hearings.[100] Leading the charge against Bush as the new director of the CIA was Democratic senator Frank Church of Idaho. Church and his committee found Bush's nomination "disturbing" because Bush had not demonstrated political independence in his previous posts.[101] Barbara sat and fumed over criticism of her husband as the hearings progressed. It was her understanding that Church was being critical of the CIA, not her husband, but she was still furious at his denunciations. After Bush was confirmed, Bethine Church, Frank's wife and Barbara's friend, told her that Frank "did not mean it personally."[102] Barbara's political education was continuing, and she came to understand the old maxim once articulated by John F. Kennedy: in Washington there are not any friends or enemies, just colleagues.

The CIA assignment was difficult for Mrs. Bush. Times were changing, and second-wave feminism radically affected expectations for women. A stay-at-home mom who had raised five children found her contributions devalued. To compound the situation, for the first time in almost thirty years, the Bushes had an empty house. George Bush worked long hours, and security restrictions at the new job made it impossible for the couple to discuss his work. Without the cushion of family and the comfort of her husband's company, Barbara plunged into a deep depression. She was lonely, unhappy, and ashamed of those emotions.[103] Her husband suggested that she get professional help, but Barbara resisted. Instead, she spent night after night weeping in his arms as she tried to explain her feelings. In her memoirs she writes, "I was just the right age, fifty-one years old, for menopause; I could not share George's job after years of being so involved and our children were gone. I was a classic case for depression. . . . I was wallowing in self-pity."[104]

Later, Mrs. Bush would wonder why she refused to consult a doctor, but at the time she was determined to fight through her sadness alone.[105] Perhaps it was Yankee self-reliance, but she discovered that work seemed to be the antidote. Barbara threw herself into volunteer work, devoting hundreds of hours to the Washington Home, a hospice where she did all sorts of chores from washing patients' hair to changing bedclothes. She assembled a slide show about China that she delivered before various audiences; her speaker fees were donated to charity. After a difficult six months, the depression lifted, but the experience gave Barbara a new understanding of those who have to deal with mental health problems. She told an interviewer, "Now when I hear of depression, instead of saying 'Oh, pull yourself together,' which is what I used to think, I now think, well that's tough and you've got to get some help."[106] Bush's tenure as CIA director came to a close when Jimmy Carter was inaugurated in January 1977. The Bushes returned to Houston.

The Bushes were both pleased and relieved when their oldest son, George W. Bush, married Laura Welch in November 1977. The young couple, both of them thirty-one, were a study in contrasts: Laura was a librarian and teacher, quiet, serious, and grounded. George had been a mediocre student at Yale and enjoyed socializing and fraternity life more than intellectual pursuits. Even though he had earned an MBA degree from Harvard Business School, he was floundering as he cast about for a career path. He had drifted from a management trainee position for an agricultural firm to working on U.S. Senate campaigns in Florida and Alabama while partying hard. The oldest Bush son had a tendency to abuse alcohol; Laura was seen as a steadying influence.[107] George W. Bush tried to emulate his father's success by founding an oil and gas exploration company; his venture failed miserably. The elder Bushes had worried about their firstborn, but they heartily approved of Laura. At the time that Laura and George W. were married, the younger Bush had made the decision to run for Congress. To have been a thirty-one-year-old unmarried male in Texas would have raised questions about Bush's sexuality, but these potential questions were laid to rest with his marriage. The next year, George W. Bush was defeated in his bid for the congressional seat he sought. Barbara, who had a special relationship with her oldest son forged during the time she was mourning Robin Bush, remained concerned about his future.

Bush biographer Herbert S. Parmet comments that after George Bush's return to Houston, there was no doubt that he was "drawing a clear bead on the presidency, testing himself, gauging his popular appeal for that most American ordeal by democracy."[108] Barbara realized, too, that her husband was planning a run for national office. He never actually told Barbara that he was running for president; she assumed it because two Bush fund-raising groups had been formed, and all her husband's actions over the past twenty years had been preparing him for this race. When she was asked if her husband had discussed the matter with her, she responded, "Did he ask me if he could run for president? . . . The answer is no, but he didn't ask me to marry him either."[109] In March 1978, she wrote to a friend, "What a man is my great George. He is getting better about 'blowing his own horn,' a thing we were taught as children never to do. But a thing you must do if you want this job."[110] During the summer of 1978, Barbara recalled a meeting at Kennebunkport with a number of influential people, including Bush friend James Baker and former Republican National Committee chairman Dean Burch, to discuss her husband's run for the presidency.

The early campaign effort moved forward. The couple had been building a national network of acquaintances and friends for years.

Annually, the Bushes sent out thousands of Christmas cards to maintain contact with their far-flung supporters. George Bush criss-crossed the country, meeting with prominent Republicans, and he and Barbara traveled to international destinations to visit with foreign leaders to bolster his claim that he had experience in foreign policy matters. Bush told a campaign aide, "I'll go anywhere and do about anything that's legal to try and win this thing."[111] Demonstrating faith in her husband, in 1977 Barbara had told George's sister Nancy Ellis that her brother was going to be president. "I just hope," said Barbara, "I am going to be able to do all that he needs and expects me to do."[112] George Bush formally announced his candidacy for president on 1 May 1979.

Though she enjoyed it, Barbara found campaigning to be exhausting. The various events were endless, and life on the primary trail could be trying and frustrating. Still, she was willing to make sacrifices for her husband's presidential bid. Barbara was hurt, then, when one of her sisters-in-law told her that she had been the subject of a family discussion. In anticipation of a national campaign they asked, "What are we going to do about Bar?" Mrs. Bush writes, "That really hurt. They discussed how to make me snappier—color my hair, change my style of dressing, and I suspect, get me to lose some weight."[113] Barbara wept until her husband told her that the whole thing was crazy, and she could just continue on as she always had.

Even though the personal criticism hurt, Barbara was optimistic about her husband's chances for election and the possibility that she would become first lady. In an interview with the *Dallas Times Herald* in October 1979, Barbara told a reporter that she thought her husband would make it to the White House, and when he did, her priority would be teaching children to read. This was one of the first announcements about her interest in literacy. She had definite ideas about the first lady's potential: "I think the First Lady has an obligation to make something happen. I will encourage Jane and John to read and in that way hope to unlock the doors that will solve other problems."[114]

Despite a surprise win in Iowa, and later victories for Bush in Michigan, Pennsylvania, Massachusetts, and Connecticut, former California governor Ronald Reagan had won enough delegates to secure the Republican nomination for president. The Bushes prepared to attend the Republican National Convention, release their delegates, and make a graceful exit from politics—or so Barbara Bush thought. Slowly, it became apparent that George Bush was being seriously considered for the vice presidency.

There was no shortage of vice presidential candidates, and Barbara wrote, "I truly began the convention thinking, Hurrah, no more politics. But as the week went on, I found myself getting very competitive. George was by far the best man for vice president."[115] The other candidates posed potential problems, and Bush, who had the background and credentials most needed by Reagan, emerged as the choice for vice president in spite of opposition from Nancy Reagan. Mrs. Reagan was still smarting over Bush's charge that Reagan's proposed supply-side economics program, tax cuts to encourage economic growth, was nothing short of "Voodoo economics."[116]

Before he would accept Bush as his vice presidential running mate, Reagan demanded Bush's firm support of the entire Republican platform. The platform contained a pro-life plank and "support for a constitutional amendment that would negate the *Roe v. Wade* decision."[117] The abortion issue was difficult for both Bushes. They had a long history of involvement in Planned Parenthood and actively endorsed family planning. It was here, however, that their positions diverged. George Bush was pro-life, but he felt abortion was acceptable if the woman in question was raped or the victim of incest, or if her health was seriously threatened. Mrs. Bush felt that abortion should not be used as a contraceptive and that *Roe v. Wade* had been abused, but she believed "abortion was a personal issue—between the mother, father and doctor. If a minor is involved, you can add parents to that list. . . . Abortion is not a presidential matter. . . . Morals cannot be legislated."[118] Mrs. Bush went on to write that she and her husband had different positions but respected each other's views.

The relationship between Reagan and Bush worked because of Reagan's bonhomie and desire to be inclusive and Bush's loyalty to his chief. The same could not be said for their wives. One writer noted that even before they left the convention, "the buzz was that the two women didn't get along."[119] A reporter asked Barbara Bush directly about the report. Mrs. Bush branded the story as silly and said that the two women had met only twice, "And from what I've seen of Nancy so far, I like her and she likes me." When asked about differences between the two candidates' wives, she responded, "Nancy is a size four and I'm a size forty-four."[120] These comments are typical of the public Barbara Bush who would go to great lengths to put a positive spin on a situation. In fact, the differences were substantial. Both had attended Smith College (Mrs. Reagan had graduated), but the two women came from different worlds and held disparate views. Though Barbara was polite and gracious, Nancy found her to be an aristocrat who seemed too sure of her place in the world. Later, Barbara told an interviewer, "Nancy Reagan and I are friends. We were never great friends. We have zero in common. I'm very family oriented. . . . She is very focused on Ronald Reagan, which is great. That's what she chose to do."[121] The two saw little of each other during the campaign and over the course of the Reagan White House years. The Reagans entertained the Bushes only a few times in the White House residence.

Mrs. Bush, who silently suffered Nancy Reagan's slights, never made any public pronouncements about her predecessor, but she enjoyed a payback at Mrs. Reagan's expense. After leaving the White House, Mrs. Reagan was the subject of a scathing, tell-all book by celebrity biographer Kitty Kelley. Mrs. Bush said that she had "no intention of reading that garbage." Shortly after making this comment, Anna Perez, Mrs. Bush's press secretary, noticed Mrs. Bush engrossed in a book by a popular author while the two were traveling. Perez observed that the first lady would "shake her head and make a comment about Nancy. Puzzled, Perez got up and peered over Barbara's shoulder. 'Behind the fake cover, she was reading the Nancy bio,' said Perez."[122]

Mrs. Bush found that campaigning for the national ticket was vastly different from primary campaigning. It was much more intense, and she had to be careful how she answered questions. Now that she was of interest to the national media, she was asked her position on various issues. For example, in her first postconvention news conference she was queried about the equal rights amendment (ERA). She had always supported ERA, but Reagan opposed it. Recognizing that she had to espouse the party line, she said, "'I'm campaigning on the Republican platform.' Asked how that squared with her previous position, she simply turned away with a smile."[123] She was uncomfortable hiding behind the platform and understood it was not the best strategy, but Barbara was determined not to do any harm to the campaign with a snap judgment or acerbic word, though this would happen in the future. Her travels took her all over the country. On Election Day, Ronald Reagan and George Bush trounced incumbent president Jimmy Carter.

By the time that George Bush became vice president in January 1981, Second Lady Barbara Bush was a political veteran. Even though she was not the first lady, she decided to focus on literacy, a cause near and dear to her heart. During Bush's eight years as vice president, Barbara participated in more than 500 literacy events all over the country. In addition to continuing her volunteer work, she performed requisite political duties: appearances before visiting groups, meetings with Republicans, official entertaining, and travel. According to an article in the *New York Times* on 8 April 1984, Mrs. Bush had traveled to fifteen countries, hosted 590 events at the vice president's residence, and attended another 715, many of them at the White House. Even though she was one of the busiest people in the administration, Mrs. Bush commented that if not for the Secret Service agents who accompanied her, "she would just be another face in the crowd."[124]

Mrs. Bush campaigned vigorously for the reelection of the Reagan-Bush ticket in 1984. Her cause and her white hair had become well known to the public. Almost universally well liked, her appearances generated larger, more appreciative audiences. One incident that occurred during the campaign demonstrated that there were limits to Mrs. Bush's good humor and tolerance, and she went back on her promise to avoid trenchant comments. She could deal with most situations and people, but when her husband or children were the targets of what she considered to be unfair criticism, she would respond. During one of the presidential debates, Democratic presidential candidate Walter Mondale needled President Reagan about his rich, elitist vice president. Mrs. Bush was already annoyed and prickly because she believed that there was a double standard for Geraldine Ferraro, the first female to be a candidate on a national party ticket, and George Bush; she lamented that her husband was "running against history in the making."[125] She also knew that Ferraro and her husband were wealthy. While talking to reporters on a campaign trip, she said, "That rich . . . well, it rhymes with rich, could buy George Bush any day." The story received almost immediate national coverage. Later, Mrs. Bush would claim that she was just kidding with reporters and believed her comments were "off the record." She telephoned Ferraro to apologize and reported: "She was very gracious about it. I certainly wasn't lying about being sorry. I would rather die than hurt George Bush in any way and what I said in jest was ugly."[126] Though Ferraro found the comment to be rude, she wrote that she told Mrs. Bush, "Don't worry about it. . . . We all says things at times we don't mean. It's all right."[127] It seems naive and unlikely for Mrs. Bush to assume, after having spent years in public life, that her comments were off the record unless she had stated this explicitly. A more likely scenario was that Mrs. Bush wanted to push the notion that Ferraro was just as affluent as the vice president, but once the idea was planted, she backed away from her statement, apologizing to Ferraro and saying that she would never do anything to hurt her husband's campaign. This Bush tactic would be used again with varying success and would result in similar reactions from Barbara Bush. The media storm blew over in a few days, but the story followed Mrs. Bush for years. In her memoirs, Mrs. Bush reflected on the way in which the incident colored her future press relations. She wrote, "I do not blame the press for reporting it because I should have known better. But they should know that I never again felt free to be relaxed with them."[128]

Her husband got into some trouble, too. During the vice presidential debate, Bush was condescending to Ms. Ferraro, at one point lecturing her about foreign policy. Mrs. Bush never had any reaction to her husband's treatment of Ferraro during the debate but justified another comment he made the day after the event. The vice president told an audience, "We kicked a little ass last night." Mrs. Bush explained that this was not her husband's personal assessment of the debate. The slogan, she said, had appeared on a sign at a Reagan-Bush rally, and her husband had repeated the line—it was picked up on a television boom microphone and, like her "rich" comment, became national news. Ferraro's supporters called the comment sexist; Barbara Bush, defender, said, "Baloney . . . as the mother of four competitive boys, I know what that expression means and, I suspect, so does Geraldine."[129] If Ferraro had boasted about her rough treatment of George Bush, Mrs. Bush might well have had an explosive reaction, but interestingly, Ferraro's only comment was that the day after the debate, Bush spent his day "cracking lockerroom jokes with the longshoremen."[130] The Reagan-Bush ticket enjoyed an overwhelming victory success in its reelection bid as they crushed Mondale and Ferraro. Mondale was able to carry only his home state of Minnesota.

Mrs. Bush titled her *Memoir* chapter about her second lady years "Around the World and Back." Building on the first four years of the Reagan administration, the 2,923 days of the vice presidency passed in a flurry of activity. She hosted 1,192 events at the vice president's residence and attended another 1,232 events in Washington. The vice president and second lady covered approximately 1.3 million miles in 1,629 days of traveling, "including visiting all fifty states and sixty-five different countries."[131]

During the second Reagan administration, George Bush laid the groundwork for his own presidential bid in 1988. There was more travel, more literacy events, more discreet political activity to pile up IOUs that could be cashed in during the upcoming campaign and election.

After George Bush officially became the Republican nominee for president in the summer of 1988, the entire Bush family mobilized for the campaign. Mrs. Bush told reporters that as a potential first lady, she would not be involved in public policy initiatives like Rosa-lynn Carter. She would tell her husband what was on her mind—she always had—but she did not feel the necessity to share differences of opinion with reporters.[132] She was reticent about addressing policy questions on the campaign trail, saying that while she did not mind discussing the issues, she did not feel particularly well informed. She was, however, very comfortable talking about George Bush.

Occasionally, Barbara became the target of media and entertain-ment criticism. In February 1988, just after the New Hampshire pri-mary, *Saturday Night Live* presented a skit, the "Pat Stevens Talk Show." The host, Stevens, turned to the Barbara Bush character and said, "I'd like to congratulate George on his startling victory in New Hampshire. He's doing well in the South. He's had a wonderful reign as vice president. Tell me, are you proud of your son?" The Barbara character said, "Pat, he is not my son. He is my husband." Stevens turned to the audience and said, "Well, she looks so much older. I hardly think it's *my* faux pas."[133] There was press speculation that Barbara Bush was not amused; however, she told an interviewer that she never saw the program. Once again, Barbara Bush was trying to have things both ways. She capitalized on her grandmotherly image as long as it worked in her favor, but when twitted about it by comedians or the media, she bristled.

On another occasion, Jane Pauley of the *Today* show asked: "Mrs. Bush, people say your husband is a man of the eighties and you're a woman of the forties. What do you say to that?" Struggling not to burst into tears, Barbara said, "Oh, you mean people think I look forty? Neat." The response worked nicely, but Pauley's pointed reference to her age and being old-fashioned in the eyes of the media was hurtful. By her own admission Barbara was devastated.[134]

Her comments prior to the 1988 Republican National Convention demonstrated that Barbara was, at best, out of touch or, more likely, insensitive to much of the suffering that surrounded her. She acknowledged that there had been many issues of concern prior to 1988, but for her, they were just coming to the fore. She said, "I'm sure someone had AIDS before 1980. I never heard of it. I'm sure we had homeless, but they were exceptions. They still are exceptions, actually, 'cause we're talking about a small number. I guess we've always had problems with affordable housing. But I wasn't as conscious of it."[135] Though she had lived a privileged life, it is difficult to believe that Mrs. Bush could utter these statements after eight years as the wife of the vice president. In spite of broad access to information and extensive travel, her words confirm that the second lady was poorly informed.

Mrs. Bush addressed the delegates to the convention, and her speech focused on her husband. She told her audience, "You should feel proud of what you've done at this convention. . . . You've nominated for the presidency of the United States a man who is as strong and caring and decent as America herself."[136] She received a rousing response. George Bush told the country in his nomination acceptance speech that his vision was of a "kinder, gentler society." To achieve this goal, he presented himself as the progenitor of a large, happy family. His values were rock solid. He was a man who could be depended upon. Barbara Bush attested to that.

Barbara Bush and Kitty Dukakis, the wife of Democratic presidential nominee Michael Dukakis, both traveled more than 50,000 miles in the ten weeks between their party's nominating conventions and Election Day. Barbara visited ninety-two cities in twenty-nine states, gave 184 interviews, and was a popular presence at seventy-seven events and fund-raisers. More than half of Barbara's events were joint appearances with George Bush.[137] She gave scores of speeches during the campaign; most addressed her husband's experience and qualifications to serve as president.[138]

No one had any doubt about Barbara's importance in her husband's campaign. Her particular role was watching the candidate's back. George W. Bush, who was working in his father's campaign, commented: "There were times [when] people did something that I think upset my mother. . . . Leaks and staff siphoning credit for ideas originating with the candidate especially infuriated her."[139] Campaign workers learned to maintain a respectful distance from the candidate's wife and do their work. One staffer remarked that when Mrs. Bush frowned, "it had the capacity to send shudders through a lot of people."[140] Watching her husband's back included monitoring the work of campaign workers and campaign advertising: she was critical when her husband was the object of negative ads, but she did not object when her husband's campaign used them.[141]

One writer has suggested that Mrs. Bush was involved in one of the more momentous decisions of the 1988 presidential campaign.[142] Following the Democratic National Convention, George Bush trailed his opponent Michael Dukakis by almost 20 percentage points. Bush was advised to attack Dukakis's prison furlough program, which had ostensibly given convicted murderer Willie Horton the opportunity to rape, sodomize, and torture a couple during his brief weekend release. Bush and his chief of staff, Craig Fuller, had shied away from the Horton situation because the convicted murderer was an African American and his victims were white; Bush did not want to exploit the inherent race issues. Campaign manager Lee Atwater, George W. Bush, and Barbara Bush agreed that the Horton issue was a way to point out to voters that Dukakis was weak, soft on crime, and too liberal. Barbara Bush helped to persuade her husband that hardball tactics had to be employed if he hoped to win the presidency.[143] Bush was persuaded: Willie Horton ads appeared on cable television but were reported in the mainstream press, and references to Horton cropped up in Bush's campaign speeches. An observer noted that Bush's campaign "virtually nominated Willie Horton as Dukakis' running mate."[144] According to one author, no one was more appalled by the ads than Dorothy Bush, George's mother, who was offended by their racism.[145]

Dukakis's numbers plummeted, and his campaign could never rebound; Bush was elected. In her autobiography, Mrs. Bush writes, "We got blamed for dirty politics and racism. Baloney. The ad was not ours, and the truth of the matter is, Willie Horton should not have been out of prison."[146] Barbara Bush was a skillful politician and expert at covering her tracks. The Bushes were principled when negative ads were used against them, but not as principled when they targeted an opponent. Years later, a dying Lee Atwater apologized to Michael Dukakis for his smarmy campaign tactics.[147] George Bush never distanced himself or apologized for the ads. A reporter who traveled with Mrs. Bush during the campaign observed that she was tougher than her public image. Publicly, Barbara Bush was given to the use of hyperbole, and her comments were peppered with words like "wonderful," "enormous," "sweet," and "precious." Privately, however, her conversations with the candidate, as demonstrated by their discussions of Willie Horton, were tough and candid.[148] Peggy Noonan corroborated the reporter's assessment: "Those merry eyes, the warmth, the ability to get the help cracking in a jolly way, and then not so jolly. A lack of pretension, a breeziness, but underneath, she is Greenwich granite."[149]

In October, just weeks before the election, rumors began to circulate that asserted George Bush had conducted extramarital affairs with his executive assistant, Jennifer Fitzgerald, and with another woman who purportedly had been his mistress while he was at the CIA. Fitzgerald had become George Bush's secretary when he was chairman of the Republican National Committee. She worked as his executive assistant in China and served on his vice presidential staff. She was highly efficient but was abrasive and not well liked. Fitzgerald brought the same type of organization and discipline to Bush's offices that Barbara brought to his home. Rumors spread about a liaison between the two. According to the tabloid *LA Weekly,* "None of this information came as a great surprise to Washington insiders, where the vice president's relationship with Ms. Fitzgerald, and his general taste in women, is the stuff of cocktail party legend."[150] When Barbara Bush heard the story, she told campaign staffers that it was ridiculous and to disregard it. When the story persisted, she labeled the charges as malicious: "It is ugly and the press should be ashamed of themselves, printing something that is a lie," she said.[151]

Historians, reporters, and observers have advanced two theories: Jennifer as mistress and Jennifer as office wife. Celebrity biographer Kitty Kelley comes down squarely on the side of Jennifer as long-term mistress and furnishes evidence to support her contention of the liaison.[152] Writer Kati Marton suggests that, at a minimum, Bush and Fitzgerald were "emotionally close" but argues for Fitzgerald as office wife. Fitzgerald, writes Marton, was doing what Bush wanted done as he conducted his business.[153] She was "one of those women found in the upper reaches of corporations as well as in politics who give their lives to great men. They work the long hours no one else will and they understand their bosses better than others."[154] Bush's biographer Herbert Parmet concurs that Fitzgerald ran an efficient, no-nonsense office: "Her imperiousness and special access to the boss also made it easy for her colleagues to resent her" and spread rumors of an affair.[155] Bush fueled speculation by being seen in Fitzgerald's company during Barbara Bush's absences from China. However, Parmet concludes, "More than a decade of probing, which became more intense during the 1992 presidential campaign, failed to uncover any evidence of a Bush-Fitzgerald romance."[156] In 1998, a writer at the *LA Weekly* observed that the paper's original 1988 story "alluded to," but never confirmed, Bush's extramarital affair: "In fact, the story had as much sourcing as the creationist account of the origins of the Earth."[157]

Whether Fitzgerald was office wife or mistress, the rumors and stories were painful for Mrs. Bush. After almost forty years of marriage and a life dedicated to serving George Bush, the depth of her hurt and anger can only be imagined. A former staff member said, "I always thought less of George Bush for having Jennifer around as much as he did. It was so 'in your face' for Barbara."[158] For his part, George Bush, demonstrating a degree of insensitivity, did nothing to distance himself from Fitzgerald and thereby put an end to the rumors.

Barbara's problems with Jennifer Fitzgerald did not dissipate until the 1992 presidential campaign, when rumors of her husband's infidelity resurfaced. George Bush was accusing Democratic presidential nominee Bill Clinton, who was dealing with his own infidelity problems, of lacking the moral fiber to serve as chief executive when the media confronted him with questions about Jennifer Fitzgerald. This time, however, Fitzgerald, who wielded influence and power and controlled access to the vice president, was too great a political liability to be ignored. She was transferred to the State Department's Office of Protocol and vanished from view. Exhibiting the steely discipline that had characterized her success and effectiveness, Mrs. Bush put a positive spin on the situation when she told interviewer Barbara Walters that Fitzgerald was a wonderful lady.[159]

The charges of marital philandering had little effect on George Bush's fortunes. On Election Day 1988, his years of being a loyal conservative, a loyal Republican, a loyal Reaganite were rewarded when he won the prize he had sought for almost three decades. He was elected president, besting Dukakis. On a cold day in January 1989, Barbara Bush rode to the White House in triumph. Roger Ailes, the presidential campaign media adviser, told a reporter, "I think America is going to go through a real love affair with Barbara Bush because she's real. She's tough. There's not one ounce of fake in the woman."[160]

For Barbara Bush, the White House marked the finish line in a long, successful journey that had started in Rye, New York. In the course of frequent uprootings and tragedy, a long political internship, and changing times, she had evolved as a formidable woman. The Executive Mansion was an invitation to opportunity. The new first lady would be able to advance literacy and other causes in public while offering her opinions to the president in private. Barbara Bush resolved to make the most of her tenure, to "do something every day."[161] On her way to fulfilling that promise, she achieved prominence and became an indispensable adviser to the president of the United States.

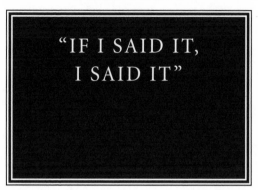

CHAPTER 2

"IF I SAID IT, I SAID IT"

In her public writing during the presidency and after, Barbara Bush does not refer to the extensive scholarly literature about "the rhetorical presidency," the use of the bully pulpit by the president to influence his audience, the American people, or the people of the world. Yet she understood that her new position afforded a special opportunity to address her issues and concerns. By the time she came to the White House, Barbara Bush was a seasoned political professional with more than twenty-five years' experience in the public arena. She was well aware of the value of frequent contact with Americans through the spoken word, the press, books, and articles. Thus, she made extensive use of various forms of persuasion during her White House years. Mrs. Bush employed her podium to advocate for literacy, practice politics, and capitalize on the ceremonial dimensions of her position. She spoke out about literacy, education, AIDS, cancer, and the Persian Gulf War. She campaigned for her husband and for Republicans running for office. She was an effective hostess at her official home and at her family's home in Maine. All these accomplishments depended on her skill as a communicator.

Careful attention to her public image was one key to Barbara Bush's success. Americans saw a good natured, sixtyish, grandmotherly woman who revered her husband but had dealt with her share of crises and heartaches. She was perceived as down-to-earth, plainspoken, a realist with an irreverent sense of humor and a penchant for self-deprecation. She seemed human and approachable and was very different from her predecessor, the distant and demanding Nancy Reagan. Part of Barbara Bush's skill was to emphasize this contrast without directly attacking Nancy Reagan and incurring her wrath.

Mrs. Reagan had been an imperious, controversial first lady. Feared by many White House staff members, the woman alternately labeled as "Dragon Lady" and "Queen Nancy" had zealously protected her husband while affecting personnel and policy decisions. Former White House chief of staff James Baker, who had dealt with her complaints and demands, said that Mrs. Reagan considered White House staff to be "hired hands."[1] During her husband's second term, Mrs. Reagan clashed repeatedly with Donald Regan, Baker's successor as White House chief of staff. Mrs. Reagan believed that Regan had assembled a staff that was loyal to him rather than the president, that he had handled the Iran-Contra affair poorly, and that his actions made the president look weak.[2] Mrs. Reagan clamored for his removal, and he was forced from the White House in 1987. In retirement, Regan published his memoirs, *For the Record: From Wall Street to Washington,* which attacked Mrs. Reagan and disclosed that she consulted an astrologer to determine the timing for certain presidential activities.[3] After leaving the White House, Mrs. Reagan launched her own salvos at Regan when she published her memoirs, *My Turn: The Memoirs of Nancy Reagan.*

During the Reagan-Bush transition, the two Republican camps drew apart in what was more like a hostile takeover than a seamless shift from one conservative Republican administration to another. Both George and Barbara Bush distanced themselves from Ronald and Nancy Reagan. George Bush wanted to make it clear that he was his own man and was not operating in the former president's shadow.[4] There was a rumor that Reagan's pictures were removed from the West Wing while portraits of Gerald Ford and Jimmy Carter remained.[5] In this setting, the underground tensions between Mrs. Bush and Mrs. Reagan provided a subtext to the events of these months. Barbara Bush was prepared to set a very different tone once her predecessor had departed.

By January 1989, the country was tired of Nancy Reagan's peevishness and the internecine warfare that it had sparked, and was ready for a change. She had been the recipient of critical press reviews for her hauteur and for her admission that she had not returned fashions that she had been loaned by designers or paid taxes on that clothing. In the days prior to the new president's inauguration, Mrs. Bush initiated her efforts to demonstrate that she was most definitely not Nancy Reagan. Appearing before a large gathering in Washington, the soon-to-be first lady poked fun at herself and in her patented sarcastic tone said, "Please notice the hair, the makeup, the designer clothes and remember, you may never see it again."[6] Actually, Mrs. Bush had been buying designer fashions for years (though she also bought "off the rack"), but to freshen up her fashion image, she relied more heavily on one of her favorite designers, Arnold Scaasi. He told an interviewer: "Her style is an American classic because she doesn't try to be something she isn't and . . . it becomes Barbara Bush."[7]

The first lady's clothes were a public means of emphasizing her power. The vivid reds favored by Nancy Reagan gave way to Barbara Bush's shades of blue. Mrs. Bush's trademark three strands of faux pearls became a popular fashion accessory; soon magazines carried advertisements for "first lady neckwear." Mrs. Bush took a shot at her svelte predecessor when she told reporters, "My mail tells me that a lot of fat, white-haired ladies are tickled pink."[8] Perhaps an even more satisfying moment for Barbara Bush came when "her image showed up on the side of a bus in Washington, D.C., for an Ikea furniture ad. It read, 'Nancy Reagan style at Barbara Bush prices.'" Mrs. Bush, the wealthy aristocrat, had emerged as a "Woman of the People."[9]

According to one source, Americans said that they would not be comfortable talking to Nancy Reagan, but they would feel very relaxed chatting with Barbara Bush.[10] This difference was emphasized in news articles and pictures of Mrs. Bush reading to groups of children. Barbara Bush promised to be a wholesome, down-to-earth, noncontroversial first lady. Maureen Dowd of the *New York Times* offered a slightly different but interesting perspective: "Someone who worked with both Nancy Reagan and Barbara Bush offered this contrast between the two first ladies: If Mrs. Bush did not like you, you felt an absence of warmth rather than a presence of coldness."[11]

Mrs. Bush and her staff thus sought to sell the new first lady to the country as "everywoman," even though she was probably better off financially than Nancy Reagan. Their first attempt took place on April Fool's Day 1989. When Mrs. Bush arrived at the annual Gridiron Club dinner, an evening during which the press and politicians make jokes about each other, she was wearing a red wig. She never indicated that her new red hair was a joke. This action caused great confusion, and many dinner guests believed that the first lady had in fact dyed her trademark white hair. Mrs. Bush commented that some people thought she was wearing the wig because she was sicker than had been reported (she had recently been diagnosed with Graves' disease) and the wig was covering hair loss from radiation treatment. Others thought that Mrs. Bush had not attended the dinner at all and wondered who was accompanying the president. Most of the attendees were too intimidated to question the new hair color and simply maintained a respectful silence.[12] Finally, when President Bush got up to speak, he said, "Luckily, Barbara has not reacted in the slightest to all the comments about her gray hair." The gag surprised everyone, and Mrs. Bush earned points as a good sport. Later, C. Landon Parvin, a speechwriter who conceived the prank, said, "It was great. She looked awful. It looked like she had Millie [the Bushes' springer spaniel] on her head."[13]

The two Bushes made a more serious attempt to establish a stronger rapport with the country when they led reporters Diane Sawyer and Sam Donaldson of ABC's *Prime Time* on a tour of the second floor of the White House, on 21 September 1989. As the tour began, Donaldson remarked that he and many other reporters had covered the White House for many years, but no members of the media had been invited "upstairs." The Bushes, ever mindful of public and press relations, corrected the oversight.

More than twenty-five years had passed since Jacqueline Kennedy had taken Americans on a widely heralded televised tour of the White House staterooms. The 1962 tour had proved to be a major public relations triumph for Mrs. Kennedy, who was thought to be a little too grand for the American people. The television special "warmed up" Mrs. Kennedy—a New York socialite who had attended exclusive private schools, Vassar College, and the Sorbonne in Paris—and showed her to be a likable, if somewhat distant, first lady.

The 1989 program did the same for both Bushes, but especially for Barbara, who came across as accessible, friendly, and funny. As they were touring the second floor hall, trailed by Mrs. Bush's dog Millie, Donaldson reminded Mrs. Bush that former British prime minister Winston Churchill, a frequent visitor to the White House during World War II, would pad around "in the buff." Would Mrs. Bush allow such a thing? Donaldson asked. She responded, "I certainly would allow it, I just wouldn't look."[14]

Later in the program, Donaldson and the first lady walked out to the Truman Balcony. The network reporter told Mrs. Bush that President Truman had experienced a great deal of opposition when he decided to build the balcony in 1948. Mrs. Bush asked, "Was it [1948]? I wasn't alive then Sam."[15] Exuding good humor, the Bushes were chatting with both reporters near the conclusion of the program when Sawyer asked Mrs. Bush, "What has been the hardest part for you, Mrs. Bush?" Mrs. Bush gushed, "It hasn't been hard for me. I've loved every minute. I can hardly wait to get up every morning. I know that sounds terrible, but I have loved it."[16]

To communicate her message and initiatives, Mrs. Bush understood that she had to have a productive relationship with the media. Her instructions to her press secretary, Anna Perez, provide insight into her East Wing operation. The first lady told Perez that she had one rule in dealing with the press: "If I said it, I said it." She did not want anyone to interpret or explain her statements. She insisted upon accuracy. If the staff did not know the answer to a question, they had to do the necessary research so that Mrs. Bush would not have to backtrack at a later date to explain to reporters why she was wrong. Mrs. Bush wanted to get things right, and she had little tolerance for shoddy work. Most important, according to Perez, she did not want her husband to have to expend any of his political capital to clean up her mistakes.[17]

Mrs. Bush did not hold regularly scheduled press conferences, but she saw reporters with some frequency. Occasionally, she would have lunch with a small group of reporters and would invite them upstairs to the family residence to join her for a conversation. The press roundtables were on the record, and reporters were sent transcripts of the proceedings.[18] Mrs. Bush flourished in this setting because she was in control, but she also realized that these intimate gatherings and direct access to the first lady might well yield positive press treatment. Years later she told an interviewer that, in her opinion, the female press corps was a little gentler than its male press counterpart while she was in the White House. She commented that the press always wanted her to say something violently opposed to her husband: "Well, if I opposed my husband, I told him in our bedroom. I tried not to say it in front of the press."[19] Most reporters liked Mrs. Bush and understood that her more candid observations were off the record. A reporter who covered the first lady for the *Washington Times* noted that she could be barbed in her comments, yet "She often was refreshingly honest."[20]

Sometimes, the relationship between the first lady and the press could be strained. Shortly after Mrs. Bush became first lady, five children were killed and twenty-nine people were wounded with an assault weapon in a Stockton, California, schoolyard. She was asked about the incident and responded that she supported banning military-style, rapid-fire assault weapons like the AK-47, used in the schoolyard massacre. She told an interviewer, "I myself do not own a gun. I am afraid of them."[21] The president, who was a member of the National Rifle Association, was opposed to such a ban because the weapons were used by hunters and sportsmen. Mrs. Bush's comment put her at odds with the president. Three weeks later, Mrs. Bush announced that in the future, she would not talk publicly about controversial issues. Perez said that the first lady made the decision because she wanted to focus instead on illiteracy, homeless women, children, and AIDS. It does not appear that there were any attempts by the president to "rein in" the first lady, but rather a concern on Mrs. Bush's part that she was publicly disagreeing with the president. Perez told reporters that Mrs. Bush was not the president of the United States: "She [Mrs. Bush] says that her opinion is not the one that people should be focusing on." United Press International White House correspondent Helen Thomas asked Perez, "What if we think her opinions are important?" Perez responded, "Shame on you!" Thomas shot back, "Shame on me for saying the first lady has a right to an opinion?"[22]

The first lady made especially effective use of the press while traveling. Mrs. Bush was aware that she could not always get media coverage when she was in Washington, but when she was away from the capital, the regional and local press was plentiful, and she was able to circulate her message supporting literacy or another cause. The press was always invited to travel with the first lady. Her office scheduled pre-trip briefings, and time was arranged for "press availabilities." Mrs. Bush would take questions about any topic but retained the right to refuse to answer any question that she deemed inappropriate. She understood that the press needed access to be able to report on her activities and occasionally went out of her way to ensure coverage. A reporter commented, "I wound up being the one-person pool on many of the occasions when only one reporter was allowed—in fact, I went undercover sometimes as a staff member when the host government didn't want any press. They didn't know who I was, and it was a collusion thing because Mrs. Bush was determined to allow the American press to know what she was doing."[23]

Mrs. Bush told an interviewer that her press relations were excellent. She believed this happened because she was not dealing with any controversial issues.[24] At the same time, she was cautious. In her memoirs she wrote that besides not putting on a hat or helmet for the cameras, "one of the first lessons someone in public life must learn is: THE PRESS HAS THE LAST WORD."[25] Deputy press secretary Jean Becker agreed with Mrs. Bush's assessment of her press relations and could recall only two times when things became rocky, both times over minor issues: "One Thanksgiving, Helen Thomas of United Press International wanted the menu that was going to be served to the Bush family at Camp David. We couldn't get it and Helen screamed at us!" The second instance concerned Doro Bush Leblond's second marriage, to Bobby Koch, at Camp David. The press wanted to cover the wedding, but Doro felt it was a private family celebration and media would not be included. Reporters were unhappy, but Doro was married privately as she wished.[26]

Mrs. Bush could, however, use the press when she thought the circumstances demanded coverage. During her first Christmas in the White House, the first lady learned that some upscale shopping malls in Washington had banned the Salvation Army from soliciting funds. Mrs. Bush wrote, "Who can think of Christmas without the Salvation Army bell ringers? So we let the press know that I was going shopping at the Mazza Gallerie because they permitted the Army to stand outside with their pots and bells." With a press pool and television cameras filming, the first lady dropped a contribution in the pot. The offending malls were chastened by the first lady and immediately welcomed back the army. According to Mrs. Bush, "We later heard from the Salvation Army that that small gesture truly filled their coffers."[27]

Reporters covering Mrs. Bush had a different view of her press relations. In the early months of the administration, they were aggravated with Mrs. Bush because the new first lady's press operation was not a well-oiled machine. They also complained because of a limited flow of information. In an effort to further distance herself from her predecessor, Mrs. Reagan, Mrs. Bush decided that she wanted to simplify things and dispensed with an advance team that was making preparations for her upcoming trip to the Far East. The chaos that followed made the first lady reevaluate her initial decision.

Mrs. Bush never developed trust in the media. Reflecting years later in her *Memoir,* Mrs. Bush took a shot at the press and accuracy when she wrote, "When reading a newspaper, you should suspect it's a rumor if it reads something like this, 'A source close to the president, who spoke off the record, said."[28] Mrs. Bush also told an interviewer that she was distressed that so much research was done on the Internet. She found the Internet to be severely lacking in accuracy and credibility.[29]

The demand for first lady discourse increased greatly during the latter part of the twentieth century because of changes in media coverage and a greater interest in the spouse of the president. Lou Hoover became the first first lady to give formal speeches in 1929. Eleanor Roosevelt gave more than 1,400 speeches during her White House tenure from 1933 to 1945, the greatest number in the history of the institution. After Mrs. Roosevelt left the White House, her successors Bess Truman and Mamie Eisenhower avoided the podium. Jacqueline Kennedy, who arrived at the White House in January 1961, understood the value of television but gave no formal speeches. Lady Bird Johnson, possibly because she was a good politician and a former college journalism major, revived the practice.

Since 1963, every first lady has given formal speeches, and every first lady has had a speechwriter or speechwriting staff.

During her eight years as the wife of the vice president Second Lady Barbara Bush gave 265 formal speeches.[30] From 20 January 1989, through 20 January 1993, Mrs. Bush gave 449 speeches, a substantial body of discourse.[31] When she was first lady, 38 percent of Mrs. Bush's speeches were ceremonial, 34 percent were political, 11 percent were devoted to literacy, 7 percent were related to education, 5 percent were delivered at college or university commencements or convocations, 2 percent discussed volunteerism, and 2 percent were devoted to the Persian Gulf War.

Public speaking had not come naturally or easily to Barbara Bush in her early years in public life.[32] When the Bushes moved to Washington in 1967 after George Bush's election to Congress, Barbara met Janet Steiger, a fellow congressional wife. Steiger used slide shows when she addressed constituents and extolled their virtues to Barbara. Having props to concentrate on helped to reduce nervousness, and Barbara became a devotee of this form of presentation. According to Mrs. Steiger, Barbara "perfected it [the slide show] to the extent that she had a series of shows, one on the gardens of Washington, another on the buildings and so on."[33] Mrs. Bush worked diligently to refine her oral communication skills. Later she developed a presentation based on her experiences in China. A former staff member recalled that Mrs. Bush's knees would knock, but she persisted, working hard on the substance and delivery of her comments.[34] By the time George Bush announced his candidacy for the presidency in 1980, Barbara Bush was an able public speaker. She had delivered scores of speeches to diverse audiences.

When she was first lady, Mrs. Bush's principal speechwriter was Susan Green, who composed most of her speeches about literacy. According to Mrs. Bush, Susan wrote lugubrious speeches, and she had to be pointed up sometimes because her speeches could verge on melancholy. Mrs. Bush said, "Dear Susan Green, she cared so much."[35] Other speechwriters included Anna Perez, who primarily wrote political speeches, Susan Porter Rose, and Jean Becker. Occasionally an outside speechwriter or one of President Bush's speechwriters would contribute ideas and prose. Clark S. Judge, a former speechwriter and special assistant to Vice President George Bush and President Ronald Reagan, wrote drafts of Mrs. Bush's speech to the 1992 Republican National Convention. Edward McNally, one of George Bush's speechwriters, contributed to the first lady's controversial speech at Wellesley College. C. Landon Parvin, a former speechwriter for President Ronald Reagan and a freelancer for the Bushes, wrote a draft of Mrs. Bush's 1992 commencement address at Pepperdine University. Parvin later wrote daughter-in-law Laura Bush's successful speech for the 2005 White House Correspondents' Dinner. During her comments, Laura Bush likened her mother-in-law to Don Corleone of *The Godfather.* She also poked fun at her in-laws by describing time at their Kennebunkport, Maine, home: "First prize, three days vacation with the Bush family. Second prize, ten days."[36] Though her comments were fully scripted like her mother-in-law's, Laura Bush was a hit in part at the expense of the former first lady.

Mrs. Bush told her speechwriters that she wanted her talks to be short and funny and to leave her listeners with something to remember. The writers relied on "Orben's Current Comedy" (Robert Orben had been a speechwriter for President Gerald Ford) and "Apple Seeds," newsletters that contained humorous material and thoughts for speeches. They occasionally borrowed ideas from the "Laughter, the Best Medicine" and "Towards More Picturesque Speech" columns of *Reader's Digest.* Although these sources did not have a great deal of intellectual firepower, she quoted from a diverse collection of people, including John F. Kennedy, Winston Churchill, writer Eudora Welty, historians Daniel Boorstin and Barbara Tuchman, and ballplayer Yogi Berra.[37]

Mrs. Bush was not afraid to make fun of herself and used self-deprecating humor frequently. Blessed with perfect comedic timing, the first lady was able to use a pause, silence, or a look to set off a prescripted punch line.[38] Speaking to a 1990 fund-raiser for John McKernan, who was running for governor of Maine, Mrs. Bush apologized for her husband's absence: "But I was delighted when George asked me to fill in tonight—I'm afraid for some of you it's like expecting to see Madonna and getting Roseanne Barr instead."[39] In 1991, the first lady addressed a mammography conference reception and referred to a recent sledding accident in which she had broken her leg. She said, "Incidentally, I'm glad to be here. You know the business about my going sledding with my grandchildren? A coverup—I was really getting ready for the next Winter Olympics."[40] During a speech to the American Magazine Conference, Mrs. Bush mentioned her brother Jim was a consultant for *Sport and Field Magazine:* "I might add one of the few magazines in America that hasn't called asking questions about my dog Millie, my hair, my weight, or my clothes."[41]

Mrs. Bush was skilled at integrating anecdotes into her speeches. She used stories to relax her listeners and draw them in to her message. Her conversational style made it seem that she was having a private talk with listeners. Speaking at the commencement ceremony at St. Louis University, Mrs. Bush said that recently she had shared a podium with comedian Bill Cosby. She recalled, "Bill talks about when his oldest daughter went to college, the tuition bill had already reached thirteen thousand dollars. He looked hard at the bill and then looking hard at his daughter said, 'Thirteen thousand dollars! Will you be the only student?'"[42] Another anecdote that found its way into her speeches concerned reading and Thomas Jefferson and his books: "Jefferson['s] personal library became the core collection for the Library of Congress. Whether he donated them, or, as another story goes, he sold them because of financial need, Jefferson did say, on the day his library was packed up, 'I cannot live without my books.'"[43]

Mrs. Bush used "jab-in-the-ribs" anecdotes and humor frequently. Receiving the Harry S. Truman Award from the American Association of Community and Junior Colleges, Mrs. Bush said, "The fact that this is the Harry S. Truman Award and I am Mrs. George Bush confirms what I've known all along: education is the most non-partisan of causes, and we are united in our concern for providing the best possible education to all Americans. Either that or Harry S. Truman was a Republican . . . and all of you too. Just wishful thinking."[44]

The White House speechwriting process began when Mrs. Bush offered certain thoughts, ideas, and ways to frame topics to be addressed in her speeches. One writer, or a group of writers, would prepare a draft of the first lady's remarks and give it to her for markup. Mrs. Bush's additions and deletions would be incorporated into a second draft, and the speech would be marked up again, until

Mrs. Bush was satisfied with the finished product. A speech might go through three or four drafts. Mrs. Bush commented that Green, Perez, and Becker knew her well and were able to write in her voice, particularly Becker. Mrs. Bush said that she did not make changes to her speeches once she reached the podium because if she did not have every word written out, "I'm apt to enlarge and talk and talk and talk."[45] However, materials in the Bush Library present a contrary picture. Some of Mrs. Bush's speeches contain handwritten notations about topical events, people, and ideas. Of particular note are her 1992 campaign speeches, which contained penciled-in emendations and additions. Although she denied it, Mrs. Bush was a good extemporaneous speaker, capable of setting aside her prepared comments and working from brief notes or a keyword outline.[46]

It is both interesting and enlightening to note the differences that existed between the president and first lady's speechwriting operations. Perhaps the most critical difference was that Barbara Bush enjoyed giving speeches whereas the president did not. According to John Podhoretz, who worked in the White House, President Bush hated giving speeches: "He usually got bored in the middle, even if it was only two pages long."[47] Charles Kolb, another White House staffer, commented that President Bush "saw little need to explain much of anything. His public remarks lacked content, depth, inspiration, and frequently, even elementary grammar. Bush abhorred soaring rhetoric and emotional speeches."[48] Marlin Fitzwater, Bush's press secretary, recommended that the president make policy statements in press conferences and informal interviews rather than give speeches.[49] Intuitively, Mrs. Bush knew that she could use the podium to educate, explain, appeal to people's pride or patriotism. Her speeches, almost dialogues, were peppered with topical references, humor, and personal touches that made the audience feel that she was speaking to each listener.

Most of Mrs. Bush's speeches were written for specific occasions, but there were four series of speeches that utilized a generic text that could be adapted for certain audiences. These included commencement addresses and the speeches that Mrs. Bush gave during the 1990 midterm elections, the 1991 Persian Gulf War, and the 1992 presidential election. The former first lady attested to this when she indicated that some speeches were "stock" in that the basic ideas stayed the same from speech to speech.[50] A good example of this practice is commencement speeches. Every year that Barbara Bush was in the White House, her staff helped her to prepare a generic commencement speech that could be adapted to virtually any academic audience. The names of those to be thanked changed, as did certain regional references, but essentially, the speech stayed the same.

Her 1989 speeches suggest that Mrs. Bush was familiarizing herself with her new position. Almost half of her speeches that year were ceremonial in nature. She spoke to the Congressional Club, the March of Dimes, the United Way, and the Kennebunkport River Club Centennial Celebration, among other organizations. There were also speeches to literacy organizations, the dedication of the George H. W. Bush Elementary School in Midland, Texas, and an education summit. Every year that Mrs. Bush was first lady, she spoke to many audiences about literacy.

Mrs. Bush's highly visible speech making continued, with her best speech in 1989 given when she received an honorary degree from Smith College, her alma mater, which she left to marry George Bush. She told her audience, "I want to be absolutely honest with you. This is not my first honorary degree, but it is the one I value *most* of all. How I wish my Dad were alive and here with me. He'd be so pleased and delighted—and utterly astonished." Mrs. Bush recounted some of her adventures and offered her philosophy of life: "I guess if I had to distill all of this down, I would say that these are the things life so far has taught me: Attitude is ninety per cent of reality, and attitude is a choice—choose a good attitude. Like what you do. Serve others, you will always get back more than you give. Laugh early and often, *at* yourself and with others."[51]

Her 1990 speeches were a mix of ceremonial, commencement, and political discourse. The first lady began the year by presenting her inaugural gown to the Smithsonian Institution. Other speeches during the year included comments at National Nurses Day, the Alzheimer's Disease Public Policy Forum, the National Endowment for the Humanities Teacher-Scholar Program, and the National Alliance to End Homelessness. One of Mrs. Bush's favorite speeches in 1990 was given at the New York Public Library's "A Decade of Literary Lions" dinner, which recognized outstanding writers. Celebrating the achievements of authors, she told listeners, "Well, Henry

Kissinger, Toni Morrison, Annie Dillard, Arthur Schlesinger and all the rest of you great authors—oh my gosh, it just occurred to me—you wanted Millie! I am sorry, but look at it this way, Millie is just a literary dog, not a lion." She continued to praise the authors and the library's role in encouraging reading.[52]

The midterm elections took place in November 1990. Rosalynn Carter had been the first first lady to campaign by herself during the midterm elections of 1978. Mrs. Bush continued the tradition by campaigning for her party's congressional and gubernatorial candidates. She was a much-sought-after speaker because of her popularity and her ability to advocate for Republican candidates and positions without being seen as extreme in her views. Her travels took her across the country as she spoke on behalf of thirty-three different office seekers. Dick Waterfield, running for Congress in Texas, John McKernan, running for governor in Maine, Ally Milder, running for Congress in Nebraska, and George Voinovich, running for governor in Ohio, were among the group of candidates receiving Mrs. Bush's endorsement. She shared with her listeners her experiences on the road. Since Labor Day, said the first lady, she had been in twenty-one cities and fourteen states: "In the process, I've learned to hula in Honolulu, pledged to read to the Girl Scouts in Miami, opened the Metropolitan Opera Season in New York City and threw out the opening pitch at the second game of the World Series. Actually, I've been on the road so much, when I finally do get home, I half expect the White House guards to bar the gates until I show them my I.D."[53]

After extolling the virtues of the candidates, Mrs. Bush would tell audiences that they were really needed in Washington or their state capitals. During her speech in support of Ally Milder, Mrs. Bush said, "I really am delighted to be here today to campaign for Ally but I want to be honest with you—I'm also here because George Bush asked me to come. George really needs Ally in Congress to fight for programs like the line-item veto, and the balanced budget amendment."[54] Mrs. Bush provided the same rationale for voting for Gary Franks, an African American running for Congress in Connecticut. She reminded listeners that Franks's opponent, Toby Moffett, "is a member in good standing of the same group that has stalled the balanced budget amendment, and has stalled George's tough Anti-Crime Bill." Gary

Franks, said Mrs. Bush, would represent the interests of the voters, "Not the special interests first." She concluded her remarks by telling listeners that Franks was "one of the finest candidates George and I have ever seen."[55]

One of Mrs. Bush's most effective speeches was given in support of Pete Wilson, who was running for governor of California. She said, "Have you ever noticed in California just how the state prospers with a Republican Governor and falls back with the Democrats?" Pete Wilson would be an able governor, said Mrs. Bush, and what he had accomplished as the mayor of San Diego was impressive: "I love what they [Democrats] say about Pete, and none too kindly. He's a resume candidate, no charisma, no fire, just a series of jobs well done—sound familiar? Yes, the pundits said all these things about—George Bush." The president's wisdom and calm had guided the country, she said, and Wilson would bring the same qualities to the office of the governor.[56] Most of the candidates that she campaigned for lost their contests, but Gary Franks was elected to Congress, and Pete Wilson was elected governor of California. Even if she experienced mixed results, Mrs. Bush was effective at rallying the troops, raising money, and providing "feel-good" moments for Republicans. Her actions also contributed to her image as someone who was willing to serve the president by traveling to any state where she could help members of her party. There were moments when Mrs. Bush became discouraged, and she lashed out—but most of her negative thoughts were written in her diary. On 24 October 1990, two weeks prior to the midterm elections, she was distressed that budget talks had come to an abrupt halt, President Bush had felt the necessity to veto the civil rights bill, and Republicans were "running, not walking away from George." The first lady wrote, "I am having to work on myself not to be bitter about those members of Congress who are acting gutless, and there are so many on both sides of the aisle. I also have to remember that he [the president] will have to work with them all again."[57]

When the election results were tallied, ten of the candidates Mrs. Bush had campaigned for won their elections, and twenty-three lost. The first lady labeled the election "something of a downer" and bemoaned her poor track record. Fiercely competitive, she was disappointed when candidates that she had campaigned for lost at the polls. Still, she extracted some positives from the defeats, writing that, historically, the party that holds the White House loses seats in Congress and the Senate during the midterm elections. Her final assessment was, "It was not the wipeout that we kept reading and hearing about."[58]

Mrs. Bush's speeches in 1991 had a more somber tone as the Persian Gulf War dominated the first months of the new year. Mrs. Bush spoke to military families waiting nervously for news of their loved ones; she appeared at rallies when the troops returned; she and the president met privately with the survivors of those killed during the war.

The ceremonial speaking requirements of her job never diminished, and Mrs. Bush addressed the Los Angeles Junior Achievement Luncheon, the National School Boards Association, the American Red Cross Conference on Volunteerism, and the Brooklyn, New York, Bureau of Community Service. Having enjoyed some success campaigning for candidates the previous year, Mrs. Bush took to the hustings once again and offered testimonials in support of Richard Thornburgh, running for the U.S. Senate in Pennsylvania, and Steve Pierce, running for Congress in Massachusetts. Speaking to the Pennsylvania Republican Party, Mrs. Bush noted, "In the last two and a half years, I've campaigned for some of the brightest, the most articulate and the most qualified men and women in America. Thirty-five candidates in 30 cities and I loved every minute!"[59] Apparently Mrs. Bush's enthusiasm and support did little for Thornburgh and Pierce, who were defeated.

The year 1992 was pivotal for the Bushes as the president was seeking reelection. The first lady's efforts on behalf of the president and other candidates boosted her total of speeches for the year to 193, more than double the previous year's total. Even though a third of her presentations were political in nature, Mrs. Bush continued speaking on behalf of various causes and concerns. She gave speeches about literacy, addressed the Leukemia Society of America, National Girls and Women in Sports, Girl Scouts Care for the Earth, and Champions of Safe Kids.

Perhaps Mrs. Bush's greatest rhetorical challenge—and her shining moment during her White House tenure—occurred on 1 June 1990, when she gave the commencement address to the graduating class of Wellesley College. In December 1989, Mrs. Bush received an invitation to serve as the 1990 commencement speaker at Wellesley College. Nannerl Keohane, the college's president, wrote to Mrs. Bush, "Your dedication to volunteerism strikes a resonant chord here at Wellesley, where we encourage students to begin a lifelong commitment to public and community service. Your work in furthering literacy also sets an example for young women who have benefitted from the best that higher education can offer."[60] President Keohane requested that Mrs. Bush share with the graduates any advice she thought would serve them well in the future. Keohane did not mention that the class's first choice, the African American novelist Alice Walker, had declined the invitation to address the class.

Mrs. Bush received approximately 100 invitations annually to address college and university graduating classes and was able to accept only a handful, but she tried to speak at colleges, universities, and high schools that represented a cross section of small and large academic institutions and geographic regions.[61] In 1990, the first lady accepted invitations to appear at Southwest Community College, in Cumberland, Kentucky; St. Louis University, in St. Louis, Missouri; the University of Pennsylvania, in Philadelphia; Kennebunkport High School, in her home-away-from-home of Kennebunkport, Maine; Dunbar High School, in Washington, D.C.; and Wellesley College, in Wellesley, Massachusetts. There is no indication that she ever envisioned the controversy that would develop as a result of her invitation to speak at Wellesley.[62]

Shortly after it was announced that she would be the commencement speaker, 150 of 600 graduating Wellesley seniors presented Dr. Keohane with a petition protesting the invitation to the first lady. The petition read in part: "To honor Barbara Bush as commencement speaker is to honor a woman who has gained recognition through her husband, which contradicts what we have been taught over the last four years at Wellesley."[63] Peggy Reid, a senior and one of the authors of the petition, wrote that the protesters meant no disrespect of Mrs. Bush: "Barbara Bush was selected because of her *husband's* accomplishments and notoriety, not those of her own. So, it is not the validity of her choices in life that we are calling into question but rather the fact that we are honoring, not Barbara Bush, but Mrs. George Bush."[64] Reid's rationale was lost in

a storm of controversy. The petition started an intense public debate that brought headlines and articles from around the country.
Many newspapers published stories supportive of Mrs. Bush. The
Atlanta Journal-Constitution carried a story titled "Wellesley Women
a Bunch of Snobs"; a *Boston Globe* story urged "Hey Wellesley,
Lighten Up on Mrs. Bush"; and the *Los Angeles Times* noted, "No
Welcome Mat for First Lady." In spite of editorial support, rumors
abounded that some seniors would boycott Mrs. Bush's talk and
leave the graduation exercises early.

Some of the seniors objected to Mrs. Bush because she was a
symbol of a Republican Party that had done little to support
women's concerns; others said that Mrs. Bush was emblematic of
wealthy white families and did not represent single-parent or extended families. One senior said, "Why wasn't my mother asked to
speak? She stayed at home and raised kids. Mrs. Bush is famous because she is married to George Bush. We wanted to hear from a
woman who had made many gains on her own." Other seniors were
embarrassed by the petition, noting that Mrs. Bush had been the
second choice of a majority of the class to serve as commencement
speaker. "I think it's disrespectful, the message that Mrs. Bush got
from students. It's unfair to expect every woman to have a career.
What's wrong with putting family first?" asked a member of the
class of 1990.[65] An alumna wrote to the seniors, offering a reality
check: "If you think a woman who can successfully raise five children while following an ambitious husband is not a woman of
achievement, then you haven't a clue as to how the real world
works. . . . Grow up!"[66]

Mrs. Bush reacted with outward calm and graciousness, and can-
celing her appearance was never seriously considered. Her patroniz-
ing comments, however ("Much ado about nothing. I understand it.
Even I was twenty once"),[67] and the suggestion that those who objected to her speech were "looking at life from a [twenty-one-year-
old] perspective"[68] may have disguised irritation. In the years since the
Wellesley speech, Mrs. Bush has admitted on a number of occasions
that she found the Wellesley seniors' response disheartening, and she
commented, "I have to remind myself that THEY invited me."[69]

In planning her generic 1990 commencement address, Mrs. Bush
and her staff decided that the first lady would focus on three themes:

"get involved in something larger than yourself; remember to get joy out of life; cherish human relationships." These ideas were at the heart of Mrs. Bush's commencement speeches to the graduating classes of the University of Pennsylvania on 14 May, St. Louis University on 19 May, and Kennebunk High School in Maine on 11 June, respectively. The three speeches had almost identical conclusions: "And who knows? Somewhere out in this audience today may even be a future president of the United States. I wish her well!"[70]

As the controversy at Wellesley raged, the first lady told her staff that she did not want to make a special speech catering to Wellesley. She gave no reason for her decision beyond writing, "I also did not want to complain, explain or apologize in any way."[71] The generic commencement text would be used with some changes and specific adaptations to the situation. The speech would dispense advice to the graduates; above all else, it would not be controversial.

At a White House news conference, President Bush commented on the opposition to his wife and told reporters that the young women of Wellesley "have a lot to learn from Barbara Bush and her unselfishness, and her advocacy of literacy and of being a good mother and a lot of other things." Perhaps most important, noted the president, was that Barbara Bush was "not trying to be something she's not. The American people love her because she . . . stands for something."[72]

Support for Mrs. Bush came from disparate quarters, including columnist Ellen Goodman, Senator Barbara Mikulski (D-MD), former president Richard M. Nixon, and a number of Wellesley alumnae who lined up behind the first lady. Humorist and columnist Erma Bombeck wrote a more serious piece when she advised dissenting Wellesley seniors to focus on the woman who had raised five children and still kept a sense of self as she and her husband led an international, whirlwind life. Bombeck wrote, "If the Wellesley students . . . can't imagine what Barbara Bush could contribute to their education, imagine your own mothers. To deny them a voice is to suggest they have not achieved anything of any importance. They gave you a voice and a seat at the commencement. How important is that?"[73] A Wellesley graduate of the class of 1989 wrote, "In my four years at Wellesley, I can never recall a time when a woman who was 'just' a wife and mother was seriously considered as a candidate for commencement speaker. And worst of all, I can never remember anyone seeing anything wrong with that."[74] Columnist Elizabeth Drew, also a graduate of Wellesley, wrote, "It is as intolerant to say that a woman must have a career to amount to something as it used to be to deny jobs to women they could handle perfectly well."[75]

Two weeks prior to the graduation, the controversy bubbled over on Public Television's *MacNeil/Lehrer NewsHour.* Wellesley president Nan Keohane, Wellesley senior Chris Bicknall, who had not signed the petition but was close to the protesters, and other guests debated the first lady's selection as commencement speaker. Bicknall sought to demonstrate that the Wellesley students had not been cranky or nasty in voicing their opposition to the first lady's selection as commencement speaker. Instead, they argued that they had philosophical reservations about Mrs. Bush's appearance based on what they had been taught over the past four years. Bicknall summed up the protesters' objections when she told host Judy Woodruff, "There is no doubt that Mrs. Bush has been a wonderful mother, and [has been involved in] advocacy and literacy and important volunteer work, but as women who have been challenged to look down [on] traditional roles, it is not surprising the members of my class wanted to hear from someone from the other side."[76] Accordingly, feminist Gloria Steinem or author bell hooks might have been more appropriate choices, said Bicknall. She also stated that the debate was not a negative for Wellesley; in fact, it had prompted an extended conversation about feminism. This, said Bicknall, was the focus of the protesters, not the speaker herself. President Keohane explained that the 150 seniors who met with her were saying "that among the many thousands of women who might be excellent role models as volunteers or mothers, she [Mrs. Bush] had been chosen by their classmates because she was the wife of the President and that is the difficulty they had."[77] Later in the discussion, Bicknall expressed concern that Mrs. Bush had not used her bully pulpit to discuss abortion, motherhood, or child care. The protesters' viewpoint came across as well reasoned and logical, even if it was not popular in the press or embraced by all of the 600 Wellesley seniors.

At the same time that points of view were being aired on the *MacNeil/Lehrer NewsHour,* Mrs. Bush announced that she would be accompanied to Wellesley by Russia's first lady, Raisa Gorbachev, who would be visiting Washington with her husband during the first week of June. Mrs. Gorbachev would also have some comments for the graduation audience. The move prompted one Wellesley senior to tell a reporter that she was looking forward to Mrs. Gorbachev's remarks: "I'm really excited . . . she might have something more interesting to say."[78] Bringing Mrs. Gorbachev along deflected some of the criticism leveled at Mrs. Bush and proved to be an excellent public relations move. The previous year, President Bush had invited French president François Mitterand to join him at Boston University, where the U.S. president was giving the commencement speech. That tandem had garnered positive press comments, and the combination of Mrs. Bush and Mrs. Gorbachev at Wellesley also promised to be successful. The invitation to Mrs. Gorbachev also served another purpose. Nancy Reagan had had a well-publicized icy relationship with the Russian first lady and on one occasion had been heard to mutter, "Who does that dame think she is?"[79] Mrs. Bush had known Raisa Gorbachev prior to coming to the White House, and the two women enjoyed a warm, respectful relationship; the striking difference was yet another reminder that Barbara Bush was not Nancy Reagan. A reporter who observed Mrs. Gorbachev commented, "Gone was the woman who once . . . practiced the art of conversation as lecture, peppering the people she met with a mixture of facts and dogma. Today, instead of simply talking, she conversed."[80] Commencement day dawned sunny and warm. Mrs. Bush reviewed her speech one more time on the plane to Massachusetts. She was encouraged by the people who lined the streets of Boston, waving and cheering as she and Mrs. Gorbachev made their way to Wellesley. At the college, Mrs. Bush looked out at more than 5,000 people who had crowded into the large white tent that had been erected for the graduation exercises.

Using an earnest tone, she began her address with comments about diversity at Wellesley. Then, with a mischievous grin, she referred to the controversy surrounding her commencement speech: "I know that you wanted [author] Alice Walker, known for *The Color Purple*—guess how I know? Instead, you got me, known for the color of my hair." The audience began to warm to the first lady.

Heartened by the positive response, Mrs. Bush built momentum as she outlined the three themes that had formed the basis of her talks at the University of Pennsylvania and St. Louis University. She was at her best when she included personal examples: "Life must have joy. It's supposed to be fun. The reason I made the most important decision in my life—to marry George Bush—was because he made me laugh. It's true, sometimes we've laughed through our tears, but that shared laughter has been one of our strongest bonds." Later, drawing on a popular movie of the day, *Ferris Bueller's Day Off,* she continued, "Find the joy in life, because as Ferris Bueller said on his day off. . . . 'Life moves pretty fast. Ya don't stop and look around once in a while, ya gonna miss it.'"

Stressing a favorite theme, the responsibility of parents and the importance of family, Mrs. Bush told the graduates that if they had children, those children had to come first. She said, "Your success as a family, our success as a society, depends not on what happens at the White House, but what happens inside your house."

Concluding her speech, Mrs. Bush declared that the controversy at Wellesley was over. She put a new twist into the line that she had used previously with excellent results: "And who knows? Somewhere out in this audience may even be someone who will one day follow in my footsteps, and preside over the White House as the President's spouse. And I wish him well!"[81]

The audience was both surprised and delighted. Much of the press expressed admiration for Mrs. Bush. NBC anchor Tom Brokaw proclaimed that the speech was one of the best commencement addresses he had ever heard. One reporter wrote, "If Barbara Bush triggered a storm of controversy on her way to the commencement podium at Wellesley College, she walked away Friday to a chorus of cheers."[82] Laughter and enthusiastic applause repeatedly interrupted the speech. Mrs. Bush rose to the challenge rhetorically and won over much of her audience. While some Wellesley students remained steadfast in their opposition, others signed a new petition commending the selection of Barbara Bush as commencement speaker and celebrated "all the unknown women who have dedicated their lives to the service of others."[83]

A few writers were dissatisfied with the speech. One *Boston Herald* reporter felt that Mrs. Bush's speech was all style and no substance. She wrote that the first lady was gracious, charming, and funny, but that was not enough: "As America's most popular symbol of family life and service to others, she might have stepped out from behind her husband's shadow and taken a position on one—any one—of the controversial issues facing women and children in America today."[84] Another columnist opined, "If Barbara Bush has her own opinions on serious public subjects—and everyone suspects she does—she is not independent enough to express them."[85]

Public opinion also supported the first lady. An analysis of White House telephone calls and messages on the day of the speech indicated that of 105 calls received, 103 were positive and just 2 were negative. A sampling of reactions included "Top notch speech"; "We need more encouragement and Mrs. Bush can give us what we need"; "Her speech brought tears to my eyes"; "I have very liberal views and I'm a Democrat, but she transcends politics"; "How generous to have shared Wellesley with Mrs. Gorbachev." One of Mrs. Bush's critics took issue with her message and told the White House that she was forty-six years old and unmarried: "I chose to be single. I don't like marriage being pushed by Mrs. Bush and others. Republican administrations seem to be pushing marriage."[86]

Mrs. Bush's speech falls into the opportunity-missed category. While it is difficult to fault the first lady for her commonsense message, she had the chance to respond to her Wellesley critics by speaking to them about what she had accomplished as a volunteer and advocate for causes. She might have told them that she deserved to be their commencement speaker because hers had been an active life, a life well lived. She might have also spoken out about some of the issues of the day. She chose not to do any of these things; rather, she wanted the audience to like her, to believe that she was above the fray. The recycled speech, while entertaining, would have resonated with more of her audience if it had been written specifically for Wellesley and if she had addressed any of the protesters' arguments. Instead, she chose style above substance and relied on her celebrity and perception as the ultimate good sport, a recurring Bush theme. Mrs. Bush must have been satisfied with her speech; she used much of the text in commencement addresses over the next few years.[87] Mrs. Bush said that Wellesley had not caused her any great discomfort.[88] She did not hold a grudge against the students for the petition or some of the statements that were made prior to her speech. She said that she understood the students' concerns. After the speech,

Mrs. Bush and her staff wrote scores of letters to Wellesley alumnae asking them not to stop giving to their alma mater. She said, "I love the school and we wrote a lot of letters to disgruntled alumni saying don't stop giving to Wellesley, keep giving to Wellesley, it's a fine school."[89]

If she missed an opportunity to write a speech specifically for Wellesley or to speak to the issues of the day, Mrs. Bush deserves admiration for her willingness to deliver the commencement address when her appearance sparked heated debate and criticism. As a final postscript to Wellesley, Barbara Bush's commencement address has become one of the most anthologized of first lady speeches and has been part of numerous collections of outstanding discourse of the twentieth century.

Faced with a situation similar to that at Wellesley, Barbara Bush's daughter-in-law Laura Bush turned down an invitation to speak at commencement exercises for the Graduate School of Education and Information Sciences at UCLA in June 2002. When it was announced that an invitation to speak at the commencement ceremonies had been extended to Mrs. Bush, both students and faculty protested her selection. There was a familiar ring to their complaints: the younger Mrs. Bush had a thin résumé; she had no merit and had been suggested as a speaker only because of her political celebrity. Unlike her mother-in-law, who chose to tough out the controversy and argue that she had thoughts and experience worthy of consideration, Laura Bush told UCLA that she would have to decline its invitation because of prior engagements.[90]

Barbara Bush was an active but cautious public communicator. Like a number of her predecessors, she was aware that every speech, news story, literacy event, and ceremonial event made her more familiar to the public. Her strategy was to project that she was "not Nancy," and a well-produced and well-received tour of the White House family quarters showed the country that she was warm and likable.

She developed into a solid speaker who was adept at analyzing her audience. Her more than 100 formal speeches per year were funny and thoughtful. The remarks prepared by her speechwriters were improved by the first lady's participation in tailoring them to fit the needs of a particular speaking situation and Barbara Bush's personal style. Though she could be caustic in private, the public saw only a graceful, irreverent, and occasionally serious Barbara Bush. That she spoke continuously about literacy strongly linked Mrs. Bush with her White House project. After comments about gun control early in the Bush administration, she did not discuss controversial topics.

Mrs. Bush was also adept at dealing with the press. She was usually good copy, and she and press secretary Anna Perez tried to get reporters what they needed. If she had to refuse a request or a question, she tried to provide other information. Her insistence on accuracy helped the first lady to step over the quagmires that had plagued some of her predecessors.

Though she may not have liked the fourth estate, she knew that the media would write about her appearances and concerns. Her post–White House statements suggest that she was frustrated by the press at times, yet she hid her irritation well.

Barbara Bush's positive image, even if slightly tarnished by the campaign of 1992, remained intact, and she enjoyed great popularity while in the White House. In the years that followed her return to private life, Mrs. Bush continued to rank high on Gallup's Most Admired Woman poll, no doubt keeping her name before the public with the publication of two books, *Barbara Bush: A Memoir* (1994) and *Reflections: Life after the White House* (2003). Barbara Bush carefully constructed and maintained a positive image. She grasped the fact that public communication efforts would project her concerns; she understood her public and what would resonate with millions of Americans. As a communicator, Barbara Bush was a success.

CHAPTER 3

"IF YOU COULDN'T BE HAPPY IN THE WHITE HOUSE, YOU COULDN'T BE HAPPY ANYWHERE"

Liz Carpenter, who served as press secretary and staff director to Lady Bird Johnson, recalled that when Lyndon Johnson was growing up, his father would wake him early and admonish him to start his day because "every boy in town is out of bed and has had an hour start on you."[1] That, wrote Carpenter, accounted for the frenetic pace at which Lyndon Johnson lived and ran his White House. George Bush, like his fellow Texan, functioned at hyperspeed, and his White House, twenty years later, reflected the same frenetic energy.

Though her pace was not as rapid as her husband's, Barbara Bush's days in the White House were fast-paced and crammed with activity. They usually began at 6:00 AM when she got up to let Millie out or take her for a walk. Sometimes she let the butlers take care of Millie and had coffee in bed with the president. The two would glance through five newspapers and share various stories. The president went to his office early. Later, Mrs. Bush would go to her own office in a small sitting room off the southwest corner of the White House where she would work for approximately three hours each day. In the spring, she moved to the beauty parlor on the northwest corner of the White House because it was cooler during the warm weather.[2] She decided not to maintain an office in the East Wing, the traditional first lady's office wing of the Executive Mansion, because space there was at a premium. In addition, she believed that the staff was happier if she stayed out of the way. She wrote, "Lucky for them, I couldn't even do a 'surprise' drop-by: Millie always preceded me by two minutes, announcing my arrival."[3]

The couple worked separately but spoke frequently on the telephone.[4] Mrs. Bush acknowledged that she had influence; her comments were reminiscent of Betty Ford, who also tended to plead her case with the president using "pillow talk," causes and concerns she brought to his attention before retiring for the night.[5] Mrs. Bush said, "I probably lobby him indirectly by telling him stories and things I've seen. He's very interested and very good about listening."[6] From time to time, Mrs. Bush commented on the president's speeches, underlining the parts she liked, and on one occasion she used her husband's ideas in her own speech. In a memo to her press secretary, the first lady wrote, "Why don't we say fathers are important in some speeches. We know they are—why not say so. Just as George says, 'every child deserves someone who knows their name' every child knows that it took two to have them."[7] After she had read the draft of the president's commencement speech to the University of Michigan (where she would also receive an honorary degree), Mrs. Bush wrote on it, "Anna—He has some very good quotes."[8]

Similar to many of her predecessors in the White House, Mrs. Bush loved having her husband nearby; working and living "over the store" offered them the chance to spend more time together. Mrs. Bush noted that if the president needed a break, he might call her and say, "Do you want to take a spin around the South Grounds?" At other times he might call and ask, " 'How about joining me for lunch?"[9]

Living up to her edict of "doing something every day," Barbara Bush was busy and involved in the White House. When materials currently closed to research are made available for study, and her appearances can be tallied, it is likely that she will be found to be among the most ceremonially active first ladies. Mrs. Bush's own tally of activities for the first 100 days of the Bush administration, 21 January through 30 April 1989, gives some sense of the "exhilarating whirlwind" that was her life in the White House. She wrote, "I hosted either alone or with George: eighteen receptions, sixteen dinners, twenty-four coffee or teas, nineteen luncheons and two breakfasts. I visited nine states and four countries, conducted twenty-four press interviews, and participated in forty-two doing and caring events and forty-one other types of events."[10]

In addition to the plethora of activities of the first hundred days, Mrs. Bush was staggered by the volume of mail she received. From January through March, she received 30,000 pieces. Most of the letters were positive, with some writers expressing opinions on various subjects and others asking for help. Mrs. Bush writes that over the years, her Correspondence Office referred 12,000 letters to government agencies that might help writers. On average, the first lady received about 100,000 letters per year.[11]

To deal with the myriad demands of her schedule and to aid in communicating her message to the American people, Mrs. Bush chose a first-rate staff. Extending a practice started by Lady Bird Johnson, Mrs. Bush's staff, which numbered fourteen, smaller than Nancy Reagan's, was broken down into offices for press, social, correspondence, scheduling, projects, and graphics.[12]

Susan Porter Rose was chosen to serve as deputy assistant to the president and chief of staff for Barbara Bush. A graduate of Earlham College, the forty-eight-year-old Porter Rose brought a distinguished résumé to her new position. She is the only woman in White House history to serve at the senior staff level for three first ladies.[13] In addition to serving Mrs. Bush, she was assistant director of correspondence for Pat Nixon and assistant director of correspondence and later appointments secretary for Betty Ford. Mrs. Bush and Porter Rose enjoyed a long and close working relationship. Porter Rose had previously served as chief of staff on the second lady's staff from 1981 to 1993. During the transition from the Reagan to the Bush administration, she was the executive manager for the Office of the First Lady. An efficient and capable manager, Porter Rose was familiar with the White House. She suggested to the new first lady that offices for scheduling and projects be added to the East Wing. The East Wing–West Wing tensions that had plagued earlier administrations were greatly reduced as a result of Porter Rose's management. She oversaw the operation of various offices while assisting in speechwriting and Mrs. Bush's literacy project.[14]

Some referred to her as Barbara Bush's Svengali, but Porter Rose saw one of her primary goals as protecting Mrs. Bush from the internecine politics of Washington and the press corps, playing "bad cop" to the first lady's "good cop." "I say 'no' because it's better for me to take the heat. . . . I try to keep her out of trouble," the chief of staff told the *Washington Post*. No major initiative or minute detail escaped Porter Rose's scrutiny. She said, "I plan, I hire, I coordinate, I smooth ruffled feathers, I schedule, I help keep a lot of balls in the air, I deal with the very big picture and sometimes I deal with the most minute detail."[15] Mrs. Bush commented that Porter Rose knew her way around the White House: "Susan has the most extraordinary sense of what is right and thinks things through with great care. I don't. Therefore, we made a great team for twelve years. Susan saved both George and me from many mistakes."[16] Porter Rose's vigilance kept Mrs. Bush popular and out of political quagmires for much of her term, a tribute to the chief of staff's attention to detail. Porter Rose told Mrs. Bush that she would need a press secretary when she went to the White House. Mrs. Bush wrote, "Obviously I had not yet realized how much had changed and that everything I said and thought would be news."[17] In an interview she amplified this thought when she said, "For eight years [as second lady] I could say what I wanted, no one paid any attention, but the minute George became president-elect, they were interested in everything I said."[18]

Anna Perez, who Mrs. Bush called "a gem," was the first African American named to serve as a first lady's press secretary. A graduate of Hunter College with a major in journalism, Perez began her career as assistant press secretary and communications director to Senator Slade Gorton (R-WA). Later, she served as press secretary to Congressman John R. Miller (R-WA). Mrs. Bush learned about Perez from Congressman Miller, who called and told her that he had the perfect person for the job. Mrs. Bush wrote that her new press secretary was "bright as a whip, tough, fair, fun to be with and has great judgment."[19] The selection of Perez also gave the first lady the chance to make a statement about her desire to expand opportunities for minorities. George Bush had always made it a point to hire African Americans, Latinos, and Asians for his office. Now his wife had her opportunity, and in Perez she had a savvy, seasoned veteran of media relations. A dynamic presence in the East Wing, Perez had a quick mind and a puckish sense of humor. In an interview after she left the White House, Perez quipped that she learned three things about her new boss from the start: "Don't mess with her man, her kids or her dogs."[20]

Deputy press secretary Jean Becker had worked as a reporter for *USA Today* for a decade and has served both the former president and the first lady as chief of staff since they left the White House. Susan Green, assistant director of projects, had worked at the Department of Education; she became Mrs. Bush's principal speechwriter. These two rounded out the core of Mrs. Bush's operation. Laurie Firestone, who had been Mrs. Bush's social secretary when she was second lady, served in the same capacity in the White House. Catherine Fenton, who had worked at the Commerce Department and spent a short time as Mrs. Bush's correspondence secretary, became Firestone's deputy. Later, Fenton would become Laura Bush's social secretary. These women, in addition to Julie Cooke, director of projects, Ann Brock, director of scheduling, and Joan DeCain, director of correspondence, completed Mrs. Bush's staff.

While she could be exacting and demanded as much current information on a subject as possible, Mrs. Bush was a good boss who commanded the allegiance of her staff members. Almost the entire staff served the first lady from Inauguration Day 1989 until President Bush left office in 1993, in sharp contrast to the turnovers for Nancy Reagan. Porter Rose, Perez, and Becker told an interviewer that they enjoyed working with the first lady.[21] Becker said that sometimes Mrs. Bush could be tough, but this was only because "she cares so darn much. You always know where you stand with her and I admire that. I love her directness. . . . All of her current and former staffs adore her."[22] Julie Cooke said that as a boss, Mrs. Bush made clear what was important to her: "She was not a micro-manager, but she wanted to be kept informed. We sent piles and piles of things to her every day, and it would all be returned the next day. She was tireless." Cooke continued, "She dealt very fairly with people, she was generous, and everyone on the staff greatly respected and loved her."[23]

An interesting contrast was offered by former United Press International chief White House correspondent Helen Thomas, who commented that during Mrs. Bush's White House years, "There was a feeling among many that she exhibited a touch of distance when dealing with her staff."[24] This observation seems to be at odds with other testaments. In an interview, Catherine Fenton said that Mrs. Bush was "open and inclusive" with the staff, and that "she was maternal too." Because of this, "we worked all the harder to please them [the Bushes]." She recalled one evening when President Bush unexpectedly invited a large number of members of Congress to the White House for dinner (something he had in common with Lyndon Johnson, who was notorious for large impromptu dinners). Fenton and much of the staff stayed late to help with the dinner. Mrs. Bush, who had been relaxing in the family quarters of the White House and was as surprised as the staff, got dressed and hurried downstairs to greet her guests. She noticed Fenton yawn and saw that she was tired. She remarked with a knowing smile, "I've been doing this for forty-four years."[25]

The senior staff's admiration for and loyalty to Mrs. Bush can be seen in another way. Porter Rose rejected the possibility of writing a book about her White House experiences, saying that it would constitute a breach of a professional relationship. Following Porter Rose's lead, in the years since they left the White House, no former staff members have written "tell-all" books that cast aspersions or raise questions about the practices or character of the former first lady. Still, Mrs. Bush could be demanding. Perez made the point that "you can't have thin skin and work for her."[26] Porter Rose commented that the Bushes "have the ability not to acknowledge the things they don't want to acknowledge."[27]

Some lower-level staffers had less positive evaluations of Mrs. Bush. They characterized both Bushes as difficult and autocratic and the first lady as domineering. The first lady was not shy about critiquing personal appearance, telling one aide, "You've got to do something about your hair." She also made suggestions to those who needed to stop smoking and those who needed to lose weight.[28]

Mrs. Bush enjoyed the ceremonial part of her position.[29] Her attendance at hundreds of events made her a familiar presence to the American people. Reading to children, celebrating the centennial of the National Zoo, lighting the national Christmas tree, lighting a candle in the White House for AIDS victims, or throwing out the first pitch at a World Series game gave people the sense that the first lady was a good sport, always working, and she traveled everywhere. She was so active that one media historian wrote that while Mrs.

Bush presented herself to the public as a homemaker, she was so inundated with public appearances that President Bush, no slouch in terms of activity, took some of the responsibility for White House entertainment.[30]

During the early days of the Bush administration, the new first lady was involved in a "caring" event that generated extensive press coverage and earned her high marks and positive evaluations in many quarters. In March 1989, Mrs. Bush visited Grandma's Place in Washington, where babies with AIDS who had been abandoned were cared for and loved. Mrs. Bush wrote, "There I held a precious baby who later died. Unbelievably, this photo made news because, even then, people still thought touching a person with the virus was dangerous."[31] Her simple gesture spoke eloquently of Mrs. Bush's concern about AIDS and brought attention to an evolving medical and social problem.

In the White House, there were the president's events, and Mrs. Bush might drop in, there were Mrs. Bush's events that she did herself, and there were joint events for the president and first lady. Fenton estimates that Mrs. Bush was involved in approximately twenty-five ceremonial events on her own per month.[32] The Bushes entertained about 40,000 people annually.[33]

The most important social events for the Bushes, as with other presidential administrations, were state dinners, which provided an opportunity for the Bushes to meet and entertain foreign heads of state in a relatively relaxed atmosphere. Fenton commented that the Bushes excelled at using entertaining as a political tool. They had had experience and did it gracefully. She recalled that when George Bush was vice president and lived at the Naval Observatory, his next-door neighbor was the British ambassador. Occasionally, the Bushes would invite the ambassador and his wife over, and they would grill salmon and have an informal meal.[34] It was here and during the years at the United Nations, in China, and at the Republican National Committee that the Bushes honed their entertaining, diplomacy, and political skills.

The preparations for a state visit might begin six months before the head of state arrived at the White House. When the visit was confirmed, a state dinner might be planned. The Department of State budget limited state dinners to nine or ten per year. If a dinner were to be planned, a date was agreed upon (most state visits ran three days in length), and the chief of protocol would officially extend an invitation to the visitors. If they accepted the invitation, elaborate planning began. Mrs. Bush was involved in all phases of planning, and both the president and the first lady had definite ideas about how things should be done.

The Department of State assembled a guest list that was submitted to the president, the first lady, and the president's chief of staff. They would make additions and deletions and tried to include guests from both political parties and the business, professional, entertainment, and sports worlds. The guests' preferences, likes, dislikes, and religious prohibitions were taken into consideration. Mrs. Bush had input into the meal that would be served, entertainment, table setup (table linen, china, silverware), and other dinner-related details.[35] The social secretary dealt with the delicate matter of seating, which took into consideration political, cultural, and ideological differences.[36]

During their White House tenure, the Bushes had state dinners for President Perez of Venezuela, President Mubarek of Egypt, President Collor of Brazil, President Sassou-Nguesso of the Congo, Prime Minister Shamir of Israel, and Prime Minister Mazawiecki of Poland. Fenton said that the state dinners that were especially noteworthy honored President and Mrs. Gorbachev of the USSR, Queen Elizabeth and Prince Philip of England, and President Corazon Aquino of the Philippines. On the night of the Aquino state dinner, 9 November 1989, President Bush was informed that the Berlin Wall had fallen; he announced this to cheers and applause, and the evening took on a special meaning.[37] Other state dinners honored governors and the members of the Economic Summit. Mrs. Bush entertained at luncheons for the Ladies of the Senate and for the wives of visiting heads of state.

Toasts, which are part of any White House ceremonial occasion, were scheduled differently by the Bush administration. The Bushes preferred to have toasts for an event take place prior to dinner (during other administrations, toasts were offered at the conclusion of dinner). After this, dinner could be served and everyone could enjoy the event. Members of the press, who were in attendance during the early part of a state dinner, could leave after the toasts to file their stories. Most state dinners were covered by a press pool of approximately three reporters; the *Washington Post* and *Women's Wear Daily* were almost always represented.[38] Following dinner, the guests would enjoy entertainment. Cellist Yo-Yo Ma, violinist Isaac Stern, opera stars Leontyne Price and Jessye Norman, and singer and pianist Harry Connick Jr. were among those who performed at the White House. Dancing frequently would follow the entertainment.

Some entertainment was much different from that which occurred in the staterooms. After many years, the White House echoed with the laughter of the large and boisterous Bush family. During their televised tour of the White House, President Bush pointed out a toy box in one of the halls that must have been the first stop for children when they came to the historic home. The numerous Bush children and grandchildren were frequent and welcome visitors in Washington and Kennebunkport. This was a striking departure from the Reagans, who had strained relations with Ronald Reagan's children, Maureen and Michael, from his first marriage to actress Jane Wyman, and with their own children, Ronald Jr. and Patti. While it was not unusual for stepparents to have rocky relationships with stepchildren, Mrs. Reagan struggled to develop a relationship with Maureen and Michael. She experienced discord with Ron and Patti and, by some accounts, received little help from her genial but detached husband. The Reagan children and grandchildren were not often seen at the Executive Mansion. If they came, comedian Mark Russell joked, the youngsters would have to wear name tags.

While their father was in office, the Bush children were busy with their individual pursuits. George W. Bush was a part owner of the Texas Rangers baseball team; his brothers Jeb and Marvin were involved in business and raising their families. Doro Bush, the youngest sibling and only girl, was married to Robert Koch at Camp David. Since she had been married previously, she wanted a low-key celebration, "definitely not a White House wedding," and settled on exchanging vows with Bobby Koch at the presidential retreat in Maryland.[39] The wedding was not a state occasion in the tradition of the White House weddings of Tricia Nixon or Lynda Bird Johnson. Rather, it was a gathering of friends and family, with no press, a request by Doro that was honored.

Although the other Bush children generally stayed out of the press, Neil Bush did not have the same luck, as he became embroiled in a major scandal. After struggling with dyslexia, Neil earned bachelor's and master's degrees in business from Tulane University. Following the completion of his education, Neil became associated with the oil and gas industry. When George Bush became vice president, Neil was offered the chance to become a director of Silverado Savings and Loan. As the son of the vice president, he had many business opportunities; some were questionable and ill-advised. One of George Bush's biographers writes, "Neil Bush was seduced by a get-rich-quick crowd and his own desire to replicate his grandfather's and father's independent means."[40]

During his tenure as a director of Silverado, Neil voted to approve loans that defaulted; he failed to inform other bank directors that some of the loan applicants were his business partners: "Federal banking regulators later followed the trail of defaulted loans to Neil Bush oil ventures."[41] Silverado collapsed in 1988, and almost 1,000 other savings and loan institutions followed suit because of changes in regulatory policies enacted during the Reagan-Bush years that led to overextension, riskier loan practices, and excess. American taxpayers would have to pay the bill for the mess, which was estimated to cost from millions to trillions of dollars.[42]

Neil Bush became the public face of the savings and loan scandal. He was charged with conflict of interest but not criminal wrongdoing.[43] He continued to maintain his innocence. Barbara Bush wrote, "Neil became the poster boy of the S & L scandal despite the fact he was just one of literally hundreds of outside directors of failed savings and loans. He was investigated by the government *and* the press, who decided that Neil was guilty before he even had his say." She went on to lament, "His whole problem is he is our son."[44] In a April 1991 interview, Mrs. Bush strongly defended Neil: "He's done nothing wrong. He's the most honest, caring, giving man I know and I think he's really being persecuted. It is just so unfair . . . it is terrible for him. Absolute outrage."[45] When a reporter asked if the first lady felt sympathy for the Kennedy family, dealing with a rape investigation of nephew William Kennedy Smith at the same time that Neil was fighting conflict-of-interest allegations, she responded with a prickly, "Of course you feel sorry. If you don't mind my saying so, I'd rather you didn't mention their latest flap in the same breath as my innocent son."[46]

Despite his mother's protestations of innocence, Neil Bush eventually paid a fine of $50,000 and was banned from banking activities because of his role in the failure of Silverado. He continued to deny any wrongdoing but dropped his appeals.[47] A Resolution Trust Corporation suit (this corporation was set up to deal with the considerable residue of the savings and loan scandal) against Bush and other directors of Silverado was settled in 1991 for $26.5 million. Insurance covered much of the settlement, and a fund established by wealthy Republicans was set up to defray Neil's legal costs.[48]

In spite of Neil's problems and other concerns, living in the White House was a joy for the Bushes. However, both Barbara and George developed medical problems during their sojourn at 1600 Pennsylvania Avenue. Mrs. Bush began to have problems with her eyes during her first few months of residence. After tests, the first lady was diagnosed with Graves' disease, an autoimmune disorder that causes the thyroid gland in the neck to produce too much of the hormone that controls the body's metabolism. Patients afflicted with Graves' disease suffer from swollen eyes, double vision, and weight loss. Mrs. Bush received radiation treatments to deal with her condition. A short time after beginning treatment, Mrs. Bush commented, "Last week was the first without seeing double."[49] A little more than a year later, the president experienced cardiac symptoms that were thought to be connected to Graves' disease. Doctors were baffled further when the Bush's dog, Millie, was diagnosed with lupus, also an autoimmune disorder.[50]

Speculation centered on the White House as a questionable health environment. Extensive tests were conducted on the drinking water in the White House; at Camp David; at Walker's Point, the Bush's home in Kennebunkport, Maine; and at the vice president's residence, where the Bushes had lived for eight years prior to moving to the Executive Mansion. The issue was never satisfactorily settled, though the disease did not slow Mrs. Bush's pace.[51] The first lady even joked about Graves' disease during the 1992 presidential campaign. She told an audience in New Orleans that Millie had been diagnosed with lupus: "One of the craziest [things that they had heard on the campaign trail] was the rumor that George had Lupus.

Let's get this straight right now, the dog has Lupus! George, Jr. says we could 'clear this all up if we'd stop drinking out of Millie's bowl.'"[52]

Mrs. Bush once told a reporter that "if you couldn't be happy in the White House, you couldn't be happy anywhere."[53] With long days and continuous demands on her time, Mrs. Bush delighted in the wonderful pleasures of living in the Executive Mansion and used her staff and available resources to help fulfill an ambitious agenda.

CHAPTER 4

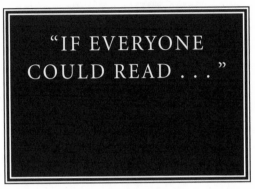

"IF EVERYONE
COULD READ . . ."

Since 1960, every first lady, with the exception of Betty Ford, who
served only a little more than two years, has had a sustained formal
White House project. Jacqueline Kennedy's decision to refurbish the
interior of the White House gave rise to the precedent. Lady Bird
Johnson brought national attention to environmentalism and high-
way beautification. Rosalynn Carter educated the country about
mental health problems. Hillary Rodham Clinton chaired the
President's Task Force on National Health Care. Nancy Reagan, Barbara Bush's immediate predecessor, was involved with the "Just say
no to drugs" program. The press now asks every potential first lady
about her proposed project. Some first ladies found their areas of
advocacy when they arrived at the White House, whereas others had
long records of involvement with an issue.

This was the case of Barbara Bush and literacy. The new first lady
had a history with the subject. Literacy was a great deal more than
her White House project; it was a convergence of personal interest
and national attention, a movement that took on a life of its own. It
predated Mrs. Bush's years in the Executive Mansion and continues
to be her focus since leaving Washington. It is her signature issue
and enduring legacy to the country. Moreover, it contributed in no
small measure to the perception that Barbara Bush was a level-
headed, wise woman, concerned about her country's ability to read,

the person charged with ensuring that the Bush administration was perceived as kinder and gentler.

In part, Mrs. Bush's interest in literacy might have stemmed from personal experience when her son Neil was diagnosed with dyslexia, a neurological disorder that makes reading, spelling, and writing very difficult. Neil was in the second grade when he was tested and his problem identified; until he was seven years old, he had successfully camouflaged his deficiencies with adaptation strategies. The disorder was not well known at the time, and Mrs. Bush constructed her own program to help her son read. Tutors were hired, and Mrs. Bush made tapes for Neil and encouraged his efforts. George W. Bush commented, "Mother worked hard with Neil . . . she was the one who really spent the time making sure that Neil could learn to read the basics."[1] For his part, Neil hated reading. Years later, however, he was grateful for his mother's intervention and said, "To this day, I don't feel handicapped. I have all the confidence in the world because of her."[2]

While her personal experiences with Neil's reading problems would certainly provide a legitimate reason for her interest in literacy, Mrs. Bush has disputed this contention. There is no evidence that she had an abiding interest in the issue during the 1950s beyond encouraging her own children to read. In the early 1960s, she was a parent volunteer for the Reading Is Fundamental (RIF) program in Washington, D.C. Her decision to embrace literacy was dictated by politics and the desire to do something to benefit all Americans. When she knew that George Bush was going to run for president in 1980, she thought about various White House projects. She wrote, "I felt the subject I chose should help the most people possible, but not cost the government more money and *not be controversial.*"[3] A number of potential undertakings might have fit that description, but literacy seemed to stand out. In addition, Barbara Bush was an inveterate reader who has had a lifelong love affair with books, and the thought that people were unable to read, and thus learn, both saddened her and called her to action. Mrs. Bush told an interviewer, "I just believe that if everyone could read, write and comprehend, we'd be a lot closer to solving many of our nation's serious problems."[4] Over the years, this has become her mantra. A historian suggested that politics could not be discounted as an important factor in Mrs. Bush's choice of project. She certainly understood that literacy was a safe choice for the wife of a potential candidate for national office.[5]

While Mrs. Bush's statement about literacy seems logical, it is just the tip of the problem. Reversing intergenerational illiteracy was both controversial and expensive. Her husband's campaign was informed that literacy was Mrs. Bush's project prior to a trip that she and an aide were making to Cardinal Stritch College in Milwaukee, Wisconsin. When they arrived, the president of the college told Mrs. Bush that she had assembled more than forty literacy experts to hear Mrs. Bush's presentation. At the time, Mrs. Bush was still learning about literacy, and she was shocked to find that she would be facing such a distinguished audience. Thinking quickly, she asked the group, "If you were married to the President of the United States and had the chance to make an impact on illiteracy, what would you do?" The experts had many ideas and opinions, and when half of the participants had spoken, Mrs. Bush's aide informed her that time was up and they had to leave. She felt fortunate to escape, but at the same time, she had begun her education in literacy.[6]

The literacy outlook in 1980, the year Mrs. Bush committed herself to her new project, was bleak. Jonathan Kozol, author of *Prisoners of Silence: Breaking the Bonds of Adult Literacy in the United States,* a seminal study of adult literacy published in the same year, sounded the alarm about the dimensions of the problem. He reported that "sixteen percent of whites, forty-four percent of blacks and fifty-six percent of Hispanic adults were 'functionally incompetent.'" Kozol pointed to data from the Office of Education that concluded that 57 million adults, or more than 35 percent of the adult population, were unequipped to carry out the most basic functions. In terms of economic consequences, the funding of welfare programs and loss of productivity was set at $6 billion per year.[7] What was required to reverse the cycle, wrote Kozol, was nothing short of a revolution, an all-out literacy struggle to teach people to read, write, and comprehend. He suggested a national commission to deal with these concerns. He concluded, "It is within our power to transform the situation; but the price will be a large one and the task will not be easy."[8] Mrs. Bush told the author, "Yes—I read the book [Kozol's book]. I read it after I decided to make literacy my cause in

1978 when I realized George Bush was truly going to run for president. I read all I could on literacy and illiteracy."[9]

Other authors had discussed and suggested solutions to the literacy problem. They included Irwin Isenberg, *The Drive against Illiteracy* (1964); Robert A. Dentler and Mary Ellen Warshauer, *Big City Dropouts and Illiterates* (1965); Wanda Cook, *Adult Literacy Education in the United States* (1977); Marc Bendick, *The Illiteracy of Welfare Clients* (1978); and Carman St. John Hunter and David Harman, *Adult Illiteracy in the United States: A Report to the Ford Foundation* (1979).

Despite his alarmist tone, Kozol was only the latest commentator in the twentieth century concerned about American literacy. Prior to World War I, the U.S. Bureau of Education published a study titled *Illiteracy in the United States and an Experiment for Its Elimination* (1913). When hostilities broke out and American soldiers and sailors headed to Europe, the discovery that many draftees could not read sparked efforts to educate these young people. A generation later, with America's entry into World War II, the same problem recurred, and in the postwar period commentators discussed "Why Johnny Can't Read." The Sputnik crisis of 1957 renewed interest in literacy that culminated in President Lyndon Johnson's Great Society programs such as the Adult Education Act of 1966. This legislation increased literacy appropriations and suggested establishing national leadership, a national resource center, and a standard reporting process. The National Right to Read program was launched to combat illiteracy on a nationwide scale.[10] By 1980, the time was right to revisit the literacy question.

While the Reagan administration was interested in literacy, more pressing concerns in defense and the economy caused a reevaluation of priorities, and appropriations decreased: "Between 1980–1991, federal funding for adult literacy programs dropped from fifty-seven percent to twenty percent—$209.35 per adult literacy student versus $5,991.00 per kindergarten–twelfth grade student."[11] To bridge the chasm between federal and private efforts, volunteer organizations were founded, including Literacy Volunteers of America and Laubach Literacy Action.

The picture was not greatly improved in 1985 when Kozol published *Illiterate America,* a follow-up to his 1980 work. The new book pointed out the disparity in education that existed between rich and poor school systems. Kozol graphically depicted what happened to the poor when they left school. Without the ability to read, people were unable to navigate society and unable to improve themselves. Stuck in low-paying and menial jobs, they were driven by desperation, in some cases, to lives of crime or prostitution.

Noting these many problems, Second Lady Barbara Bush focused on adult literacy. Benita Somerfield, the executive director of the Barbara Bush Foundation for Family Literacy, explained that in 1981, adult literacy was a serious problem without a champion. "By putting the considerable force of her personality and her visibility as wife of the Vice President behind it, she put literacy on the map."[12]

Mrs. Bush invited government personnel, literacy experts, academics, and researchers to breakfasts at her home, the Naval Observatory. Among those who took part in the literacy discussions were Sharon Darling, president of the National Center for Family Literacy; Peter Waite, president of Laubach Literacy Action; Jinx Crouch, president of Literacy Volunteers of America; Professor David Harman of Columbia University; literacy consultant Tom Sticht; and Jack Harr and Anderson Clark of Project Literacy US. Julie Cooke, who coordinated projects for Mrs. Bush, also attended the meetings. Mrs. Bush was also aided by Susan Green, whom she described as one of her mentors in literacy: "She [Green] was there with me in the beginning, when few people were really paying attention to literacy."[13] Somerfield believes that the breakfasts were successful because the assembled group discussed the scope of the problem, innovations, the latest research, and how to effectively teach English as a second language. Mrs. Bush became more knowledgeable about literacy, and the people in the field got to know each other.

Marie M. Adair, executive director of the New Jersey Association for Supervision and Curriculum Development, credits Mrs. Bush with making literacy a priority of the country. She said, "Mrs. Bush helped us to take the first giant step." Adair observed that when Mrs. Bush began her advocacy, the field was not yet labeled literacy; it was called reading or reading and language arts. "Literacy is the big picture: reading, speaking, writing and critical thinking are major elements," said Adair. "Mrs. Bush understood that literacy was key and chose an excellent message. She affirmed literacy's central place in learning."[14]

Mrs. Bush visited scores of literacy programs around the country. While visiting, she would speak with the students and inquire about what they were learning and their goals. She wanted the students to know that she was passionate about learning to read and that it could make a critical difference in their lives and in the lives of families where parents were learning to read for the first time.

Mrs. Bush spoke to corporations and businesses to raise funds. She participated on panels and wrote articles. She worked with state literacy councils and convened meetings of governors' wives and got them to lend their support to literacy efforts in their states. Capital Cities/ABC and the Public Broadcasting System launched Project Literacy US (PLUS), programs and public service announcements that highlighted reading tutors, adult learners, and a literacy hotline. The Newspaper Publishers Association published supplements about literacy, and major foundations announced new literacy program funding.[15]

Thousands of letters arrived at Mrs. Bush's office, and rather than forwarding them to the Department of Education for responses, she hired a specialist to deal with queries. Though they did not have particular expertise in literacy, Louisa Biddle and later Mary Peacock assisted Mrs. Bush in her work. Able and efficient, Biddle and Peacock answered correspondence, accompanied Mrs. Bush to literacy events, and helped her to learn more about the issue. The second lady's office became a clearinghouse for literacy questions, and she and her staff became accepted as part of the literacy field.[16]

Mrs. Bush received hundreds of letters about literacy concerns and replied to many writers. Her letter to a teacher letter dated 21 June 1988 was typical of her responses and reflected her feelings about books: "In my opinion, the best value for the money, on any given day, is a book. One can learn a new skill, travel, be diverted or amused by reading. Books have been my lifelong companions."[17]

In 1984, Mrs. Bush wrote *C. Fred's Story,* a series of observations on life with Barbara and George offered by the Bush's buff-colored, male cocker spaniel. C. Fred, a birthday gift from Marvin Bush to his mother, was named for C. Fred Chambers of Houston, George H. W. Bush's best friend. C. Fred's observations covered the Bushes' years in Washington, in China, and back to Washington during

George Bush's vice presidential tenure. One of the devices that Mrs. Bush used in her book was to have Fred describe an event or situation; then, in italics, she would add her own feedback. For example, C. Fred writes, "Some people call me 'Siegfried.' Others call me 'See Fred' as in 'See Fred run.' Mr. Justice Stewart calls me 'J. Fred.' My name is Charles Frederick Bush, C. Fred for short." Barbara Bush writes, *"I have never dared tell C. Fred that J. Fred Muggs was a chimpanzee."*[18] Later in the book, C. Fred commented on his food: "I have been on a diet since the day I arrived. For ten years, Bar has fed me half a can of diet dog food every morning and the other half every night. I like table scraps very much—but she won't let anyone feed me. . . . Bar and George . . . eat all the time—wonderful, rich, varied food." In her role as respondent, Mrs. Bush commented that she did not see much gourmet food while on the banquet circuit or campaigning or traveling the country on behalf of literacy: *"Are you kidding? Who gets rich food on the rubber chicken circuit?"*[19] The last section of the book is composed of photos of the famous people that Fred met, including Happy Rockefeller, actor Charlton Heston, Prime Minister Yitzak Shamir of Israel, Prince and Princess Sadruddin Aga Khan, and Prime Minister Margaret Thatcher of England, among others. The goal of the book was to raise funds for literacy organizations; it sold 15,000 copies and raised $100,000. All profits were donated to Literacy Volunteers of America and Laubach Literacy Action, two organizations with which Barbara Bush worked.

The success of *C. Fred's Story* led to a media tour and an invitation to appear on NBC's *Today Show.* As host Jane Pauley was preparing for the telecast, she suggested to Mrs. Bush that they make the interview fun and not discuss literacy. Mrs. Bush's reaction was immediate and emphatic: "Not talk about literacy? No way. That was what I was there for. Her first question was, 'Mrs. Bush, why would a dog write a book?' Knowing that this might be my only chance, my answer was that he was worried about illiteracy in our country, and then I got in as many facts as possible before I let her get another word in edgewise."[20]

In the same year, Mrs. Bush shared alarming statistics about illiteracy with the Texas Library Association. She said, "As you know, up until now, everything has not been all right in my chosen field . . . that of helping to wipe out illiteracy. An estimated 23 million

Americans cannot read or write at a very elementary level. Another 23 to 40 million adults are defined as functionally illiterate . . . they are not proficient enough to read instructions, forms, signs." These people were not able to function as contributing citizens in society, said Mrs. Bush. The problem was especially worrisome among minorities, she told her audience, which evidenced greater percentages of illiteracy: "An estimated 56% of Hispanics, 47% of Blacks and 17% of Whites in America are functionally illiterate."[21] She went on to discuss her role in the fight against illiteracy: "I am not an expert but a cheerleader. I encourage reading, the teaching of reading, the necessity of reading and the job of reading. And I encourage the giving of time and money from individuals and corporations to this end."[22]

Literacy problems did not improve significantly over the next two years. There were still tens of millions of Americans who were unable to read, write, and compute in America's technologically advancing society. Unemployment, crime, poverty, and unrealized tax revenues were some of the costs of not confronting the problem, Mrs. Bush said.[23] Speaking to the Evansville, Indiana, Public Library Friends, she warned, "The poor basic skills of so many adults threaten our very future because the literacy of parents is directly related to the educational chances of their children. Literacy affects our entire way of life, because a democracy's vitality depends on an informed populace."[24]

A great deal of Mrs. Bush's time as the wife of the vice president was devoted to her project. In her *Memoir,* Mrs. Bush wrote, "I participated in 537 literacy-related events and another 435 events related to volunteerism. At times it was exhausting but it was always exhilarating. I always felt like I got more out than I put in."[25] According to an index prepared by archivists at the George Bush Library, Mrs. Bush gave 265 speeches during her eight years as second lady. Forty-eight of these speeches were definitely identified by the author as having discussed literacy or literacy-related topics.[26] Currently, only a handful of Mrs. Bush's speeches from this period are available for research.

Benita Somerfield believes that Mrs. Bush's role in literacy evolved as a result of a combination of her sense of who she is, her forthrightness, her formidable intelligence, and a wicked sense of humor. The efforts of her chief of staff, Susan Porter Rose, and a very well planned agenda that stressed substantive activities rather than "photo ops" greatly enhanced her effectiveness.[27] An interviewer commented about Mrs. Bush's passion for her work in literacy and noted the first lady's concern for "those who live out of reach of the pleasures of books. The implications of multigenerational illiteracy . . . struck her with great force."[28]

By the time she became first lady, literacy was on the nation's agenda, but Mrs. Bush used the White House "bully pulpit" to give the issue even greater visibility. She told her staff that literacy was her "major," and encouraging people to volunteer in literacy programs was her "minor." She cared deeply about the volunteerism aspect of the program and believed that it was consistent with "the kinder, gentler nation" her husband described in accepting the 1988 Republican presidential nomination.[29]

In March 1989, Mrs. Bush launched the Barbara Bush Foundation for Family Literacy, whose mission is "to establish literacy as a value in every family in America, by helping every family understand that the home is the child's first school, that the parent is the child's first teacher, and that reading is the child's first subject and to break the intergenerational cycle of illiteracy."[30] The *New York Times* reported Mrs. Bush's announcement of the formation of her foundation on page one. The first lady told the press, educators, corporate figures, and community leaders that 23 million Americans were illiterate and another 35 million were semiliterate. She had been involved in literacy for almost ten years and had visited literacy programs, libraries, single-parent classes for high school dropouts, public housing projects. "You name it—I visited it—it has become very apparent to me that we must attack the problem of a more literate America thorough the family. We all know that adults with reading problems tend to raise children with reading problems," said Mrs. Bush.[31]

In a piece that he wrote after the launch of Mrs. Bush's foundation, nationally syndicated columnist William Raspberry commended the first lady's efforts. Raspberry wrote that Mrs. Bush was the inspiration for renewed interest in literacy. She already had an impressive résumé, with eight years devoted to the issue: "She [Mrs. Bush] understands the need for a full-scale attack on joblessness, poverty, adolescent parenting, drug use and all the other ills that afflict society. But she would agree . . . the conquest of illiteracy comes first."[32]

The foundation began to publish materials, including *First Teachers*, which described ten pioneering programs that had been successful (one of the programs highlighted was Hillary Rodham Clinton's program in Arkansas) and *Barbara Bush's Family Reading Tips*. Later, the foundation published *Successful Strategies in Family Literacy* and *Lessons Learned: A Review of the First Lady's Literacy Initiative for Texas*. A national grant program was established, and since 1989, the foundation has funded more than 500 literacy programs in forty-seven states and the District of Columbia. Mrs. Bush did not participate in the grant decisions, leaving those determinations to peer review panels. Almost $16 million has been disbursed to date.[33]

A month later, Mrs. Bush spoke to the annual conference of the American Newspaper Publishers Association. She praised the newspaper industry, telling listeners, "One of the most important things you do is tell the very human stories of literacy.... Newspapers are giving hundreds of local literacy programs so much of the help they need so badly, help with recruiting students and tutors, space for classes and tutoring."[34] The newspaper industry also supported Mrs. Bush's efforts by proclaiming that 8 September 1989 was International Literacy Day, "Newspaper Literacy Day." Special sections were published about the topic. "The Mini Page," a regular insert aimed at children that is included in many newspapers, devoted most of its edition to literacy. Under the headline "Read, Says Mrs. Bush," there was an interview with the first lady, who explained literacy to children in simple terms: "Try to imagine your life without being able to read. You wouldn't know what to order in your favorite restaurant, you couldn't check the box scores of your favorite team ... or the TV listings." There was also a literacy puzzle, a story about Millie, and some concluding thoughts from the first lady.[35]

Mrs. Bush employed a many-pronged attack in raising the country's consciousness about literacy. In addition to supporting the work of her foundation, she made speeches and visited literacy programs. She read stories to children over the radio, and later the tapes of her books were sold in retail stores. She appeared on television to discuss literacy. In her travels, she never missed a chance to mention her project.

She welcomed the opportunity to speak to the press about her project. Her increasing involvement with literacy led the *New York*

Times Book Review to conduct an interview with the first lady that was published a few months after the creation of her foundation. The interview began by saying that Mrs. Bush's choice of literacy as her White House project "has the ring of genuine, abiding commitment." The first lady discussed her favorite books, reading to her children and grandchildren, and cultivating good reading habits. She told the interviewer, "We can pass along our good traits as well as our bad ones." She went on to say that "children who are read to are likely to become good readers themselves and later read to their own children as a matter of course."[36] The interview conferred legitimacy on the project and introduced Barbara Bush and her cause to a wider, more diverse and influential audience. The complementary tone of the piece contributed to the image of Mrs. Bush as the nation's grandmother and point person for literacy.

In her four years as first lady, Mrs. Bush gave 449 speeches. Eighteen percent of those speeches focused primarily on literacy and education. Many more speeches that did not principally discuss these topics mentioned literacy. For example, in May 1990, addressing the graduating class of the University of Pennsylvania, she spoke about Benjamin Franklin, the founder of the university, his love of words, and her White House project. Illiteracy, she said, affected as many as one out of five Americans: "And it's part of the drug problem, part of ignorance and AIDS, part of homelessness and alienation. When Ben Franklin was dining in Paris, one of his companions posed the question: 'what condition of man most deserves pity?' Each guest proposed an example. When Franklin's turn came, he offered: 'a lonesome man on a rainy day who does not know how to read.'" Mrs. Bush encouraged the graduates to be lifelong readers and to encourage others to cultivate the habit. Quoting from Robert MacNeil's book *Wordstruck,* she said, "If you love the language, the greatest thing you can do to ensure its survival is not to complain about bad usage, but to pass your enthusiasm to a child."[37] In her widely heralded commencement speech at Wellesley College a month later, Mrs. Bush took advantage of the extensive media coverage and told her listeners that if they had children, they had to read to them. She repeated her mantra, if people could read, many of the problems plaguing society could be eradicated. Literacy informed almost everything she did.

Another major success for Mrs. Bush was *Millie's Book*. Buoyed by the reaction to *C. Fred's Story*, Mrs. Bush saw the second volume as an opportunity to raise money for her new foundation. Mildred "Millie" Kerr Bush was the English springer spaniel who became the newest member of the Bush family upon the death of C. Fred in 1987. Millie was a gift to Barbara from George Bush in 1987. *Millie's Book* focused on Millie's adventures at the home of the vice president and, later, the White House. Millie shares history and personal impressions rather than a list of visitors who came to call on the presidential family. Commenting on the White House Green Room, Millie tells readers that this "is where Bar receives the spouses of the heads of state after their formal arrival ceremony for a cup of tea and a little get-to-know-each-other chat. The chair I chose was the one where the spouses sit. The Prez says that this is just one reason why he does not want me to attend formal receptions."[38] Another entry, from an earlier part of the book, describes a visit from another famous dog: "Several months after I arrived at the V.P. House, we got a letter from Benji, the famous dog movie actor, asking if he could come by for a courtesy call. You can imagine my excitement . . . and then I discovered the awful truth. Benji turned out to be an aging (twelve-year-old) female."[39] At a *Millie's Book* event in Houston, Mrs. Bush told her audience that Millie sent her regards; the dog was keeping an eye on the White House while Barbara and George were away. The first lady said that Millie had designated the profits from her book to go to the Barbara Bush Foundation for Family Literacy, "not because of its name, but because Millie is a very good mother herself, and she knows that parents are children's first and most important teachers. Although she prefers chasing squirrels, Millie knows that reading is essential to the welfare of America."[40] The first lady was more than surprised when *Millie's Book* debuted at number one on the *New York Times* best-seller list and spent twenty-three weeks on the *Publisher's Weekly* bestseller list. The profits from *Millie's Book* would eventually top $1 million, all of which were donated to Mrs. Bush's foundation.

Mrs. Bush spent the fall of 1990 signing thousands of books. She made the rounds of the morning talk shows, appearing on *Today*, *Good Morning America*, and *The CBS Morning Show*. Millie received such a positive response that a staff member was assigned to answer her fan mail. Even the president took notice and quipped to an audience, "Who would have thought . . . Millie, would write a book that was the number one on the bestseller list last week . . . ? Give her Alpo and she wants to see the wine list."[41]

The first lady even championed literacy in the speeches she gave for candidates vying for office during the 1990 midterm elections. She would declare her support for a candidate and then go on to tell audiences that she was always asked about Millie. She was great, said Mrs. Bush, and her book had been on the *New York Times* and *Washington Post* best-seller lists. "Nobody is more surprised than Millie and nobody more pleased than me, because the proceeds from *Millie's Book* go to family literacy programs and projects around the country."[42]

The country was enmeshed in the Persian Gulf War when the first lady took a brief break from the unending pressure to honor the U.S. Commission on Libraries on 23 January 1991. She underscored the importance of public libraries: "Someone once said, 'it is not true that we have only one life to live; if we can read, we can live as many more lives and as many kinds of lives as we wish.' . . . There's no adequate way to express my conviction about the importance of libraries. I truly believe they are among the American people's greatest gift to themselves."[43]

Two months later, Mrs. Bush spoke to the Florida Literacy Conference. She lauded the organization's success in reaching great numbers of recent immigrants to the United States and said, "You know that literacy is more than basic skills. It's programs that help new Americans. . . . It's family programs that break the cycle of intergenerational illiteracy. Community based literacy programs bring people together, for a common goal, toward a shared understanding."[44]

Recalling her parents' influence on her and stressing the importance of encouragement to read at home, Mrs. Bush told the White House Conference on Libraries and Information Services, "More and more I've become convinced that it all begins at home, all our learning, about work and freedom and the joys of literacy. . . . Like many of you, I learned to love to read in the arms of warm, reading parents in the rooms of warm, inviting libraries. And libraries have helped sustain my learning ever since."[45] In an interview Mrs. Bush remembered, "I think of my dad sitting in his chair by the fireplace and my mother on the couch, and after we children could read everyone was curled up with something."[46] Her advocacy of parents reading to children was rooted in personal experience.

Mrs. Bush took part in hundreds of literacy events. A speech she gave to the San Antonio Commission on Literacy on 20 September 1989 is typical of her scores of appearances. She called the fight against illiteracy "the worthiest cause there is." She was pleased with private sector efforts in her project and told listeners, "We need your know-how. We need your man-hours. And we need your money."[47] Benita Somerfield said that there was not one particular speech about literacy that was more prominent than the others. She explained, "The consistency with which she gets that message out and the strength of the message are what, I believe, have made it so powerful and long-lasting."[48]

Mrs. Bush traveled to schools, Project Head Start locations, day care facilities, and General Education Development (GED) graduations. When Mrs. Bush and her entourage arrived at an out-of-town location for a literacy event, she would ask her hosts and hostesses to highlight literacy or education, not Barbara Bush; she wanted people to know what was going on in their community. Then she would ask what her sponsors wanted her to tell the press, since they were the people who would write the local stories. Did the program need volunteers or contributions or greater publicity? Mrs. Bush would help in any way she could. In addition, Mrs. Bush always spotlighted one or more new readers: men, women, and children who had joined the ranks of the literate.[49]

Like many first ladies before her, Mrs. Bush found that sometimes it was easier to generate press coverage of her events outside of Washington than in the capital city. This was a source of irritation for the first lady, who worked unceasingly for her project. A reporter who covered the first lady wrote, "Her literacy campaign was a public service but also did not get a lot of publicity."[50]

In September 1990, Mrs. Bush began hosting a ten-part Sunday evening radio show titled "Mrs. Bush's Story Time." The idea for the series originated with the Children's Literacy Initiative in Philadelphia. The goal, wrote Mrs. Bush, was "to get families back to reading together and to spread the message about reading aloud to children."[51] The first program of the series, which aired on ABC radio and many of its affiliates, began with a call-in show about literacy hosted by Peter Jennings. In the sixteen weeks that followed, Mrs. Bush, celebrities, and cartoon characters read books over the air. The programs were scheduled for early evening so that young children would be likely to hear the stories. A typical promotional announcement for one of the programs, heard over radio, stressed the importance of parents reading to their children: "This week Mrs. Bush will read *The Empty Pot* by Demi. It charmingly illustrates that honesty is always the best policy. Experts agree, reading aloud is one of the best ways to help children learn to read. So check your listings for Mrs. Bush's Story Time and make a date of it with your children."[52]

Mrs. Bush's programs, "Read Me a Story," were recorded on audiotape and later copied and sold at large retail outlets. The tapes were boxed and sold at a nominal cost along with a copy of *Barbara Bush's Family Reading Tips;* all profits from the tapes were donated to the foundation.

A year later, after completing the second round of programs, Mrs. Bush told her sponsors and many of the people connected with the production of the series that she was overjoyed that this children's literacy initiative was flowering. Project Literacy US was distributing her foundation's reading pamphlet, and audio cassettes would be available shortly. She complimented her audience, saying, "I hope every single one of you feels as proud and good about our story time as I do. Think of it this way: you've made yourselves a very special group of interior decorators for children. You've helped adorn the insides of their minds and hearts with the most lasting kind of beauty."[53]

Mrs. Bush tried to employ all the available means of persuasion in highlighting literacy. She visited the *Oprah Winfrey Show* on 23 October 1989 and 13 March 1990 to discuss literacy with the popular talk show host. The president and Mrs. Bush hosted two National Literacy Honors ceremonies at the White House, on 11 February 1990 and 22 November 1992; the events were broadcast as a television special on ABC. In October 1990, Mrs. Bush wrote an article for the *Reader's Digest* titled "Parenting's Best Kept Secret: Reading to Your Children."

The first lady suggested that parents (1) get started now, (2) make reading aloud a habit, (3) involve the whole family, (4) keep books handy, and (5) choose good books. "Get a child hooked on reading," wrote Mrs. Bush, "and its joy will last a lifetime."[54] The appearance on Oprah Winfrey's program, hosting the literacy honors ceremonies, and the article in *Reader's Digest* reached huge national audiences.

Mrs. Bush acknowledged that she had an effect on one major piece of legislation, the National Literacy Act of 1991.[55] She found an unlikely ally in Democratic senator Paul Simon of Illinois. Known for his trademark bow tie, Simon had long been interested in literacy. In the late 1970s, as a member of the U.S. House of Representatives, he saw that some of his constituents who were seeking his help were unable to read and sign the forms that would authorize him to look into their federal records. He later recalled: "A husband or wife would have to sign. I see the lack of literacy as a massive deterrent to people enjoying the richness of life and taking advantage of the economy."[56] Reacting to these problems, Simon held the first ever congressional subcommittee hearings on the question of illiteracy. After the hearings, Simon suggested to Secretary of Education Ted Bell that they hold a series of breakfasts with a few concerned people who might offer suggestions for dealing with the issue. One of the attendees at the breakfast meetings was Barbara Bush.[57]

In Barbara Bush, Simon found a kindred spirit, and the two forged a bipartisan literacy effort to discuss what could be done. They already knew each other, having volunteered at the same public school twenty years earlier. Mrs. Bush had discussions and meetings with Simon about literacy at the Department of Education. On 13 July 1989, Simon introduced S. 1310, "a bill to eliminate illiteracy by the year 2000, to strengthen and coordinate literacy programs, and for other purposes."[58] The bill had a long legislative history. It was referred to the Committee on Labor and Human Resources and the Subcommittee on Education, Arts and Humanities before being amended twelve times. At first, the White House was opposed to the bill. Then Simon called Mrs. Bush to explain the situation and, according to Simon's account, "the administration position suddenly reversed itself 180 degrees, supporting the measure."[59]

The bill was passed by a vote of 99 to 1 on 6 February 1990. The National Literacy Act was signed into law as H.R. 251 by President Bush on 25 July 1991. It provided for a multiagency-supported National Institute of Literacy that would serve as a national clearinghouse for literacy efforts, a National Workforce Literacy Assistance

Collaborative, improvements to the Even Start program, and support for state literacy programs in correctional institutions.[60] In his comments at the signing, President Bush acknowledged that he had been educated about literacy by his wife: "Education is not just about making a living; it's about making a life. And literacy is where education begins. I first understood the truth of that statement by watching Barbara in her work that still continues, working her heart out for literacy."[61] The president gave the pen used to sign the National Literacy Act to his wife. Mrs. Bush commented in her autobiography, "I must say that I got more credit than I deserved. . . . It [the National Literacy Act] was the first piece of legislation—and to date, the only one—ever enacted specifically for literacy, with the goal of ensuring that every American adult acquires the basic literacy skills."[62] Of Simon, Mrs. Bush wrote that the senator was a champion of literacy: "We disagreed on the means to solve the problem—he wanted to pump more money into everything—but his heart certainly was in the right place."[63]

Though she only acknowledges having her imprimatur on the Literacy Act, Mrs. Bush may have influenced other legislation. The Adult Education Act, which increased federal funding for adult literacy, and the Even Start Act, which funded intergenerational literacy programs, were both enacted during the Bush administration. It is not a stretch to imagine that Mrs. Bush was also an advocate for these bills. When the National Adult Literacy survey was conducted, it was the first time in twenty years that literacy in the United States had been measured. President Bush convened an education summit that produced Goals 2000, establishing national education goals. This was the impetus for the charter school movement.[64] Marie Adair believes that Mrs. Bush's support of the National Literacy Act was especially important. She said, "Without the pressure of legislation it may or may not have gotten done." Moreover, Adair believes that the legislation was the foundation for the No Child Left Behind initiative of President George W. Bush.[65]

When President Bush ran for reelection in 1992, his campaign stressed his administration's many accomplishments in literacy. In addition to the National Literacy Act of 1991, he proposed funding for literacy programs during fiscal year 1993 of $443 million, a 127 percent increase since the beginning of his administration. With the president's encouragement, private sector companies including General Motors, Motorola, Texaco, and the Energy Company of New Orleans were donating funds and personnel to address literacy needs in the workplace. The U.S. Army was working with public school systems to increase literacy levels in its ranks. In association with the nation's governors, the president endorsed a national goal for reforming education: by 2000, every American adult would be literate.[66]

Following the president's loss to Bill Clinton, Mrs. Bush offered an assessment of her husband's efforts on behalf of literacy: "I'm so deeply proud of George Bush for more reasons than I can ever count and one of them is for putting literacy up front, with the national goals . . . with Head Start and Even Start and that unprecedented act (National Literacy Act of 1991)."[67]

Not everyone was enthusiastic about the president's support of literacy. Charles Kolb, who worked in the Department of Education and later in the Bush White House, wrote that although Mrs. Bush had made literacy her signature initiative, "it remained essentially rhetorical, and every time efforts were made to tee up a substantial literacy effort—in the White House, with the Department of Education, or through working with various groups—things went nowhere."[68] During a 1997 conference on the Bush administration held at Hofstra University, a historian took a different approach in assessing Mrs. Bush's literacy program, saying the initiative was "symbolic cover for George Bush when his policies on the nation's pocketbook would not suffice."[69] Benita Somerfield, one of the participants in the conference, took issue with the statement, saying Barbara Bush had not only used the bully pulpit but had constructed that particular pulpit. After recounting the literacy and education legislation that was passed during the Bush administration and the accomplishments of those literacy programs, Somerfield observed, "If we were to survey policy makers on both sides of the aisle . . . you would find great agreement that Barbara Bush is indeed 'the first lady of literacy.' That is her place in history. I do not believe that was her intent but that has been the result. And this role has only deepened and expanded since the White House years." Somerfield concluded, "No, I will never accept . . . that Barbara Bush's advocacy of literacy was cover for anything."[70]

Ever the adroit politician, Barbara Bush knew that literacy was a safe project, but her activity in the area dated back to the pre–vice presidency period. It was not symbolic cover for underperforming initiatives of her husband's administration but was definitely one of the achievements of his presidency.

Mrs. Bush said that literacy was her legacy to the American people. Perhaps the change wrought by Mrs. Bush is summarized in a comment made by a reporter who covered the first lady during her years in the White House: "I think one of her lasting legacies may be . . . lists of books on a refrigerator."[71]

Adair points out that progress has been steady: "We haven't reached the performance level we want, but we've made great strides in literacy. We're in a good place. As a multi-lingual society our task is more complicated than other countries. Mrs. Bush promoted literacy and her message with her high visibility. She's seen as a role model."[72] Adair's comments are supported by *A First Look at the Literacy of America's Adults in the 21st Century,* the report on the National Assessment of Adult Literacy (NAAL). The survey results, published in late 2005, indicate that the average quantitative literacy scores of adults increased 8 points between 1992 (Mrs. Bush left the White House in 1993) and 2003.[73]

The former first lady is still out on the hustings telling parents to read to their children early and often and urging those who cannot read to get help. Literacy was not a project for Mrs. Bush, wrote Somerfield; it was a commitment that has continued with many and varied activities.[74] Her advocacy shone the spotlight of national attention on an area that needed publicity, funding, and discussion, and it provided Barbara Bush with the opportunity to make a significant difference in the lives of Americans.

Barbara Pierce, circa 1929.

Barbara Pierce in her late teens, circa 1941.

Barbara and George Bush on their wedding day.

Barbara Bush plays with her son George W. Bush, Easter, 1948.

Barbara and George Bush, Midland, Texas, circa 1948.

The Bush family in front of the U.S. Capitol, circa 1967.

Mrs. Bush talking to the press aboard Air Force 1, 30 May 1989.

Barbara Bush and Raisa Gorbachev at Wellesley College, 1 June 1990.

Mrs. Bush stands before a poster for Millie's Book, *12 September 1990.*

Mrs. Bush reads to children in the White House Library, 2 July 1991.

President and Mrs. Bush stand on the rocks outside their home at Walker's Point, Kennebunkport, Maine (Millie is in the background), 10 August 1991.

Mrs. Bush records a story for "Mrs. Bush's Storytime," 9 July 1991.

Mrs. Bush reads to children in Missouri with Governor John Ashcroft, 10 October 1991.

Mrs. Bush works the phones for the Bush-Quayle reelection campaign, 29 February 1992.

The President and Mrs. Bush greet supporters, 23 August 1992.

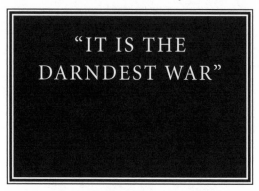

CHAPTER 5

"IT IS THE DARNDEST WAR"

Barbara Bush was happily anticipating her family's yearly sojourn in Kennebunkport during the summer of 1990. These visits meant time at the beach, the opportunity to walk and read, and extended visits with her grandchildren. The first lady was still basking in her triumph at Wellesley College, and her poll ratings, 80 percent approval, compared with 61 percent for her husband, attested to her popularity with the American people.[1] With the rigors of the congressional elections ahead, in which she intended to play an active role, and the presidential contest two years in the future, the Bushes stood at a midpoint in what they hoped and expected would be the first of two terms in the White House.

Then a foreign policy crisis erupted. In the ensuing Gulf War against Iraq, Barbara Bush used the tested techniques that she had practiced before college audiences with American military personnel to bolster their morale and advance the priorities of the administration. Her success at this task further enhanced her popularity. Just as this crisis showed her husband as an adept world leader and crisis manager, so too did Barbara Bush's role demonstrate how effective she had become as a supportive first lady.

On 2 August 1990, Iraq invaded Kuwait. The powerful army of Iraqi dictator Saddam Hussein swept aside resistance from the outnumbered Kuwaiti forces within a few hours. Iraq soon seized control of the oil-rich nation. The enmity between the two countries had been percolating for years. Hussein charged that Kuwait was illegally drilling in the nearby Rumaylah oil fields, thus costing Iraq billions of dollars in lost revenues. He announced that Kuwait has ceased to exist, and he annexed it as Iraq's nineteenth province. Hussein now controlled 21 percent of the world's oil supply. Iraq seemed poised to sweep into Saudi Arabia and threaten the oil supplies of the industrialized West; if that incursion were successful, fully 40 percent of the world's oil supply would be in the hands of Iraq.[2]

George H. W. Bush faced the greatest crisis in the twenty months of his presidency as he sought to mobilize international resistance to Iraq's act of aggression. For Barbara Bush, this sudden turn of events meant that her personal plans for an idyllic summer had to be scrapped. The president decided that he ought to join his family in Maine for what would be a working vacation. Not wishing to emulate the precedent of Jimmy Carter, who became a virtual prisoner in the White House during the Iran hostage crisis a decade earlier, President Bush chose to go north. That meant, for his wife, a complete change in the texture of the vacation and her own role.[3] The White House moved to Maine, and Barbara Bush juggled the many demands of her husband's crisis management style.

Barbara bridled at the criticism directed at her husband for deciding to take his prescheduled three-week summer vacation at Walker's Point. She told an interviewer, "He just wanted to put [things] in the right perspective. You know, this is not the United States against Saddam Hussein, this is the world against Saddam Hussein. I think occasionally we forget that. George stayed in Maine because it sent the right message."[4] Moreover, George Bush and his family had always found strength and solace at their summer home at Walker's Point in Kennebunkport. About eighty miles from Boston, the property had been purchased by Dwight Davis Walker (George H. W. Bush's great-grandfather) and his son, George Herbert Walker, known as Bert (George H. W. Bush's grandfather) in the late 1890s. At the time, Kennebunkport was a small but important fishing village on the southern Maine coast. The two men built a large Victorian house on the peninsula and named it Surf Ledge. From the turn of the century, the Walkers would travel to Maine to escape steamy summers in their native Saint Louis, Missouri.

Dorothy Walker and Prescott Bush were married in Kennebunkport in 1901; a smaller house, called the Bungalow, was built next to Surf Ledge and given to Dorothy and Prescott as a wedding gift. Prescott Sheldon Bush Jr. was born in Kennebunkport in 1922. Though the family would eventually settle in Greenwich, Connecticut, Prescott and Dorothy began to bring their own children to Maine during the 1930s. It was here that Dorothy taught her children sailing, tennis, and bridge. It was also here that George H. W. Bush acquired his love of the sea. His sister Nan has observed that for George Bush "spending time in Kennebunkport became a deep and important thing in his life, a real touchstone place."[5]

When George Bush wanted to introduce Barbara Pierce to his extended family, he invited her to spend seventeen days at Kennebunkport. Barbara, too, fell in love with the estate. Later, she and George brought their growing family to Maine to spend summers swimming, boating, hiking, and picnicking.[6] Just prior to becoming vice president, Bush bought the former Surf Ledge, now known simply as "the Big House." Barbara lovingly refurbished the house. Their children and grandchildren continue to spend some part of the summer at Kennebunkport. During the summer of 2007, President George W. Bush met with Russian president Vladimir Putin at the Bush family home as the two mixed high-level talks with speedboat rides and fishing.[7]

The six-acre Bush estate differed from the more ornate Kennedy compound in Hyannisport, Massachusetts, and it bore no resemblance to the "cottages" of the Newport, Rhode Island, rich, but it was exclusive and offered privacy and comfort. In a 1989 magazine interview, Barbara Bush said that her home in Maine was a "hodgepodge'—a house grandchildren are more than welcome in." The lifestyle was relaxed and informal. Lunch, said Mrs. Bush, was usually soup, with sandwiches or salad. "The children eat dinner early, but the two older grandchildren usually eat with us. . . . Most of our meals are cooked on the grill, swordfish being my favorite and lobster a close second." The family did a fair amount of entertaining. Bedtime varied for different people, but George and Barbara turned out their lights around 9:30 PM after active but satisfying days.[8]

During his tenure as president, Kennebunkport became George Bush's summer White House. It was at Kennebunkport that the president announced his controversial selection of Clarence Thomas to serve as an associate justice of the Supreme Court. The compound became the center of power, and it played a role in the pre–Persian Gulf War negotiations of summer 1990.

In a busy series of events, George Bush held meetings with aides, spoke to world leaders by telephone, and welcomed heads of states, including King Hussein of Jordan and Prince Saud al-Faisal of Saudi Arabia to his summer home. Twelve Bush grandchildren arrived to spend some part of the vacation with Barbara and George. Always the good sport, Barbara never complained publicly about the extra people or extra work that was required of her. Her diary entry of 16 August 1990 provides some sense of how strenuous those requirements could be: "We had all the little kiddies cleaning out their rooms, straightening their drawers and then I had room inspection. We made a picnic lunch and sent Ellie, Sam, Jebby, Barbara and Jenna to the beach for the day. At twelve noon His Majesty King Hussein (of Jordan) arrived with his entourage. . . . The group of twelve had a lunch of half a lobster, chicken salad and muffins."[9] Shortly after the Jordanians departed, His Royal Highness Prince Saud al-Faisal arrived with *his* entourage.

Some days, Mrs. Bush noted, would begin in the middle of the night with telephone calls and hurried conferences. Whenever he could find free time, President Bush would play a round of golf, play horseshoes, fish, or while away the hours piloting his cigarette boat through the waters of the Atlantic. Though busier than usual, many days in the summer of 1990 were filled with the comings and goings of the famous and family.[10]

The president worked along with the United Nations to assemble an international coalition of countries that opposed the invasion and asked and later demanded that Iraq's leader, Saddam Hussein, withdraw his forces from Kuwait. Thousands of American troops and troops from coalition countries were sent to Saudi Arabia as part of an operation called Desert Shield. The change of locale did not affect the president's work. The international coalition that President Bush had helped build eventually numbered twenty-three countries and included, most notably, the Soviet Union.[11]

Barbara spent time with Raisa Gorbachev during a hastily called summit in Helsinki, Finland, between President Bush and Russian president Mikhail Gorbachev on 9 September 1990. The two women had developed a warm relationship during Mrs. Gorbachev's visit to Washington and Wellesley College a few months earlier. In Helsinki, they visited the library at the University of Helsinki and then greeted a crowd of well-wishers that had gathered across the street. Mrs. Gorbachev gave a sumptuous tea in Mrs. Bush's honor at the Russian embassy. Both women advocated a peaceful solution to troubles in the Middle East. Mrs. Bush told reporters, "There is a peaceful solution. I hope our husbands, along with the rest of the free world, will work hard to make peace."[12]

Presidents Bush and Gorbachev were less optimistic, and in a joint communiqué said that "nothing short of a return to pre–2 August status of Kuwait can end Iraq's isolation. Nothing short of the complete implementation of the United Nations Security Council resolutions is acceptable."[13] Neither man ruled out possible military action. Mrs. Bush returned to the United States hopeful that war with Iraq might be averted; she also commented about her counterpart: "Each visit with Raisa made me like her more and understand her a little better."[14]

Mrs. Bush told Reuters News that the standoff over Kuwait was the most serious crisis that her husband had faced in twenty months in office. He was maintaining a positive disposition, but it was always on his mind. When reporters asked her if she was offering the president advice on the crisis, she responded in a manner typical of Barbara Bush. No, said the first lady, she was not dispensing advice; however, she would advance an idea if she had something to offer: "I think wives in my case, under our system, do very well to aid and comfort their husband and keep trying to make life as peaceful as you can at home, not needle, not give suggestions. Of course, if I had a good idea I'd say 'Would this work?' and they said, 'We've done it' usually."[15]

The first lady was outspoken in her criticism of Saddam Hussein. The "dreadful man," as she labeled Hussein, was asserting that United Nations economic sanctions were killing children in his country. Mrs. Bush argued that this claim had no basis in fact. "That's not what's killing children. He went into a country and attacked it, and we can't forget that."[16] If Hussein was really concerned about the children of Iraq, she said, "he should pull his troops out of

Kuwait and end the crisis" that could plunge the whole region into war.[17] Her greatest concern was for the young men and women of the military who were living in the desert, waiting for a peaceful resolution of the crisis or the beginning of war. She would like to send them a message and "tell them we want them home and that we're doing everything we can for peace."[18] If her own children were in the Gulf, Mrs. Bush continued, "I'd feel like every other American mother. I'd be sick with worry, but I would also feel very proud."[19] In another interview with Helen Thomas, she acknowledged the difficulties faced by female troops sent to Saudi Arabia who had to live within a restrictive Muslim culture that forbade them to drive, show their faces, or make purchases by themselves. Mrs. Bush said that they should "stick with the customs in the country and we'll get them home as fast as we can."[20] Even if she was bothered by the restrictions that female troops had to endure, Mrs. Bush said little. The Bushes had a long and warm relationship with the Saudis that began during George Bush's years in the oil business; they rarely, if ever, criticized members of the House of Saud.

In the midst of diplomacy and troop movements, *Millie's Book* was launched at the Pierpont Morgan Library in New York City and provided a welcome respite from war talks. In her comments on the occasion of the book's publication, Mrs. Bush lamented that Millie could not join the assembled group: "Millie sends her thanks and sincerest regrets, but she thought it was important for one member of the family to be home when the Prez gets back to the office today. It was no sacrifice for Millie, that's just the kind of dog she is, as anyone who reads her moving life story cannot deny."[21] At a *Millie's Book* event a few days later, Mrs. Bush told the audience about Millie and George and Barbara's concern for the troops in the Gulf: "She's [Millie] deeply concerned, just as George and I, about the well-being of our men and women in the Gulf, and she shares our great empathy for their families, but she knows, as we do, that we're doing the right thing."[22] A few days later, another literacy initiative, "Mrs. Bush's Storytime," was launched nationwide on ABC radio. *Millie's Book* and "Mrs. Bush's Storytime" provided two of the few lighthearted moments that fall.

Mrs. Bush devoted a good deal of time over the course of the autumn to campaigning for twenty-three Republican candidates across the country. While her speeches extolled the virtues of various Republican candidates, she also included references to Operation Desert Shield. In one speech she told listeners about the letters that the president had received from the young men and women who were serving in Saudi Arabia, on ships at sea and in the air. She said, "The [letters] are so touching and so supportive. George worries about each and every one of them as we all do. And he is proud of these brave young men and women, as we all are."[23] Speaking to another campaign audience, she said of the fighting men and women, "They are as dear to him as his own and he is working his heart out for a peaceful solution to this awful problem."[24] She was capable of discussing policy and did, but the first lady was always at her best talking about her husband in a personal manner: "I'm going to offer an unsolicited and completely unbiased testimonial. After watching him handle the crisis in the Middle East, navigate the Helsinki Summit and deal with a Congress that seems to be more interested in politics than policy, I thank God every day that George Bush is President of the United States."[25] Mrs. Bush may have been enthusiastically received by campaign audiences, and they might have appreciated her comments about Operation Desert Shield, but their approbation did not translate into votes. Of the ten congressional candidates for whom she campaigned, only two were elected.

Just prior to Thanksgiving, the Bushes left on an important overseas trip that would take them to Czechoslovakia, France, and Germany for talks with respective leaders about Iraq. Finally, the Bushes arrived in Jeddah, Saudi Arabia. In her diary, Mrs. Bush wrote, "Thanksgiving Day, 1990—The best we ever had."[26] On Thanksgiving Day they traveled to Dhahran to visit U.S. and allied troops. The president spoke to the troops and met with reporters. He was asked what he had learned on his trip to Saudi Arabia, and he said, "I learned a lot about the kids just from looking them in the eye. And I learned once again something I already knew: how lucky we are to have this all-volunteer force as strong, as well-trained, and as highly motivated as they are."[27] When the president finished his statement, he and the first lady plunged into the crowd of well-wishers for handshakes, pictures, and autographs. Mrs. Bush recalled that every serviceman and servicewoman seemed to have a camera, and she and the president were asked to sign pictures, uniforms, and pieces of paper. The next stop was the Army Tactical Location, where the president spoke again, and then the Bushes went through the chow line and shared the troop's holiday meal. After lunch, the president and first lady took a helicopter to the USS *Nassau* and participated in a Thanksgiving Day service on the ship. They finished their day with a visit to the Marine Tactical Location. Mrs. Bush was impressed by the spirit and commitment of the young people she met. She concluded, "Our day in the desert with the men and women in the military was a highlight of George's presidency. What a privilege it was for us to share their Thanksgiving Day."[28] The day in Saudi Arabia was used to improve morale among the troops who had been living in the desert for months anticipating engagement with Iraqi troops.

The United Nations voted on 29 November 1990 to give the international coalition permission to use any means to remove Saddam Hussein's troops from Kuwait if Iraq did not comply in withdrawing its forces by 15 January 1991.[29] Barbara concluded that her husband would have an easier time dealing with Hussein because of the UN vote. She also noted somewhat bitterly that the U.S. Congress did not seem to be quite as supportive: "As is often the case, the rest of the world backs George more than our own (Congress) and press. The House and Senate have been having hearings. Many of the Congress members have plenty of criticism, but no solutions."[30]

There was vigorous debate of antiwar resolutions in both houses of Congress. In the House, the vote was 253 to 183 against an antiwar resolution; in the Senate the vote was 52 to 47; both resolutions were defeated. Later, both houses supported a resolution to use force against Iraq.[31] Polls by seven different national polling organizations reported between 68 percent and 84 percent of Americans approved of the decision to go to war, a wide range of opinion which demonstrated that many people remained unconvinced about the necessity for combat.[32]

In an undated diary entry from early January, Mrs. Bush was annoyed with the press's handling of events that seemed to be leading up to war. She wrote: "The press has a disproportionate part to play in this battle of waiting and nerves. As an example, Dick Cheney [secretary of defense] and Colin Powell [chairman of the Joint Chiefs of Staff] came . . . to see George and reported that we were ready for anything. . . . Then a member of the press reported we were not ready. Think of the message that sends to Hussein, not to mention our allies!"[33] As a precautionary measure, the White House was closed to tourists, and security was increased.

There were protests around the world. In New York City, those opposed to war gathered in Times Square and chanted, "Hell no, we won't go—we won't fight for Texaco."[34] Protesters picketed the White House, chanting peace slogans. One person chained himself to the White House fence. The Bushes could not hear the chanting in the residence, but Barbara could hear it when she was in her office. She was sympathetic to those who were morally opposed to war, like religious leaders or Senator Mark Hatfield of Oregon, who had been an outspoken critic of U.S. involvement in Vietnam. She drew the line, however, with regard to some of the people picketing outside her window: "I cannot understand sitting back and letting one country invade another and ravage its people. The reports coming out of Kuwait were so nauseating and brutal that after reading about ten pages of the Amnesty International report, I had to stop or get sick."[35]

To escape the pressures of Washington, Barbara and a group of family members and friends went to Camp David. It had snowed recently, and the group decided to go sledding. Mrs. Bush realized too late that the snow had turned to ice, and her saucer was out of control. Whizzing down a hill at a high rate of speed, she collided with a tree. At first she felt a little shaky but fine; however, she sustained a hairline fracture of the fibula. Her next weeks were spent in a wheelchair or using a cane as she healed. Mrs. Bush was feeling well enough to tell an audience a few weeks later in another one of the jokes that her ghostwriters provided for her, "You may have read, Arnold Schwarzenegger was up there with us. That's the last time we'll invite any actors to Camp David. The last thing I heard as I was racing down the hill was 'Break a Leg.'"[36]

Just after the New Year, on 5 January 1991, President Bush gave a radio address to update the country on the Persian Gulf crisis. He warned that Saddam Hussein had eleven days to meet the United Nations deadline for a full and complete withdrawal from Kuwait or military action might commence. Mr. Bush said that Saddam posed a threat to Egypt, Saudi Arabia, Turkey, Israel, and Syria. In an eerie foreshadowing of his son's arguments prior to the Iraq War that began eleven years later, he noted that there were even higher, more deadly stakes: "Each day that passes brings Saddam Hussein further on the path to developing biological and nuclear weapons and the missiles to deliver them." Concluding his remarks, Bush referred to the meal he and Barbara had shared with American troops in Saudi Arabia: "These men and women are America's finest. We owe each of them our gratitude and full support. That is why we must all stand together, not as Republicans or Democrats, conservative or liberals, but as Americans."[37]

The 15 January deadline established by the United Nations passed without any movement of Iraqi troops out of Kuwait. Her diary on 16 January gave some sense of Barbara's foreboding: "For the last twelve hours I have known something so dreadful that I can't even imagine it. I have the feeling I'd like to go to bed and pull the covers over my head and stay there for six weeks and then see if it is all over. . . . George told me last night that they decided that it would start tonight."[38] That evening at 7:30 PM eastern standard time, 2:30 AM in Baghdad, coalition forces began bombing targets in Iraq and Kuwait. Operation Desert Shield became Operation Desert Storm. Mrs. Bush wrote, "I remember feeling so frightened for our men and women who were there *and* for all the civilians in Iraq."[39] Iraq launched SCUD missiles at both Israel and Saudi Arabia, with the hope of provoking a retaliatory strike by the Israelis. This never happened as American Patriot missile batteries attempted to intercept and destroy the SCUDs.

Months later, George Bush told an audience that on the night before the invasion, he and Barbara had prayed for those who were going to war. Bush said, "For me, prayer has always been important but quite personal . . . and like a lot of people, I have worried a bit about shedding tears in public . . . but as Barbara and I prayed before the air war began, we were thinking about those young men and women overseas. And I had tears start down the cheeks and I no longer worried how it looked to others."[40]

Like most Americans and people around the world, Barbara watched the war unfold on the Cable News Network (CNN). The twenty-four-hour all-news network would establish itself as the front-runner of continuous coverage with eyewitness accounts

from correspondent Bernard Shaw in Baghdad. The reality of constant coverage became apparent to Barbara when her granddaugh-
ter Ellie rushed into her bedroom to announce, "Ganny, we are
being bombed. I'm scared." Barbara saw that Ellie had watched a
CNN report of a strike by SCUD missiles in Israel. She feared for the
children of Israel and the children watching and wrote, "I hope parents are monitoring what their children are seeing on the television
and helping them over this brutal time."[41] She advised parents to sit
down and talk to their children about what was happening and what
they might be seeing.

She was disgusted when Iraq paraded captured coalition pilots
before television cameras. In increasing frustration, she wrote, "It is
the darndest war, fought over the tube. CNN covers everything and
tells us that they are only able to show us what the Iraqis want us to
see and hear." When she learned that Hussein had put children and
elderly people in a command post that might be a strategic target,
she called the Iraqi dictator an animal.[42] As the allies increased the
bombing of strategic targets in Iraq, the Iraqis retaliated by setting
Kuwaiti oil refineries afire.

The opposition that the Bushes had experienced at the White
House fanned out across the country. Dissent was expressed on a
number of college campuses. Most students had been born after
1970, and to them the antiwar movement that had influenced public
opinion about Vietnam was little more than paragraphs in a history
book. Many students found themselves in a quandary: the military
buildup in Vietnam had occurred over a period of years; the conflict
with Iraq developed over five months. A professor pointed out, "In
the 60's, rightly or wrongly, a lot of people felt sympathetic to the
North Vietnamese. Virtually no one defends Iraq."[43]

Though casualties were low and television images of "weapons delivery" (a term used by General Norman Schwarzkopf in describing
the bombing of an Iraqi building) reassuring, a week after the bombing began the nation's enthusiasm turned to apprehension. Feelings of
foreboding could be traced to a statement by Secretary of Defense
Dick Cheney, who suggested that the war could last for months.[44] Reporters asked Mrs. Bush if the war was going on longer than people
had expected. Mrs. Bush said, "Nobody thought that the war was
going to be over in a week. We didn't." The reporter's second question,

did the first lady think that people were too impatient, provoked a stern reply that included resolve to win and a reprimand to the media: "No, I think you [the press] are impatient. I think people understand that we have a big project. . . . The public is willing to wait 'as long as it takes' and we're going to win."[45] Perhaps the public was willing to wait, but the administration was keeping a tight cap on the release of information, and members of Congress were critical of the policy. Congressman Les Aspin, chairman of the House Armed Services Committee, complained, "We haven't got the specifics and that's causing heartburn in Congress, as well as it has in the press corps." Senator Bob Kerrey (D-NE) added his voice: "People like myself in Congress need to have information so we can make judgments about what the policy ought to be. It's not healthy to have so much silence."[46]

Possible terrorist actions against domestic airline flights had a negative effect on travel. To try to bolster the industry, President Bush asked the first lady to take a commercial flight when she traveled to Indianapolis to visit a Veterans Administration hospital. She was happy to oblige and told reporters, "I want people to know the airports are secure. I'm trying to say to the public that our airlines and our airports have a lot of security and we're safe."[47] The trip got positive press coverage, and over time, ridership increased. The excursion to Indianapolis and her statement also marked the beginning of Barbara Bush's personal role in the Persian Gulf War.

A number of first ladies found themselves dealing with war while living in the White House. During World War II, Eleanor Roosevelt served as the associate director of the Office of Civilian Defense before resigning because of a lack of progress and press criticism. She visited American troops in Great Britain and the South Pacific.[48] Lady Bird Johnson, first lady during the early years of the Vietnam War, never addressed the war in speeches or visited soldiers, but she worried a great deal about her two sons-in-law, who were serving in Southeast Asia. Years after leaving the White House, reporter Barbara Walters asked Mrs. Johnson if she and her husband had differed on his war policies. Mrs. Johnson ignored the question but certainly had opinions and replied that "the black boxes—the coffins" coming home were the worst part, and it was "a bad time." Of the Vietnam War she said, "You got stuck, you couldn't get loose."[49] Pat Nixon, first lady during the latter part of the Vietnam War, visited wounded troops and an orphanage near Saigon.[50] Barbara Bush's visit to the troops in Saudi Arabia was reminiscent of both Eleanor Roosevelt and Pat Nixon; her speeches to military audiences were a first lady first.

Both the president and Mrs. Bush traveled to meet the military and their families. President Bush made his first visits to marine, air force, and army bases on 1 February. He admitted to having difficulty maintaining his composure when he saw crying faces or children mouthing the words "Bring my Dad home safe."[51] Barbara Bush delivered ninety-three speeches during 1991: between 12 February and 27 March, she made visits to and gave speeches at nine military installations. Her Gulf War–related discourse thus accounted for approximately 10 percent of her speeches for 1991. As was her practice with commencement speeches, Mrs. Bush's staff prepared a generic speech for delivery to military audiences. There were two different versions of the speech. In the first version, given from 12 February through 28 February, Mrs. Bush's objective was to support the military and their families as they dealt with the uncertainties of war. She was the president's cheerleader, bringing the regards of the commander in chief.

Mrs. Bush's first Gulf War speech was delivered at Griffiss Air Force Base in Rome, New York, on 12 February. The next five speeches followed the formula of the first. The first lady began her comments by explaining that she would have come sooner, however, "there was this little matter of a sledding expedition at Camp David." She was fine, said Mrs. Bush, but "I still wince every time the grandchildren sing 'Over the river, and into the tree to grandmother's house we go.'" She was visiting the air force base because she cared so much about those serving in the Gulf, and the president felt the same: "George feels so strongly about all our service men and women. He has been one, and he has never forgotten what it's like to fight for this great country of ours." She was proud, said Mrs. Bush, of everyone's effort, both military personnel and family and friends: "For those of you who are troops, I know you are pulling double time to fill in for our soldiers in the Middle East. . . . You are serving your country too, and we couldn't make it without you. And the same goes for families and friends of soldiers in the Gulf. You are doing the most essential service of all, by tending to daily life."

Mrs. Bush recalled her own wartime experience, waiting for a loved one to come home from combat: "Years ago, when our country was fighting another war, I was a college girl in Massachusetts. But my heart was not in the classroom, at least that's how I explained my grades to my parents. My heart and thoughts were somewhere in the Pacific with a wonderful young Navy pilot, to whom I happened to be engaged." Unlike many of her scripted humorous lines, this sentiment could resonate with audiences because Mrs. Bush had endured the same uncertainty with which they had to live. The unspoken questions were, Will my loved one return home? If he or she does return, when will that happen, and would the person return whole in body and spirit?

Acknowledging the difficulty of trying to live a normal life while the people they loved were in harm's way, the first lady told the audience on the base that they were the people responsible for making sure dentist appointments were kept, mortgage payments made, Little League games watched. People needed to support each other, and she used an anecdote to illustrate that point. She recalled a story about a friend who called a good friend of hers to see how she was doing—her husband was serving in the Persian Gulf. Her friend had an awful migraine headache, the children were home from school, the dishes were not washed, and the laundry was piled high. Mrs. Bush's friend responded that she would be over to help; she would do the laundry, wash the dishes, and take the children to the park. She then asked, "'By the way, Sam's alright, isn't he?' 'Sam? Who's Sam?' came the answer. 'Sam, your husband,' said the caller. 'My husband's name isn't Sam,' said the poor woman. 'Oh dear,' said my friend. 'I'm so sorry, I must have dialed the wrong number.' There was a long pause and then a sad voice said, 'Does that mean you won't be coming over?'"

The speech concluded with Mrs. Bush reading an excerpt from a letter that she and the president had received from a young woman in the U.S. Air Force serving in Saudi Arabia. Looking out at the desert, wrote the young woman, "I see a land I do not claim as my own, but out of respect and compassion for those who do, I am here. We share a common friend—peace. We see a common enemy—terrorism. When we speak in these terms, all boundaries cease to exist. I am afraid of what it might cost. But *far* more afraid of what it would cost if we elected not to invest at all."[52] Mrs. Bush told the audience that the woman believed in the justness of the military endeavor, and that both she and the president were proud of all these young Americans.

Her speech at Grissom Air Force Base in Peru, Indiana, on 14 February, was almost identical to her earlier comments at Griffiss Air Force Base. Mrs. Bush's next speech was given on 22 February to families of the 101st Airborne Division based at Fort Campbell, Kentucky, which had sent 28,000 troops to the Gulf. Understanding the need for humor, Mrs. Bush expanded on her sledding story and added that the president, who disliked broccoli, had not been very sympathetic about her accident: "I'm going to be honest, George wasn't very sensitive or sympathetic. Last weekend (he) asked me how I'd like to go skiing? I asked him how he'd like to eat broccoli every day for the rest of his life!"[53]

Mrs. Bush went on to praise the base's neighbors in Clarksville and Hopkinsville and the newspaper *Kentucky New Era* and television station Channel 43. The latter two organizations had put together "Operation Helping Hand" to encourage and support those at Fort Campbell. "There are so many ways your community can— and will—reach out to help you, I hope you will keep reaching out to each other,"[54] said the first lady.

Later that day, at the 161st Air Refueling Group of the Arizona Air National Guard in Phoenix, Arizona, Mrs. Bush paid tribute to the first Arizona National Guard unit to be called to duty in the Gulf. In her memoirs, Mrs. Bush wrote that this visit was different from some of the others that she made during the war. She had private meetings with the families of four soldiers, one who was a prisoner of war, one who was missing in action, and two who had been killed in action.[55] Mrs. Bush recalled that these visits were difficult, but the families always seemed appreciative of her efforts.[56] The first lady listened to the families, and there were hugs and tears.

After more than a month of bombings, Iraqi troops still had not withdrawn from Kuwait. On the evening of 23 February, George Bush gave the command to begin the ground war. Hussein had predicted that the ground war would be "the Mother of All Battles."[57] He assured everyone that his troops "would inflict such heavy casualties that the coalition forces would withdraw in dismay."[58] According to General Norman Schwarzkopf, the coalition commander, Hussein overestimated Iraqi fighting power. The Iraqis had the largest army in the Gulf, the fourth strongest in the world. Yet, much to the surprise of Hussein and many observers around the world, the coalition savaged the Iraqi troops, taking 8,000 prisoners in the first few hours.[59] The air war had exacted a greater toll on Iraqi forces than expected. Marines arrived in Kuwait City within three days. One hundred hours later, the war was over.

On 27 February, President Bush announced the cessation of hostilities and the end of the war. Newspaper headlines announced, "We win!" The war lasted forty-two days; 148 Americans were killed in action, but the coalition's victory was absolute. Mrs. Bush wrote in her diary, "All the pundits said it would be a long war, that we would have thousands dead, that it would cost billions of dollars more than it did."[60] The next morning however, the Bushes were startled to hear Saddam Hussein claim victory. Barbara, never one to mince words, wrote, "It makes you want to go in and bomb the whey out of him."[61]

One historian suggests that the outcome of the Gulf War was never in doubt because Saddam's forces were outnumbered and they had no air support. The dictator's sole strategy was to literally dig in and hold on long enough for Americans to become disillusioned with the war. Intelligence pinpointed the location of trenches and bombed Saddam's forces or rolled over them with tanks.[62]

Mrs. Bush continued giving speeches at military installations, but the focus of her post–ground war comments was that the United States and the coalition had been victorious and, hopefully, the troops would be home soon. Her speech on 28 February at Fort Meade in Maryland was intended originally to rally the troops. Instead, it was part of a victory celebration. Mrs. Bush said, "A crucial part of the success of Operation Desert Storm has been the reservists who were called to the Gulf. Forty-four of those Reserve units, from around the country, were trained by you, right here at Ft. Meade. You should be very proud of your stunning contribution to this effort. I know your president is." She went on to compliment coalition commander Norman Schwarzkopf, who was enjoying military success and great personal popularity in the United States: "Speaking of stunning efforts, how about that Stormin' Norman

Schwarzkopf! He's like a cross between General Patton and Fozzy Bear."[63] She was cautiously optimistic, she continued, about the future. She knew that servicemen and servicewomen would not be coming home immediately. Families had dealt with long months of uncertainty, and Mrs. Bush acknowledged that the wait had been unending and worrisome: "We do understand a little of what you are going through. The news from the Gulf is good—Now. But I know you have coped with uncertainty, loneliness and fear during the last several months."[64] Always, there were references to her time waiting for George Bush to come home from World War II, which confirmed her credibility with the audience.

Iraq accepted the terms of a cease-fire offered by the coalition nations on 3 March. On the deck of the USS *Forrestal*, docked at the Mayport Naval Air Station in Florida three days later, Mrs. Bush commented, "Your continued presence here in port, will be a welcome signal to the world that the peace process in the Gulf is going well. For your families, having you here at home is quite literally an answer to their prayers."[65] She understood that some servicemen and servicewomen were disappointed not to have experienced combat, but they had still made important contributions to the war effort: "However disappointed some of you may be that you won't be shipping out, please know that wherever you served, you are members of the coalition forces that liberated Kuwait. You have contributed mightily to an honorable and lasting peace."[66]

The first lady was effusive later in the day speaking to an audience at the Mayport Naval Air Station. After noting that 9,000 men and women from the Jacksonville, Florida, area were serving in the Gulf, she said, "Your loved ones have played a crucial role in the extraordinary success of Operation Desert Storm. Now that it's almost over . . . I think it entirely appropriate for you, their family and friends, to shout your heads off with joy!" Mrs. Bush told her audience that she and the president loved each and every sailor and soldier like their own: "With all the joy and pride we feel today, we also feel a deep sorrow for those precious young men and women who won't be coming home. We will never forget them and we must dedicate ourselves to protecting the peace."[67]

Mrs. Bush's final wartime speech was given on 27 March at a "Welcome Home" program at the Marine Corps Air-Ground

Combat Center in Twentynine Palms, California. She reminded her listeners that she and the president had shared Thanksgiving lunch with some of them in Saudi Arabia; she was relieved that they were celebrating Easter in California. Operation Desert Storm worked, said Mrs. Bush: "In this just war, 33 coalition nations stood against the aggression of Saddam Hussein. White fought alongside black, women along with men, Arab with Jew. And it worked!" She and the president were thankful that the troops were coming home: "Just as your absence inspired a nation to wrap itself in yellow ribbon, so your return brings an optimism of spirit and new confidence in our country."[68]

Mrs. Bush rarely missed an opportunity to trumpet her husband's successes. Meeting with reporters in April 1991, Mrs. Bush expressed admiration for her husband and his handling of the war. She told her listeners that she knew her husband of forty-six years very well, but she found herself in awe of him during the Persian Gulf conflict. She said, "I have enormous respect for his ability. I knew he had it, but these were very difficult times. Yet he managed to stay on a very even keel with absolutely no blips." She added, "I had an occasional flare-up."[69]

President Bush may have paid a price for staying on an even keel in the face of adversity. In early May 1991, he was jogging at Camp David when he experienced shortness of breath and tightness in his chest. He was immediately flown to Bethesda Medical Center and diagnosed with atrial fibrillation, a cardiac abnormality. Medication relieved his symptoms. A few days later he was also diagnosed with Graves' disease, which may have given rise to his heart problem. Like his wife, who was also treated for Graves' disease, the president began a course of radioactive iodine to treat his condition. Ever his protector, Mrs. Bush told reporters that she believed the president's illnesses had been triggered by the stress of the Persian Gulf War. Stress, she said, was a possible contributor to Graves' disease, and her husband had been deeply affected by the difficult decision to send young people off to war to possibly die in battle: "The fact that you send other people's children to war . . . don't let anyone ever underestimate that."[70] The president made an uneventful recovery, but questions about his cardiac health lingered and resurfaced during the 1992 presidential campaign. In the future, Mrs. Bush would field numerous questions about her husband's health and would respond with public statements and comments in speeches about his physical fitness to continue as chief executive.

The formal cease-fire agreement was signed in June, and the Bushes took part in a wreath-laying ceremony at Arlington National Cemetery that was followed by a parade to honor the troops that had fought in the Gulf War. Speaking to the Pennsylvania Republican Party later in the month, Mrs. Bush said, "It was glorious to join tens of thousands of grateful Americans to welcome home the troops of Desert Storm. Each of those young men and women deserve our thanks—and our commitment to the promise of a nation that is, as George says 'whole and good.'"[71] Mrs. Bush also noted that things had returned to normal at the White House as tourists were once again permitted to visit, a relief after the preceding months.

The president's approval rating fell precipitously in the months after Desert Storm. By the time he was running for reelection, he had lost momentum, and the heady days of January 1991 were a vague memory. Though historians and reporters would suggest later that the war was fought for oil, the president felt that he had been part of an international coalition that had been morally right in confronting a brutal dictator.

The Bushes visited Kuwait in April 1993 at the invitation of the government. They were moved by the gratitude of the small country for America's leading role in forming the international coalition. Two years after Iraqi troops had left Kuwait, stories abounded about supposed atrocities that had occurred during the Iraqi occupation, and devastation was still evident. In the last weeks of the war, the Iraqis had purportedly burned, plundered, and tortured Kuwaitis. However, Mrs. Bush noted in her memoirs that building was going on all over the country, and things were returning to normal.

After the trip, the Bushes were shocked to learn that a group of Iraqis, possibly under the direction of Saddam Hussein, had planned to bomb their car. The plot was discovered and conclusively traced back to the Iraqi intelligence service. President Clinton ordered the firing of twenty-three Tomahawk missiles into Iraq's intelligence headquarters in retaliation for the plot. His hope was that the attack would be a deterrent to further Iraqi terrorism.[72] The Bushes, along with General Norman Schwarzkopf and former prime minister Margaret Thatcher, returned to Kuwait again, in 2001, to celebrate the tenth anniversary of the liberation. Mrs. Bush noted many positive changes, most notably continuing efforts to rebuild the country, but prisoners of war were still unaccounted for, and the memories of atrocities were still clear.[73] Barbara Bush's opinion of Saddam Hussein remained unchanged. She told reporters, "I'd like to see him hung . . . if he were found guilty. . . . I'm sure all of you have talked to people who came back from Kuwait. But it's just horrible, the stories they tell."[74] President Bush said later, "I seldom differ with my wife. I doubt if I'll differ with her here."[75]

The Persian Gulf War prompted rhetorical and public policy responses from Barbara Bush. Though she did not have input into any war-related decisions, she was well informed about the war and outspoken about Saddam Hussein, the welfare of military troops, and the way in which war news was disseminated to the American public. This was a departure for a first lady who publicly tried to steer clear of the president's initiatives and agenda. Barbara Bush excelled at connecting with people, and hers was the face of the comforter-in-chief during the war. Speaking to military personnel and their dependents, demonstrating that airplane travel was safe, visiting wounded veterans, and comforting those who had lost family members, she put a compassionate face on the conflict. She never missed an opportunity to call attention to her husband's achievements and, while acknowledging the stress he had been under, argued that he was a healthy and fit president.

The victory in Desert Storm was a high point in the presidency of George Bush and in Barbara Bush's tenure as first lady. Patriotism enveloped the country, and it seemed that George Bush, whose own approval ratings stood at an almost unbelievable 91 percent, would sweep to a second term in the White House.[76] After early 1991, however, things began to go downhill for the presidential couple. Barbara Bush, who had aided the administration in the important public relations aspects of the Persian Gulf War, emerged as a major asset and would play an integral role in the presidential campaign of 1992.

CHAPTER 6

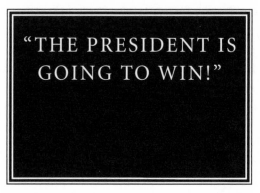

"THE PRESIDENT IS GOING TO WIN!"

For three years, Barbara Bush had been a nonpartisan first lady, whose deft speeches and well-managed media image had boosted her poll numbers. During 1992, in the heat of her husband's reelection bid, she became a defender of George Bush and his policies. Mrs. Bush had mixed feelings about another four years as first lady. She had watched the presidency age her husband; she had noted the daily slights and disloyalties directed against him "and had taken them hard—harder, some thought, than the president."[1] She worried about her husband's health. The first lady hoped to leave politics and was looking forward to retirement; she wanted to have more time with her family and wanted to have George Bush sail her down the inland waterway while both were able to enjoy the experience.

If the president wanted another four years in the White House, she would certainly contribute her best effort. A political realist, she understood that George Bush's bright prospects for reelection that the Gulf War had produced had turned gloomy by the end of 1991. A worsening economy and falling poll numbers plus the prospect of Republican dissension over his renomination worried the first lady. "I don't know if George will survive this political year or not," she wrote, "but I do know he is the only stable person running. He has the Congress, top labor leaders and the press against him. They smell blood. . . . My only concerns are for the country and I'd hate

George to lose for his sake."[2] She and George Bush would wage a tough, aggressive campaign to retain the presidency. In the course of helping her husband, Barbara Bush encountered controversies of her own that made her a more partisan figure than she had been during her first three years in the White House.

The year 1992 began on a sour note. To cement his claim that he was a president strong in the area of foreign affairs, George Bush, along with the first lady and their entourage, visited Australia, Singapore, Korea, and Japan from 30 December 1990 to 10 January 1991. The ostensible goal of their ten-day trip was to foster goodwill and explore possibilities for boosting U.S. exports to Japan; the unspoken objective was to burnish George Bush's image on the international stage. The early part of the trip progressed without incident, yet the president's health was still shaky and the potential for a setback was real. The previous year he had experienced heart problems that were associated with Graves' disease, an autoimmune disease that attacks the thyroid. Mrs. Bush too, had been diagnosed and treated for the same illness.

In Japan, both Bushes had particularly hectic schedules. Together they visited the Kyoto Imperial Palace and a newly opened Toys "Я" Us store and paid a courtesy call on Emperor Akihito. The president, who was accompanied by a number of prominent U.S. automakers, attended meetings to try to persuade the Japanese to relax strict barriers to the importation of American cars. Mrs. Bush, accompanied by Mrs. Miyazawa, wife of the prime minister, visited the American Trade Fair at the Mitsukoshi department store. During the late afternoon, Mrs. Bush had tea with Empress Akihito, and then the women watched President Bush and U.S. ambassador to Japan Michael Armacost play the emperor and crown prince in tennis; the Americans were badly beaten. After the game, the Bushes returned to their rooms at the Akasaka Palace, the Japanese guest house.[3] The president told Mrs. Bush that he did not feel well, but not too bad.[4] He took a long nap and then prepared for the evening's event, a state dinner given in honor of the Bushes by Prime Minister and Mrs. Miyazawa. While on the receiving line, George Bush felt ill and knew that he should leave but persevered. Unable to eat, he maintained a brave front. "I remember breaking out into a cold sweat, and the next thing I knew. . . . I realized I was lying flat on the floor, having thrown up all over Miyazawa,"[5] recalled the president. Initially, Mrs. Bush was frightened, but doctors who were in attendance at the dinner examined the president and diagnosed a nasty intestinal flu. According to Mrs. Bush's press secretary, Anna Perez, the first lady knew the president was all right when he sat up and said to Prime Minister Miyazawa, "Why don't you just roll me under the table and let me sleep it off."[6] He was taken back to the Akasaka Palace.

As soon as the president had left the dinner, Prime Minister Miyazawa rose and asked if Mrs. Bush would like to say a few words. Nonplussed, the first lady thanked her hosts for a wonderful visit and said: "You know, I can't explain what happened to George because it never happened before, but I'm beginning to think it's the ambassador's fault. He and George played the emperor and crown prince in tennis today, and they were badly beaten. And we Bushes aren't used to that. So he felt much worse than I thought."[7]

By the time she had finished her short remarks, Mrs. Bush had the initially uneasy audience laughing. Her quick response won almost universal praise. A reporter who was present at the dinner wrote, "The First Lady accepted the mission, and she fulfilled it in an ad-libbed presentation that was marked with old-fashioned Yankee virtues: stoic calm in crisis, a gentle eloquence, a self-effacing wit."[8] Another source wrote, "The one person who came out ahead in the local press coverage was Barbara Bush. By not losing her calm and underplaying the seriousness of her husband's collapse, she certainly proved she was a worthy first lady."[9] The only naysayer was the *Washington Post*'s Tom Shales, who wrote that while Mrs. Bush had been "trotted out to make light of the president's illness by cracking a few jokes . . . the play fell flat and she came across not as bolsteringly positive but as inappropriately giddy."[10] The incident, though relatively minor, cast a pall over the trip and raised questions about the president's overall health that would continue to plague him throughout the presidential campaign. During an interview years later, Mrs. Bush commented that a number of people in the White House party had come down with a similar stomach flu, a fact the press did not report.[11]

The medical situation did not augur well for the coming year. The trip to the Pacific Rim was something less than a resounding success; a CBS poll found that only 18 percent of those polled rated the trip a success.[12] The reelection campaign was in disarray and got a late start because of the president's indecision. George Bush was a decent man and a capable crisis manager, but he had no vision for the country. The economy was in the doldrums, Bush was still reeling from a broken promise not to raise taxes, and the campaign itself seemed to have no message. A reporter who covered Bush for many years commented that despite assurances from the president that he was healthy and primed for the campaign, he seemed listless, tired, if not ill.[13]

Later that month in his 1992 State of the Union address, the president acknowledged his wife's popularity. He told his worldwide audience: "You know, with the big build up this address has had, I wanted to make sure it would be a big hit, but I couldn't convince Barbara to deliver it for me." He also tried to make light of his medical problems in Japan: "I see the Speaker and Vice President are laughing. They saw what I did in Japan, and they're happy to be sitting behind me."[14] Both comments provoked laughter, but it was obvious that the president's health would be an issue and Barbara Bush would be an important person during the upcoming election.

In December 1991, in testament to her growing popularity and importance and George Bush's declining political fortunes, Mrs. Bush flew to Concord, New Hampshire, to file the papers declaring her husband a candidate in the New Hampshire Republican primary "because nobody would dare to boo Barbara Bush."[15] In that state, the incumbent faced a challenge from conservative columnist Patrick J. "Pat" Buchanan. A month later, Mrs. Bush granted an interview to the *Washington Post* while campaigning prior to the first primary. She was asked whether she thought *Roe v. Wade* would be a critical issue in the presidential campaign. In a preview of things to come, she skillfully avoided answering the question and said instead that Americans had to do a better job of educating their children: "It's very important to be disciplined, to wait, to abstain. We're doing a really lousy job as parents."[16]

Like her husband's late-starting, incumbent campaign (he did not officially announce his candidacy until mid-February), Barbara Bush underestimated the challenge that Bill Clinton would pose to George Bush's reelection chances. As she recalled later, "I wrote over and over again that Bill Clinton did not have a chance."[17] She also did not grasp the problems that Clinton's wife, Hillary Rodham Clinton, would pose for the first lady during the campaign. The Bushes had known the Clintons before 1992, largely through their involvement with education issues in their home state of Arkansas. Mrs. Bush recalled that she had been impressed with Mrs. Clinton during the White House's Education Summit held at the University of Virginia on 28 September 1989. As first lady of Arkansas, Mrs. Clinton spoke about a program she had instituted in her state, Home Instruction for Pre-School Youth (HIPY), an innovative initiative that went into homes and worked with young children and their families. Mrs. Bush commented, "She is a lawyer and very bright and articulate."[18] Mrs. Clinton's previous experience did not send up any red flags, but like the rest of the nation, Barbara Bush was not prepared for the media feeding frenzy about Hillary Rodham Clinton that erupted during the first half of the election year. The forty-five-year-old Clinton became a focus for controversy and a tempting target for Republican critics. For Barbara Bush, the question was how to handle this aspirant for her position without alienating suburban women and other voters.

Hillary Rodham Clinton was unlike any other candidate's wife that Barbara Bush had ever opposed. A graduate of Wellesley College and Yale Law School, Mrs. Clinton had worked for the Children's Defense Fund and had served as a staff attorney on the House Judiciary Committee, considering charges against President Richard M. Nixon. At the time of the 1992 presidential campaign, she was a partner in Little Rock's prestigious Rose law firm and had been named one of the hundred most influential lawyers in America. Mrs. Clinton had always served as a political adviser to Bill Clinton. Many credited her with saving Clinton's presidential candidacy in 1992 after Gennifer Flowers came forward just prior to the New Hampshire primary to announce that she and the governor of Arkansas had been involved in a twelve-year affair. The Clintons decided to confront the allegations on national television. They appeared together on CBS's well-respected news show *60 Minutes* following the 1992 Super Bowl, thus guaranteeing a huge viewing audience. While Bill Clinton squirmed and tried to evade questions, Hillary was forthright in declaring her support for her husband: "I'm not sitting here like some little woman standing by her man like

Tammy Wynette. I'm sitting here because I love him, and I respect him and I honor what he's been through, and what we've been through together. And . . . if that's not enough for people then heck, don't vote for him."[19] The bullet was dodged, and Bill Clinton finished second in the New Hampshire Democratic primary. Clinton's success signaled that Barbara Bush would have future clashes with her Democratic counterpart. Yet the first lady, like her husband's campaign, did not devise a coherent strategy to handle Mrs. Clinton.

Before he had to deal with the Clintons, though, George Bush had to win his party's nomination, and to that end, his wife proved a valuable asset. At the time, Barbara Bush was the most popular Republican in the country; her ratings were three times those of her husband.[20]

A savvy politician and solid campaigner, she was also a good speaker who adjusted easily to audiences. In 1976, popular first lady Betty Ford, who also enjoyed higher approval ratings than her husband, had been pressed into presidential campaign service to energize Gerald Ford's campaign. Buttons and bumper stickers reading "I'm Voting for Betty's Husband" and "Keep Betty's Husband in the White House" appeared around the country. In 1992, Betty's name was replaced with "Barbara," and she took to the hustings to assist in saving her husband's presidency by giving speeches, stirring up enthusiasm among the Bush faithful, and participating in Bush-Quayle fund-raisers.

Patrick Buchanan would provide George Bush with his first challenge. Buchanan had worked as a White House adviser and speechwriter to President Richard Nixon; he also wrote speeches for Vice President Spiro Agnew. Buchanan briefly served in the same capacities during the Ford administration but resigned in 1974. He became a syndicated political columnist before serving two years as White House communications director in the Reagan administration. A far right-wing Republican, Buchanan made provocative statements: he called Adolf Hitler "a man of courage," labeled AIDS as nature's retribution against gays, and ridiculed the Gulf War. Though Buchanan was not deemed to be a serious threat, for the president, the first lady, and their campaign staff, Buchanan was a headache that would not go away.

Barbara Bush stumped in New Hampshire prior to the country's first primary election against Buchanan. She visited Chichester, Farmington, Wolfeboro, Hampton Falls, Manchester, Derry, and Bedford. Signs of political troubles for her husband dogged her. At one stop she saw a placard that read, "We Like You Barbara! But You're Sleeping with the Enemy."[21]

In the past, Mrs. Bush had been most comfortable speaking about the George Bush she knew. Her primary speeches were now more partisan, examining accomplishments and taking the Democrats to task for inaction. The speech she gave at the Farmington town hall was typical of her primary discourse. After telling her audience that her husband had been a superb president leading the country through the Gulf War, she reviewed his legislative successes, then said, "George Bush is working hard for you. But he needs help. You certainly are doing your part. But what about Congress? For three years, George has sent an economic growth package to the Hill, and for three years they sat on it. A vote for George on Primary Day will not only show support for him, but will also send a message to Congress that you want them to do their job now."[22]

In a speech at Hampton Falls, Mrs. Bush reverted to a more personal approach as she told listeners: "After 47 years of marriage, George Bush is still the finest man I ever met. And I believe he has been a superb president. First, thanks to George, you and I and our children and grandchildren awake to a safer, freer world. He led America and the world through 'Desert Storm.' And he *will* lead this nation through these tough economic times."[23] Mrs. Bush gave a total of thirty-six political speeches during the primaries and the period that ran up to the beginning of the Republican National Convention. She spent more time in New Hampshire than the president.

Mrs. Bush had one misstep in New Hampshire. During an interview with a reporter from television station WMUR in Manchester, she was asked about condom distribution in schools. The usually fluid first lady seemed lost and responded, "I'm too old to believe that's right." The reporter's next question was about parental consent for AIDS tests. Again, Mrs. Bush seemed stymied by the query and said, "Parental consent. Never even thought about that." It was a baffling performance from a woman who was rarely guilty of public lapses. The incident also demonstrated that Barbara Bush did better in "scripted" situations and would have to improve to aid the reelection effort.[24]

George Bush survived the New Hampshire primary; Patrick Buchanan garnered a third of the vote. Though he later made respectable showings in Georgia, Maryland, and Colorado, Buchanan was never a serious threat to capture the nomination. However, Buchanan caused Bush to spend more money on advertisements in the primaries than previously planned, and this left the campaign strapped for cash as the general election campaign began.[25] Buchanan's robust showing in Republican primaries earned him the opportunity to address the Republican National Convention in August. The Buchanan insurgency illustrated the depth of Republican disaffection with Bush, a problem that plagued his wife's efforts to rouse support for her husband.

The Bushes soon confronted another threat to reelection. H. Ross Perot, an eccentric and outspoken billionaire entrepreneur, told the audience on *Larry King Live* during March 1992 that he was dissatisfied with both of the major parties and that he would run for president as an independent if volunteers could get his name on all fifty state ballots. For those dissatisfied with Bush or Clinton, Perot offered an intriguing prospect.[26]

A native of Texarkana, Texas, Perot had graduated in 1953 from the U.S. Naval Academy, where he was both class president and chairman of the honor committee. Perot became disillusioned with the navy and resigned his commission after serving the required five-year commitment following commissioning. After a few years with International Business Machines (IBM), he left to found his own company, Electronic Data Systems (EDS). In 1979, two EDS employees were imprisoned by the government of Iran, charged with bribery. Perot personally organized and funded a rescue attempt led by a retired U.S. Army officer. Perot said he was "more lucky than smart," and the two EDS employees were freed when an anti-Shah mob stormed the prison. The rescue was chronicled in the book *On the Wings of Eagles,* written by author Ken Follett. In 1982, Perot sold EDS to General Motors for $2.5 billion.[27]

Perot had always maintained an active interest in politics and government. He headed a state commission to overhaul the Texas public schools. By the late 1980s, he had become critical of the United States and was preaching that government gridlock stood in the way of innovation. Perot was no admirer of George H. W. Bush; he contended that the vice president had not done nearly enough to search for Vietnam-era MIAs. His enmity increased when he strongly opposed American involvement in the Persian Gulf War.[28]

Perot's prescription for American malaise took the form of a brief volume titled *United We Stand: How We Can Take Back Our Country: A Plan for the Twenty-first Century.* The book decried what Perot saw as shaky economic policies and an ever-growing federal debt that could lead to a severe depression. He advocated the elimination of the deficit by overhauling the political system that had created it. Perot's privately financed "informercials" presented his economic plan to the country in clear language. Perot's message resonated with millions of Americans, and he caught fire and led both Bush and Clinton in the polls.[29]

The Bush campaign seemed to sag. According to one source, the president had no message, no agenda for prosperity.[30] When pressed for the message of the campaign, the best Bush could muster was, "I care." Those brief words gave the first lady little to work with, yet she soldiered on. By the end of March 1992, it was becoming increasingly clear that the president would be facing Governor Bill Clinton in the fall election. Clinton's message of change resonated with voters affected by the poor economy and fears about the growing federal deficit.

George Bush was going to be a tough sell for another reason. On 8 July 1991, the president nominated Clarence Thomas to succeed Associate Justice Thurgood Marshall on the U.S. Supreme Court. Many organizations, including the American Bar Association, the National Organization for Women, and the Urban League, opposed Thomas's nomination, but he was progressing through Senate hearings on his nomination when Anita Hill, a professor of law at the University of Oklahoma and a former employee of Thomas's at the Equal Employment Opportunities Commission, accused Thomas of sexual harassment. From 11 October to 13 October 1991, the country watched as Thomas vehemently denied Hill's allegations.

In her diary, Mrs. Bush condemned sexual harassment but expressed doubts about Ms. Hill's veracity: "Is this woman telling the

truth? . . . I will never believe that she [Hill] a Yale Law School graduate, a woman of the '80's, would put up with harassment for one
moment, much less follow him from job to job, call him when she
came back to town and later invite him to speak to her students. . . .
It just makes no sense to me."[31] When the nomination was brought
to the full Senate, Clarence Thomas was confirmed as a justice of the
high court by a vote of 52 to 48. Many women were disgusted with
the "old boy" network that pervaded the Senate and confirmed
Thomas. One of the outgrowths of the Thomas hearings was "The
Year of the Woman," an increased interest in gender politics and political participation. Another consequence was that EMILY's List
(Early Money Is Like Yeast), an organization founded in 1985 to elect
pro-choice Democratic women to office, experienced a 600 percent
growth in membership.[32] A year later, repercussions were felt when
four women were elected to the Senate.[33]

Putting Thomas and Hill behind her, the first lady focused on the
economy as she campaigned on behalf of her husband in Metairie,
Louisiana, on 5 March 1992. Mrs. Bush said, "The number one solution, of course is jobs—more jobs and better jobs. There's not a lot
that a robust, growing economy won't cure."[34] With sluggish times,
it was tough going.

Her speech to a Bush-Quayle fund-raising dinner on 21 April 1992
veered away from the economy and provided some sense of the hectic
pace of the campaign. It gave Mrs. Bush a chance to make fun of herself, which always played well with campaign crowds: "We've had some
day! Houston, Texas this morning, a fund raiser in Davenport [Iowa],
a plant opening in Cedar Rapids, a visit to the most comprehensive lit-
eracy/job training program right here in Des Moines. I understand
that the National Hot Air Balloon Championships will be held here in
August. Well, I don't want you to think this is the preliminaries."[35]

In addition to campaigning for the president, Mrs. Bush spoke in
support of Republican candidates. In March 1992, she was in Irvine,
California, to rally Republicans for Senator John Seymour's long-
shot bid for the U.S. Senate against Democrat Diane Feinstein (Seymour had been appointed to the U.S. Senate to fill the vacancy left
by Pete Wilson, who had been elected governor of California). After
extolling Seymour's virtues as a businessman, she said, "The President knows that John won't agree with him all the time. But John

has the President's wholehearted support in this race. George and this former businessman *do* agree on the need to stimulate our economy, cut the federal deficit and hold the line on taxes."[36] On Election Day, Seymour lost to Feinstein, another beneficiary of "The Year of the Woman."

Prior to its national convention, Mrs. Bush was feted by the Republican Party of Texas on 19 June 1992. In her speech she conceded that the president faced a tough race in the fall. She encouraged her listeners to become actively involved in working for their candidate. They were fighting for all the positive achievements of the Bush administration, and the first lady stated the major themes of the upcoming Republican campaign: "We believe in government that is smarter and smaller. We believe families are the backbone of our society and that if America is to become stronger, families must become stronger. We see good schools and good jobs as the answer to many of our problems. We believe in strong law enforcement at home and a strong defense abroad."[37]

Ross Perot dropped out of the presidential race on 16 July 1992, telling reporters that the Democratic Party had become much stronger and there was no way in which he could win the election. "When we started in early summer, there was a climate where we could win outright. The Democratic Party has revitalized itself. They've done a brilliant job," he said.[38]

Now Mrs. Bush faced a great challenge, her anticipated speech at the Republican National Convention. Press secretary Anna Perez drafted a core speech for the months of July and August that could be used with any size audience of Republicans and Bush-Quayle supporters at luncheons, dinners, receptions, or rallies. It opened with an acknowledgment that Mrs. Bush had done a great deal of traveling and included the comment, "It really made me look forward to retirement—in four more years." Mrs. Bush went on to speak about her husband as "the most qualified, decent, caring, wisest, experienced, steadiest man to ever hold the toughest job in the world." Seizing on Bill Clinton's message of change, she would say, "These days, we all keep hearing about change. Well, real change is more than a campaign slogan." She celebrated her husband's success in passing major legislation, the Clean Air Act, the Americans with Disabilities Act, a civil rights act, a transportation act, and a comprehensive child care act. She said that the president was fighting hard for the people: "A reporter asked me recently, what was George's passion? I really do believe that he is passionate about making sure that everyone has an equal shot at the American dream. George is passionate about fair play. Play hard, play well, play fair."[39] The first lady carried this message to dozens of communities.

Despite Barbara Bush's efforts, her husband's reelection campaign struggled. She wrote in her diary on 17 July 1992: "There is a new poll out this morning that shows Bill Clinton 23 points ahead of George. . . . Somehow it seems impossible for George to win, a Congress that bucks you at every turn, a tough press corps, 5 Democrats, 1 Republican and 1 independent railing against him for months. . . . I am hiding my head like an ostrich. It hurts too much to see George and the children so lied about."[40]

Complicating matters for the first lady was the controversy surrounding her rivalry with Hillary Clinton. Just prior to the nominating conventions, *Family Circle* decided to sponsor a chocolate chip cookie recipe contest between Mrs. Bush and Hillary Clinton. "The Great Cookie Controversy" had started in the middle of March. Hillary Clinton was asked if she could have avoided the appearance of conflict of interest when her husband was the governor of Arkansas and she was a lawyer at the Rose law firm in Little Rock. She responded, "You know, I suppose I could have stayed home and baked cookies and had teas, but what I decided to do was fulfill my profession," she replied. Critics pounced and assailed her for her insensitivity to housewives. Mrs. Clinton realized that she had made a political blunder, and she told reporters, "I had made an awkward attempt to explain my situation and to suggest that many women who juggle careers and lives are penalized for the choices they make."[41] Her explanation was lost in a storm of criticism. The quote dogged her for months and seemed to provide an opening for the GOP.

As for Mrs. Bush, who was asked about Mrs. Clinton's comment at a Bush-Quayle fund-raising dinner in Little Rock, Arkansas, she said she was too busy to bake cookies.[42] Mrs. Bush then assumed that the controversy was dead until the *Family Circle* article appeared. The first lady and her office did not know about the competition until the results were published in the magazine. The recipe that appeared was not Mrs. Bush's—and she lost. She was very surprised when serious columnists began writing about the cookie contest; a few even called it antifeminist. The cookie episode illustrated how much celebrity defined the way in which first ladies were viewed.[43]

Personal issues also confronted Mrs. Bush. A week prior to the opening of the Republican National Convention, the tabloid *New York Post* resurrected rumors that had surfaced in 1988 of a long-term affair between George Bush and his former aide, Jennifer Fitzgerald. When he was asked by a CNN reporter at a Kennebunkport news conference if he had ever had an affair, Bush responded angrily, "I'm not going to take any sleaze questions. You're perpetuating the sleaze by even asking the question and . . . I'm not going to answer the question."[44] Barbara Bush vigorously defended her husband, telling reporters that the allegations were "disgusting" and "hurtful."[45] She told the *Houston Chronicle* that the stories were "sick," and in her opinion, "The mainline press has sunk to an all-time low."[46] She denounced the press at every opportunity. Reporters countered that their questions were justified, since the president had made family and character major issues in his campaign. Later, Vice President Dan Quayle charged that the goal of the allegations, particularly those printed by the right-wing *New York Post,* was to hurt the president and help Bill Clinton.[47] The rumors seemed to fade, but their existence made it harder for the Bush campaign to argue that Bill Clinton was morally lax. Eventually, Mrs. Bush airily dismissed the charges of infidelity by telling audiences, "George Bush sleeps with two girls, Millie and me."[48]

Much to Mrs. Bush's chagrin, abortion loomed as a key issue in the campaign. A precondition of George Bush's Republican nomination for vice president in 1980 was abandoning his moderate stand on abortion. He had to accept the pro-life platform endorsed by presidential candidate Ronald Reagan. Bush acceded to Reagan's demand, but Barbara Bush had to swallow hard. Over the years she had quietly supported a more moderate view of abortion while her husband had embraced a pro-life stance as vice president and president to hold on to the conservative wing of his party. Barbara Bush now appeared to be dissenting from GOP orthodoxy. In an interview on 14 August 1992, just prior to the convention, she said that abortion had no place in the Republican Party's platform. She told the *New York Times,* "I'm not being outspoken or pro or con on abortion. I'm saying abortion should not be in there, either pro or con." Abortion, she said, was a "personal thing."[49] For George Bush, trying to survive an onslaught by pro-life forces, the first lady's stand was dynamite. In her memoirs, Mrs. Bush explained her own feelings: "I hate abortions, but just could not make that choice for someone else.

And contrary to the platform plank, which was opposed to *all* abortions, George was against abortions with the exception of rape, incest, and where the life of the mother was threatened."[50] Pro-choice Republicans celebrated the first lady's suggestion to drop the pro-life plank from the 1992 platform by printing up T-shirts that read "Finally Barbara." Barbara Bush had been pro-choice all along.

During the same interview in which she discussed abortion, Mrs. Bush criticized Republican Party chairman Rich Bond for attacking Hillary Clinton. Bond had been critical of Mrs. Clinton, disparaging her as a wife and mother. Bond had seized upon some of Clinton's legal writings from the 1970s to argue that she believed children should be permitted to sue their parents and that marriage was a form of slavery. Other Republicans joined the chorus against Clinton, and the issue seemed likely to become salient during the convention.[51] Mrs. Bush deplored the tactic, commenting, "I don't like it. She is not running for office."[52] The first lady thought it was bad politics to attack a woman. Democratic strategists who noted that the Republicans had resorted to criticizing Mrs. Clinton believed that women voters found the tactic distasteful. Bond heeded Mrs. Bush's admonition, but other Republicans, including Dan Quayle, Pat Buchanan, and Pat Robertson, found the Democratic candidate's wife to be a tempting target. So, too, did merchants in the "Spirit of America" shop next to the convention hall, which sold literature that called Mrs. Clinton, in the words of right-wing talk show host Rush Limbaugh, a "Feminazi."[53]

The Republican National Convention opened in Houston on 17 August. On the first night, former Republican candidate Pat Buchanan addressed the delegates. Mrs. Bush was worried about Buchanan. Anna Perez, her perceptive press secretary, told the first lady that Buchanan was a racist: "He was saying all the 'code' words that tell her that. I think her exact words were 'a mean spirited racist.'"[54] Mrs. Bush's concerns were justified; Buchanan railed against the

Democratic ticket of Bill Clinton and Al Gore as "the most pro-lesbian and pro-gay ticket in history." He lambasted Hillary Clinton as a radical feminist: "The agenda Clinton and Clinton would impose on America—abortion on demand, a litmus test for the Supreme Court, homosexual rights, discrimination against religious schools, women in combat—that's change, all right. . . . And it is not the kind of change we can tolerate in a nation that we still call God's country." The opening-night theme of the convention was supposed to be "Unity Night," but as Buchanan came to the end of his remarks, his strident tone left unity in tatters. He told the convention, "My friends, this election is about . . . what we stand for as Americans. There is a religious war going on in our country for the soul of America. It is a cultural war, as critical to the kind of nation we will one day be as was the Cold War itself."[55] Reporters commented that the speech opened the convention "on a note of intolerance, a smallness of spirit from which they [Republicans] never wholly recovered."[56] Later, George Bush would write that Buchanan's statements were mean and ugly.[57] Though he did not realize it at the time, Bush had lost control of the convention. A moderate Republican in a rapidly changing party, he and his wife seemed hopelessly out of touch.

Nonetheless, Mrs. Bush maintained a busy schedule at the convention. She attended events with the president, did media interviews, and was present at convention sessions. On 19 August, the day she was scheduled to speak at the convention, Mrs. Bush visited Texas Children's Hospital. Reporters asked her about her upcoming remarks. She quipped, "The most overrated speech by the most overrated person being given tonight." When reporters suggested that she was the most popular Republican in the country, Mrs. Bush responded, "Baloney." A few minutes later, the first lady responded to a question about health care, which had emerged as one of the important issues of the campaign. With her trademark tartness she said, "The president has a health care program before Congress and has had it there for quite a while. Why don't you get on your Congressmen about it? Senators too."[58]

Mrs. Bush's most important responsibility occurred on the third night of the convention, dubbed "Family Night." The feel-good evening had been planned long before Buchanan's divisive discourse.

Later, "Family Night" might have been perceived as a way to counteract the probable damage to the Republican cause by Hillary Clinton. The main speakers of the evening were AIDS activist Mary Fisher, Second Lady Marilyn Quayle, and, finally, Barbara Bush.

Marilyn Quayle followed Mary Fisher's plea to give AIDS a higher priority in the Bush social agenda. Perhaps convention planners hoped that Mrs. Quayle and Mrs. Bush's speeches would moderate the tone of the gathering. Unfortunately, it seemed as if Marilyn Quayle was perpetuating the harshness started by Buchanan. She told the convention, "Not everyone joined the counterculture. Not everyone demonstrated, dropped out, took drugs, joined the sexual revolution, or dodged the draft."[59] Mrs. Quayle said that she had made a conscious decision to put aside her law practice, work in her husband's political campaigns, and raise their children. She struck a dissonant note when she said, "They're [liberals] disappointed because most women do not wish to be liberated from their essential natures as women."[60] The speech was a thinly veiled attempt to point out the differences that existed between the second lady and Hillary Rodham Clinton. Though she spoke with enthusiasm, many listeners found Quayle's tone both peevish and combative. Mrs. Bush was disappointed with the reception given the second lady's speech: "She is a great wife and mother and a very bright woman. Unfortunately her speech did not convey her warmth or caring and she was very much criticized for it."[61]

Finally, Barbara Bush strode to the podium amid enthusiastic cheers. She continued a tradition of first ladies addressing national party nominating conventions that began in 1940 when Eleanor Roosevelt addressed the Democratic National Convention. Loved by many Americans, Mrs. Bush was perceived in a nonpartisan way as both smart and wise. She was going to carry much of the burden of campaigning in the fall. A good speech would do damage control in the aftermath of Buchanan's speech and appease those annoyed by Marilyn Quayle's comments. In addition, it would quiet the delegates and set the stage for her husband's presentation the next evening when he accepted the convention's presidential nomination.

Mrs. Bush's prose had been carefully crafted for the occasion. With the exception of her commencement address at Wellesley, no speech had received as much attention. The convention presentation, which went through at least five drafts, was written with great attention to form and content. Handwritten notes in the "Family Night" file read: "Establish identity with broad section of the American family; different kinds of families. ArchITYPAL [*sic*] images of the American spirit. Mesh this with the Bush's [*sic*] life."[62] The speechwriters, Clark Judge, Richard Moore, Jean Becker, Julie Cooke, and Susan Porter Rose, tried to integrate those ideas into their drafts. A note on one draft reads: "The introduction will have to be written at the convention so it's fresh, play off current happenings."[63] The speech's length was cut to six pages in the second draft, and in the same revision, Mrs. Bush inserted the thought that she did not want to give a speech but instead wanted to have a conversation with her audience. Brevity and the shift in intimacy from formal speech to conversation among friends was an excellent way to proceed.

The first lady exuded warmth as she began, telling the audience, "You make me feel wonderful, but then I always feel wonderful when I get to talk about the strongest, the most decent, the most caring, and yes, healthiest man I have ever known—George Bush."

Mrs. Bush began with her family-oriented theme. She and her husband had "met so many different families. And yet, they aren't so very different." Families in the 1990s—single-parent, grandparent, Gulf War veterans—were facing tough challenges. There was more violence, more crime, more promiscuity. Still, the families she had spoken with around the country had heartened her. She said: "The parents we've met are determined to teach their children integrity, strength, courage, sharing, love of God, and pride in being an American. However you define family, that's what we mean by family values."

Warming to the task, Mrs. Bush told the audience about her experience, moving to Texas and raising her own family. She had carpooled, attended hundreds of Little League games, and was a Cub Scout den mother. One of the strongest segments of the speech concerned the young Bush children and their father: "Thank goodness George didn't expect our children to be perfect—they weren't. Once when one of the boys hit a baseball through the Vanderhof's second story window, I called George to see what dire punishment should be handed out. All he said was, 'The Vanderhof's second story window! What a hit!'" She went on to say that her husband had rarely been forced to punish their children: "He had a quiet way of making them want to do right and give reverence to God. And it made such a difference having his wise hand guiding them."

Mrs. Bush recalled that an interviewer had asked the president to name the accomplishment that made him proudest. She wondered if he would say his career as a public servant, the fall of Communism, the reduction of the threat of nuclear holocaust, the Americans with Disabilities Act? "What would he answer? Well, it's the same answer George Bush always gives. That our children still come home."

Mrs. Bush asked to have a word with some special people, the parents who sacrificed for their children. She acknowledged that some parents were perpetually exhausted, that some worked two jobs, that some had put their careers on hold. She concluded the speech by saying: "You may wonder, as I did every now and then, am I really doing the right thing? Yes you are. For where will our country find leaders with integrity, courage, strength—all the family values—in ten, twenty, thirty years? The answer is that you are teaching them, loving them, and raising them right now."[64] As she finished her speech, Mrs. Bush was joined at the podium by her children and grandchildren, a physical testament to the importance of family.

The conciliatory and gentle words of the speech seemed to act as balm for the convention. The *New York Times* noted that Mrs. Bush "struck an inclusive and tolerant tone. She recounted her own traditional life, but pointedly reached out to parents who followed a different path."[65] Republican strategist Mary Matalin commented that the speech was low-key and healing and gave the national audience reasons why they should vote for George Bush.[66] A reporter contrasted the speeches by Mrs. Quayle and Mrs. Bush: "There is a paradox in tone. Mrs. Bush who cared for her family and never pursued a profession, sounded inclusive. Mrs. Quayle who is a lawyer but gave up her profession seemed to criticize women who disagreed with her choice."[67] Women interviewed after "Family Night" had mixed reactions. Many enjoyed the speeches, "but several women interviewed found the evening irrelevant or worse. 'They talk about family values, but it's really just a way to bash the other guys and cover up what they haven't done on the real issues,'" said one interviewee.[68]

If the press had compared Mrs. Bush's 1992 remarks with those she had delivered at the 1988 Republican National Convention, they would have noted a number of striking similarities. In both speeches, Mrs. Bush used the anecdote about her son hitting a baseball through a neighbor's upstairs window, the important jobs George Bush had held, his caring and decency, and an almost verbatim retelling of Bush's proudest accomplishment ("Our kids still come home"). Though sections about presidential experiences were added, the 1992 speech was a derivative version of 1988 and might be seen as evidence of the Bushes unwillingness to break new ground even before the friendliest possible audience. Rarely did Barbara Bush use her position to extend the boundaries of American public life.[69]

Hillary Clinton rode a backlash after the Republican convention, where she had been painted as a "dangerous, rogue feminist." Pollsters found that large majorities were rejecting the case against her, and 73 percent of those who had listened to criticisms of Mrs. Clinton disagreed with them.[70] Hillary bashing backfired on Republican strategists.

Benefiting from a modest postconvention "bounce" in the polls, the Bushes set out from Houston to begin the fall campaign. Barbara Bush was sent out on her own, talking to campaign audiences about the difference between Bill Clinton's Arkansas and George Bush's America. The *New York Times* commented that Mrs. Bush's postconvention swing through California produced "some of the most partisan remarks of her political life" as she attacked congressional Democrats: "Ever since Democrats took over the Senate, it's just been an enormous fight. And what we're hoping is going to happen is they're going to clean the House and clean the Senate and give us a Republican President with a Republican Congress. Then watch how things grow."[71]

In spite of her conciliatory remarks at the convention, the first lady became tougher on Hillary Clinton, telling reporters that the wife of the Democratic nominee was now fair game because Clinton had spoken about a copresidency. She referred to the slogan he had used earlier in the election cycle—"Buy one, get one free"—as justification for greater scrutiny of Mrs. Clinton's previous professional activities.[72] For her part, Mrs. Clinton had no comments about Mrs. Bush's change in direction or the media's attempts to construct a rivalry between the two women. Mrs. Bush is mentioned a few times in Mrs. Clinton's autobiography, *Living History,* but none of these references concern the campaign of 1992. Either Mrs. Clinton made the decision not to share her thoughts about the first lady, or she did not deem Barbara Bush a problem of any consequence.

In a decided shift from years past, the first lady addressed public policy issues. Although this was her husband's purview, she wanted to be taken seriously as his surrogate.[73] She always seemed more comfortable talking about George Bush and was at her best when giving testimonials and sharing anecdotes with her listeners that humanized the presidential couple. However, she was not bashful about taking a shot at her husband's opponent with rhetoric that relied on Republican talking points. In a speech three weeks prior to the election, she reacted to Bill Clinton's economic message by asking her audience, "Do you really believe our economy will benefit from a 150 billion dollar tax increase? And do you really believe the federal government will be better, smarter and more efficient if we just spend 220 billion more tax dollars? George Bush doesn't think so, his opponent does."[74]

From 21 August through 3 November 1992, the first lady gave sixty-one speeches in support of the Bush-Quayle ticket. From 1 January to 31 December 1992, more than half of her speeches were devoted to the reelection of the president and support for other Republican office seekers. While there is no evidence that Mrs. Bush planned any of the strategy or made decisions for the 1992 presidential campaign, she was up-to-date and well aware of poll numbers and day-to-day changes. A reporter who regularly covered the Bushes commented on the importance of Barbara to her husband's campaign or to anyone running for office: "If you're running for office, you want Barbara Bush—you want her out there, showing up at your rally, you want her working the room, you want her name on your leaflet that you're mailing out to potential fund-raisers. When people saw that it was a correspondence or a phone call or an inquiry from Barbara Bush, they were prone to take this seriously."[75]

In a 2 September 1992 speech, Mrs. Bush told a Raleigh, North Carolina, audience that the press often asked her to identify the worst thing that ever happened in the White House. She recounted that a White House visitor sat on a buffet table full of food and it collapsed. The first lady continued, "I *used* to say that was the most embarrassing thing that ever happened to us and then we went to Japan! I got an adorable letter from a little girl who wrote, 'tell Mr. President not to be embarrassed that he threw up on national television. I once threw up on my dog.'" But it got worse, said Mrs. Bush, during a state dinner for Boris Yeltsin of Russia. "During dinner Boris leaned over and, through an interpreter, said 'Barbara, I don't know the protocol. What should I do? A lady has her foot on mine!' I looked over at the beautiful woman sitting on his other side and just as I was about to say that I had no idea, he lifted his foot and mine shot up through the table! Poor man, I guess I had been grinding his foot into the ground."[76] The audience response was so positive that the stories found their way into other speeches.

Mrs. Bush visited phone banks, cheered on the volunteers, and made a few calls herself. During a visit to a Fort Worth, Texas, phone bank, she called a local resident and said, "Hi, this is Barbara Bush calling, and I'm calling for the Fort Worth Bush-Quayle campaign. I hope we can count on you to vote for George Bush and Dan Quayle." Some recipients did not believe they were talking to Barbara Bush; most were delighted with the phone calls.[77]

An additional concern for the Bushes was H. Ross Perot's reentry into the presidential campaign. Speaking on *CBS This Morning,* Perot said that he had been disappointed that neither President Bush nor Governor Clinton had engaged in "a serious debate on the Federal budget deficit or ways to stimulate the economy." He asserted that he had been wrong to leave the race, and he chided both Republicans and Democrats for not facing the issues.[78]

Mrs. Bush's campaign speeches followed a formula, with occasional variation. The introduction consisted of thanking federal, state, or local officials, program organizers, and/or fund-raisers for their efforts in organizing Mrs. Bush's appearance, and then a few paragraphs were devoted to the merits of office seekers. The body of the speech would discuss public policy issues, President Bush's successes in office, or the Bushes' time in the White House, their travels, or their family. The conclusion would contain an exhortation to go out and elect the aforementioned office seekers—and re-elect President Bush. Mrs. Bush concluded her speech in Raleigh,

North Carolina, by saying, "Please work your hearts out this fall to elect Republicans on all levels. George and I are going to, that's for sure. We won't let you down!"[79]

She could be serious and underscore the campaign's message: George Bush was the man to lead America through the 1990s: "With change comes opportunity and things *are* getting better. Despite our problems, thanks to George Bush's steady, experienced leadership, we have avoided the wild economic tremors plaguing our friends in Europe and Asia."[80] The president, said Mrs. Bush, was dealing with a great deal in trying to navigate a steady course; he was up against "a Democrat controlled, scandal ridden Congress."[81] In spite of this, the Clean Air Act, the Americans with Disabilities Act, the Transportation Act, and the National Literacy Act were passed on his watch. This laundry list of achievements worked its way into many speeches. It is interesting to note that former first lady Rosalynn Carter, who carried much of the burden for her husband's 1980 re-election campaign, had been roundly criticized by the press for elucidating his achievements in the same laundry-list fashion.

Mrs. Bush and her staff had access to "Talking Points," a collection of ideas and points to be made in speeches, and "The Daily Line for Republican Newsmakers" and "Clinton Facts," which followed the Democrats closely and also provided suggestions for media appearances, speeches, and press statements.[82]

Mrs. Bush received a memo from staffers regarding questions she might be asked after the second presidential debate at Richmond, Virginia. The prescripted answers, typical of modern campaigning, included responses to the queries, How do you feel the president did tonight? and What are the important differences between the candidates? Possible answers were also provided for questions about the president's domestic achievements, his proposed health care plan, the progress of the campaign, Barbara Bush's popularity, the role of the Bush family in the campaign, and reasons that the voters should reelect the president. The last section of the memo reads: "On the following questions it is very important not to take reporter's bait. Stick to guidance." Responses were provided to questions about abortion ("a deeply personal issue. My views are irrelevant. I'm not running for office. The President's views are well known"), gay bashing, support of working women, economic security for women, strengthening the family, women's health, the debates, Ross Perot (who had reentered the presidential race on 1 October 1992), and the Iran-Contra affair. With the final debate just days away, Mrs. Bush scrawled a quick answer to the query, "How do you feel the election is shaping up?" She wrote, "I've been all over the country and it feels good out there."[83]

During the middle of October, Mrs. Bush took part in the "Viva Bush" tour that was designed to attract Hispanic voters as it made its way through Texas. She told a campaign audience in Austin, "American issues are Hispanic issues and Hispanic issues are American issues. Our home state is crucial to this election. . . . We have a lot at stake here." Mrs. Bush was accompanied by her grandson George P. Bush, a fluent Spanish speaker, who was the keynote orator in many locations. The presidential campaign was a Bush family effort.[84]

Mrs. Bush campaigned continuously, sometimes visiting multiple states in one day. Good news would be followed by discouraging assessments. In her memoirs, Mrs. Bush wrote, "The weeks leading up to Election Day almost seemed like a game we played as children where we'd take one step forward and two steps back."[85]

On 22 October, a Fox News reporter told Mrs. Bush that press sources said the president had lost his will to fight. Mrs. Bush responded crisply, "That's so nutty. You know, it's going to make the victory a lot sweeter. . . . The president's going to win. . . . He's going to win, first of all, because he's done a superb job. And he's going to win . . . because of character, and character does count."[86] Public opinion polls continued to indicate that the president was lagging behind Bill Clinton. As Bush's situation became more desperate, he took greater advantage of Barbara's popularity by telling audiences, "Barbara and I think . . . "[87]

A few days prior to the election, Barbara gave perhaps her hardest-hitting speech of the campaign at Leisure Village in Lakewood, New Jersey. After telling the audience that her husband had had almost a year of being beaten up by five Democrats, one Republican, one independent, and the news media, it was time to tell the story of George Bush's tenure as president. She drew contrasts between George Bush's America and Bill Clinton's Arkansas: "George Bush's America has a new Clean Air Act that protects the environment without sacrificing jobs. Bill Clinton's Arkansas ranks dead last in environmental protection. . . . In George Bush's America, federal funds to local law enforcement have tripled; Bill Clinton's Arkansas ranks dead last in per capita spending on police protection."[88] She continued to hammer at the differences between the two men: Bill Clinton talked and talked and talked, but George Bush got things done. Nearing the end of her remarks, she asked, "And Bill Clinton wants to do for America what he did for Arkansas? . . . We don't need another Democrat governor promising another 'miracle.' *We need George Bush's America!*"[89]

Barbara Bush continued to give speeches and campaign, but the death knell of her husband's presidency sounded on 30 October 1992, when it was announced that Laurence Walsh, the independent counsel investigating the Iran-Contra affair had obtained a federal indictment against former secretary of defense Caspar Weinberger based on a note dated January 1986 (Weinberger had been indicted a few months previously for perjury). Bush had steadfastly maintained that during his tenure as vice president he was "out of the loop" on the Iran-Contra affair. Iran-Contra was *the* political scandal during the 1980s, when members of President Ronald Reagan's administration secretly agreed to sell weapons to Iran to win the release of American hostages in the Middle East; the profits from the arms sales were then funneled to the Contras, who were fighting against the Sandinista government in Nicaragua. The indictment against Weinberger said that he had handwritten notes from a January 1986 Oval Office meeting that proved the former vice president was very much involved in the decision-making process: "President [Reagan] decided to go with Israeli-Iranian offer to release our five hostages in return for four thousand TOW's [missiles] to Iran by Israel. . . . VP favored," wrote Weinberger.[90]

In desperation, the president lashed out at his opponents: "Today is Halloween, our opponents' favorite holiday. They're trying to scare America. If Governor Taxes and the Ozone Man [a reference to Democratic Vice Presidential candidate Al Gore] are elected, every day is going to be Halloween. Fright and Terror. Fright and Terror."[91] Even Barbara Bush thought this was excessive and along with the Bush campaign staff urged the president to tone down his personal attacks.[92]

On Tuesday, 3 November 1992, the country went to the polls. The Bushes returned to Houston and voted in their local polling place, then settled back to await the political verdict. Mrs. Bush wrote, "I did not believe we would win, but I'm not sure I believed it. . . . In late afternoon, George W. told us that based on exit polls, it was over, we would lose."[93] Bill Clinton garnered 43 percent of the popular vote and 370 electoral votes; though he won no electoral votes, Ross Perot carried 19 percent of the popular vote. George Bush won 37 percent of the popular vote and 168 electoral votes. At 10:20 PM that evening, George Bush gave a gracious concession speech; Barbara was not forgotten in the president's acknowledgments: "Of course, I want to thank my entire family, with special emphasis on a woman named Barbara. She's inspired this entire Nation, and I think the country will always be grateful."[94]

In the election postmortems, one historian wrote that "Barbara Bush and Hillary Clinton were more central to the campaign than any pair of dueling first ladies had ever been."[95] This was a precursor of things to come as succeeding pairs of first lady aspirants squared off as they traversed the country hunting for votes for their husbands. Barbara Bush had given her best effort in a losing cause, but the desire for change, a weak economy, and a vulnerable candidate were too much to overcome. George Bush became the first single-term Republican president since Herbert Hoover, 1929–1933.

In her *Memoir* she was hunting for reasons: "Why did we lose? George Bush says it was because he didn't communicate as well as his predecessor or successor. I don't believe that. I think we lost because people really wanted a change. We had had twelve years of a Republican presidency . . . people were worried about jobs and the economy." Then she focused her fire on the news media: "And the press. I honestly believe that most of them wanted Bill Clinton to win. He was one of them—baby boomers."[96] She went on to say that the strong media preference for the Democratic nominee had skewed their reporting. To further prove her point, Mrs. Bush recalled that on Bill Clinton's Inauguration Day, she and the former president were preparing to fly home to Houston when reporters complained to her that a press pool would not be permitted to accompany the Bushes. She writes, "That amused me, and I told them that any of them who voted for George should speak up. . . . The silence was deafening."[97] One Bush scholar agrees with Mrs. Bush's assessment and writes that the press was "not only virulently anti-Bush, but openly flaunted that fact." He points out that according to the Bush people, 89 percent of the election correspondents personally cast their votes for Clinton.[98] The Bush campaign clung to the hope that the media would report on Clinton's involvement with various women and this would turn the tide in favor of the president. The campaign kept waiting for stories that never appeared.

Like his wife, George Bush had believed that he would pull out the election. He thought that Americans would recognize Bill Clinton's alleged lack of character and his own devoted service to his country and adherence to the time-honored concepts of honesty and loyalty. Unfortunately, voters were more interested in their pocketbooks and responded to Clinton's message, "It's the economy stupid!" and the chances for change. Barbara Bush was disappointed for her husband but relieved to be finished with politics and looking forward to life in Houston, the city from which the Bushes had set out twenty-five years before.

Undoubtedly, 20 January 1993 was a difficult, sad day for the Bushes, but the events of 20 January 2001 neutralized what Barbara saw as the rejection of her husband by the American people. On that day, Barbara Bush became only the second woman in history to be the wife of one president and the mother of another president. The family had come full circle as George W. Bush took his oath of office. It had to be satisfying to Barbara Bush to see that the sacrifices she had made for her husband and family had led to this moment.

CHAPTER 7

"THERE IS LIFE AFTER POLITICS! HURRAH!"

Months after leaving Washington, Barbara Bush was still frustrated with the country's rejection of George Bush for a second term as president. She told *People* magazine, "The last campaign killed me. It was so painful."[1] Former press secretary Anna Perez tried to put a moderate spin on her employer's ire when she said that Mrs. Bush "had seen wins and losses in elections, she'd been through a presidential resignation, four assassination attempts, four national campaigns and two defeats. There was an ebb and flow to politics and life would go on."[2] Barbara Bush, like former first ladies Rosalynn Carter with Ronald Reagan, and Lou Hoover with Franklin D. Roosevelt, seemed to be more upset by her husband's defeat at the hands of Bill Clinton than George Bush was. Both Bushes believed that George H. W. Bush deserved or was entitled to another term as president because of his hard work on behalf of the American people. Former president Richard Nixon, a Bush mentor, underscored this when he wrote, "Bush honestly believed that he had been a good president and that since he had given the country such honorable and lengthy service, he deserved a second term." Nixon also recalled that Bush "could not get over his low poll numbers . . . and exclaimed, 'I've worked my heart out as President!'"[3]

Former ABC reporter Sam Donaldson advanced an intriguing theory about the motivation and future of the Bush family in politics:

"Barbara Bush was supposed to have said, 'Get over it, just get over it' (the 1992 loss). Now what she meant was not, let's forget it, we had our turn, but it was one variation on the Washington rule, 'don't get mad, get even.' And from that moment, I think, both of her sons, her senior sons (George W. and Jeb Bush) said, 'We'll do it.'"[4] George W. and Jeb Bush's successful entrances into the political arena were still two and six years off, respectively; in the interim, in spite of their feelings, George and Barbara made a promise not to criticize the Clintons.[5]

The Bushes returned to a rented house in Houston that would serve as their home until the new house they were building was completed. The transition to private citizens required some adjustment. The Bushes had to get used to shopping, cooking, and driving for themselves. "As it turns out, driving is something you never forget. Now, cooking is a little different. I never loved cooking, just eating," Mrs. Bush wrote.[6] She recalled that a few nights after returning to Houston, her son George dropped by and requested pasta for dinner because he was running in the Houston Marathon the next day. Mrs. Bush commented: "I had not cooked in twelve years, so it was not surprising that my pasta was NOT too good. In fact, it was dreadful."[7]

Many former first ladies have been busy and involved after leaving the White House. Barbara's four immediate living predecessors, Nancy Reagan (1981–1989), Rosalynn Carter (1977–1981), Betty Ford (1974–1977), and Lady Bird Johnson (1963–1969), were a case in point. All four women penned memoirs, but this was only part of their post–White House activity. Nancy Reagan shared her recollections of her years in the White House in *My Turn*. She cared for her husband, former president Ronald Reagan, who had been diagnosed with Alzheimer's disease. For almost ten years, Mrs. Reagan remained near her husband's side as he was ravaged by the illness. She became a vocal advocate for stem cell research, and it was thought that she might support Democrat John Kerry in 2004 because of his pro–stem cell position. This never happened, but the Reagans' son Ron, also a stem cell advocate, spoke at the 2004 Democratic National Convention. Rosalynn Carter wrote a best-selling memoir, *First Lady from Plains,* and traveled extensively with her husband, former president Jimmy Carter, overseeing democratic elections around the globe. She was also actively involved in

Habitat for Humanity, the well-known organization that builds and rehabilitates homes for those unable to afford a private residence. Betty Ford, the author of *The Times of My Life* and *Betty: A Glad Awakening,* spearheaded the founding of the Betty Ford Center in Rancho Mirage, California. "Betty Ford" is the most popular and successful center for the treatment of drug and alcohol addiction in the world. Mrs. Ford's work and commitment to the center have been so noteworthy that a patient said, "That woman is going to be long remembered—and not as the wife of the President of the United States."[8] Lady Bird Johnson wrote *A White House Diary* and worked on the founding of the Lyndon B. Johnson Library. In 1982, along with actress Helen Hayes, she helped establish the National Wildflower Research Center in Texas. In 1998, on the occasion of her eighty-sixth birthday, the center was renamed the Lady Bird Johnson Wildflower Center. All the former first ladies served as good role models for Mrs. Bush.

Mrs. Bush, too, had a book to write, and she began work on her memoirs with the help of former deputy press secretary Jean Becker. Her recollections were published in 1994 as *Barbara Bush: A Memoir.* Any autobiographical writings by a first lady provide readers with insight into life in the White House and personal reactions to personalities and situations. Mrs. Bush's memoirs, like Lady Bird Johnson's, were drawn from a diary that she kept faithfully during the vice presidential and presidential years.[9] In 535 pages, Mrs. Bush traced her life from Rye, New York, to the White House with stops in Odessa, Midland, and Houston, Texas; Huntington, California; Kennebunkport, Maine; Washington, D.C.; New York; Beijing, China; and back to Washington again. The book is filled with descriptions, examples, names, and self-deprecating humor. Always, Mrs. Bush was aware that she had a good life. In the preface to her memoirs, she wrote, "I have loved writing this book and know that it is a story of a life of privilege—privilege of every kind. If I didn't know it before, I know it now."[10]

Barbara Bush: A Memoir quickly climbed to number one on the *New York Times* best-seller list and remained there for four weeks. The former first lady went on a national book tour, even appearing on *The Tonight Show* and *Late Night with David Letterman.* Mrs. Bush was pleased that her book dramatized the problems of illiteracy, and the profits helped a number of literacy organizations. Most of the reviews were positive. "Mrs. Bush's account is not meant to be a treatise on world affairs, and no one will mistake it for one, though it may well be confused at times with a back issue of *Town and Country,*" wrote Michael Wines in the *New York Times.* However, wrote Wines, "None of these criticisms undermine the book's real value—that the occupants of the White House are quite human."[11] Critic Maureen Dowd enjoyed *A Memoir* and commented, "Some critics have dismissed her book as gushy society stuff, devoid of serious content or historically valuable commentary. . . . That's exactly why I liked it. I found this tour through a parallel universe intriguing and often amusing." That said, Dowd wrote, "Mrs. Bush is not Eleanor Roosevelt."[12] Other reviewers were less charitable: Eleanor Clift, writing in *Washington Monthly,* said of the book's length, "Inside this 532 page tome is a lean and mean 170 page book struggling to get out." Later in the review Clift observed, "The book reveals Barbara to be a master of the sly put-down, sometimes covered up with an excess of superlatives about whomever she is simultaneously slicing and dicing."[13] The most negative appraisal came from Frank Rich of the *New York Times,* who commented: "One of the dullest memoirs ever to lay waste to a forest." He suggested that Mrs. Bush was so self-absorbed that the people she encountered were interchangeable and that, after a while, her niceness wore on the reader. In addition, some of her comments seemed odd and insensitive: she remembered Martin Luther King leading "the most awful garbage strikes" in Memphis and donated the free toiletries she collected in hotels to a shelter, "because 'a clean piece of soap all of your own must be nice' for the poor." Rich concluded that Mrs. Bush was hopelessly out of touch.[14] His evaluation was cruel: Barbara Bush's book revealed a woman still smarting from the 1992 loss and eager to settle some scores while disclosing the passion with which she viewed her husband's career. Her observations about politics, literacy, and the Persian Gulf War made her book a worthwhile read.

In addition to her memoirs, Mrs. Bush contributed to other writing projects that interfaced with her interests. In 1996, she shared her thoughts in Andrew Gulliford's volume *Note to America's Country Schools;* a year later, she wrote the forward to *First Families: An Intimate Portrait from the Kennedys to the Clintons,* edited by Harry Benson. In 1998, she wrote an afterword to Tricia Tusa's *Bunnies in My*

Head, published by the M. D. Anderson Cancer Center of Houston, Texas. The year 2001 saw her write the foreword to *Grassroots Women: A Memoir of the Texas Republican Party,* by Meg McKain Grier. She also wrote the introduction to a 2003 book by Jill Kimball titled *Drawing Families Together: One Meal at a Time.*

Writing was only part of Mrs. Bush's postpresidency activities. She became a speaker for hire and traveled all over the country addressing various organizations. Barbara Bush, who was once so terrified of facing audiences that she would not think of speaking to a group without her slides, now commanded a hefty fee for her comments. She found that she was being paid for something she had done for free for twelve years. While on the speaking circuit, Mrs. Bush encountered former presidents Gerald Ford and Jimmy Carter, Elizabeth Dole, and former generals Colin Powell and Norman Schwartzkopf. She observed, "Most of us agreed that speaking qualified as 'white collar crime' . . . after working for years for the government, it seemed like stealing to be paid half a year's salary for one speech."[15]

In addition to writing and speaking, Mrs. Bush was busy with charitable activities. She joined the board of the Mayo Clinic and became ambassador-at-large for AmeriCares, a relief organization that delivered medical supplies to countries around the world. She lent her name and support to the Barbara Bush Children's Hospital in Maine. She continued to attend literacy events and support the work of the Barbara Bush Foundation.

Perhaps giving credence to Donaldson's theory, George W. Bush, who had drifted from business endeavors to working on his father's presidential campaign to part ownership of the Texas Rangers baseball team, asked his parents in 1993 if they thought he should run against Ann Richards for the governorship of Texas. Mrs. Bush wrote, "I told him that he should NOT run against the very popular Ann Richards. I did not think he could win." George H. W. Bush, always more moderate than his wife, commented on her advice, "I view this as an expression of love and worry and concern for her little boy."[16] Her little boy/eldest son ignored his mother's advice and mounted a campaign against Richards. At the same time, the Bushes' second son, Jeb, announced his intention to run for governor of Florida. Mrs. Bush was surprised that either man wanted to be involved in politics.

"Both of them had worked hard in the campaign [1992 presidential campaign], and both of them had seen the tough, dirty side of politics—the lies and negative campaigning,"[17] she wrote.

George W. Bush had run unsuccessfully for Congress in 1978. He had attended a "candidates school" set up by the Republican Party to provide background and training in the nuances of politics and campaigning for hopeful office seekers. At the program, Bush had a conversation with a fellow participant which seemed to suggest that George and Barbara's son was both coddled and naive: "Bush announced a brainstorm. 'I've got the greatest idea of how to raise money for the campaign . . . have your mother send a letter to your family's Christmas card list! I just did, and I got $350,000.'"[18]

Both Barbara and George campaigned and were active fundraisers for their sons and other Republican candidates in 1994. Occasionally, Barbara would campaign with George W. or sometimes with Laura Bush. Mrs. Bush confessed to being unable to watch either of her sons debate their rivals. She commented, "I had not realized how much worse it seems when your children run than when your husband runs. And that's pretty stressful."[19] Mrs. Bush thought that Jeb would win and George W. Bush would be defeated, but the opposite happened; Jeb lost his race; George W. Bush won a decisive victory.[20]

Looking back on 1994, Mrs. Bush noted that she had finished her memoir, gone on a nationwide book tour, signed thousands of bookplates, traveled extensively by herself and with her husband, campaigned for her two sons, and spent time with her family. She recalled it was an enjoyable and fulfilling year but commented, "I sometimes find retirement so exhausting that I think I'll get a job."[21]

In a letter written in January 1995, three days after his inauguration as the governor of Texas, George W. Bush expressed his debt to his parents, "I am where I am because of you. You should always know this."[22] Mother and son had always had a close relationship, particularly after the death of Robin Bush. George W. Bush remembered that his mother could be a stern disciplinarian. He told an interviewer, "I've been reprimanded by Barbara Bush as a child and I've been reprimanded as an adult, and in both circumstances, it wasn't much fun."[23] He made another point about his mother in a 1999 commencement address at Southern Methodist University:

"Remember that no matter how old you are or what your job is, you can never escape your mother. I know."[24]

A few months later, prior to a debate with Senator John McCain, Bush received an e-mail from Barbara that advised him to "stand up straight."[25] Speaking with *Time* magazine after he received the Republican nomination for president, Bush was asked what was most important about his family legacy. He responded, "The unconditional love I got from my family liberated me. It gave me a sense of security."[26] He went on to say that he was a lot like his mother: "Yes, I'm more like my Mom sometimes. I'm quick with a quip. Dad gives me advice when I ask for it, my Mom when I don't. She can be blunt, like me. She says what she wants. My Dad's always gracious." Bush concluded his comments by saying, "It's a great blessing to be raised by George and Barbara Bush."[27]

The Bush family's political fortunes brightened further in the late 1990s; George W. Bush was reelected governor of Texas in 1998, and Jeb Bush was elected governor of Florida. Buoyed by his victory, George W. Bush began to consider a run for president in 2000. During a church service prior to Bush's second inauguration as governor, the pastor spoke about a calling for public service. Barbara Bush, who heard this exhortation, "leaned over and said to her son, 'He's speaking to you.'"[28]

Two years later, George W. Bush declared his candidacy for the 2000 Republican presidential nomination. *Time* devoted its Republican convention week cover story to the birth of the Bush political dynasty.[29]

A month prior to the Republican National Convention, with the nomination assured, Barbara and George Bush spoke to the *New York Times* about their eldest son. Reporter Frank Bruni, who covered George W. Bush during the presidential campaign, wrote that both George and Barbara Bush pointed out that their son's candidacy was not a product of revenge or redemption. Yet, wrote Bruni, the Bushes' words and demeanor, especially Barbara's, "suggested that they had not left 1992 completely behind them."[30] The former president said that he thought his son would win the general election because "people are beginning to see . . . what he's really like, that he's a decent person . . . has done a good job in his state."[31] Mr. Bush also felt that the country was ready for a change after eight years of a Democratic administration, and Vice President and Democratic nominee Al Gore would not be able to present himself credibly as a fresh start after the various Clinton administration scandals.[32] A few times during the interview, Mr. Bush spoke to his wife about her "acidic interruptions" and comments about Mr. Gore. When she made a reference to an awkward toast offered by Gore during a visit to China in 1997, the former president reprimanded his wife, saying, "What are you doing? You're not going to be in this interview if you're going to start talking like that. George will call and he'll be furious."[33] Later, both Bushes had kind words for Gore, whom they had known as a U.S. senator. Mrs. Bush sat and smiled, but, as usual, she had made her point.

With the help of political consultant Karl Rove, who had directed his gubernatorial campaigns in 1994 and 1998, George W. Bush ran an aggressive, well-paced campaign. He told an interviewer about the upcoming election, "I may have to get a little rough for a while, but that is what the old man had to do with Dukakis."[34] Barbara Bush's disdain for the media seemed to be inculcated in her son. Even though he liked some reporters personally, he commented, "The best way to get objective news is from objective sources. And the most objective sources I have are people on my staff who tell me what's happening in the world."[35]

Though they helped their son in his campaign, George and Barbara kept a low profile because they did not want to overshadow him, make statements that could be perceived as controversial, or open the candidate to charges that he was using his family's name and reputation to succeed.[36] George H. W. Bush traveled extensively, talking up his son's candidacy. George W. seemed to understand intuitively something that his father had discovered many years earlier: that his mother was a potent political weapon. Mrs. Bush refused to watch television or listen to comments that were made about her son. Instead, she focused on fund-raisers and took part in "W Stands for Women," a tour that focused on trying to get more of the female vote in the battleground states of Michigan, Wisconsin, and Pennsylvania. The group on the tour included Barbara Bush, Laura Bush, Lynne Cheney, Bush foreign affairs adviser Dr. Condoleezza Rice, and Cindy McCain, the wife of Senator John McCain. The tour kicked off in Michigan, and Barbara Bush was its star. As always, Mrs. Bush's disarming candor impressed her listeners. She said, "I have to confess that I feel funny talking about women's issues. . . . You see, I think women care about the exact same thing that men care about." Laura Bush differed with her mother-in-law and said the issues of the tour were education, tax cuts, Social Security, and Medicare. "I think these issues we're talking about are bigger issues for women," she said.[37] There was no mention of abortion. The tour drew sizable audiences in the three states visited.

During the weeks of crisscrossing the country, Mrs. Bush spoke to a reporter about her daughter-in-law as a potential first lady. She commented, "I think she would rather make a positive impact on the country. And I'm not criticizing Mrs. Clinton. . . . They're two different people. Laura thinks of others." Perhaps catching herself and realizing that her comment reflected mean-spiritedness, she added that Laura would be a much better first lady than Barbara Bush because Laura would not "be a fat, white-haired old lady."[38]

On 7 November, the country went to the polls. What happened over the next few weeks made history. At first, it seemed that Al Gore had squeaked by with a razor-thin margin of victory; then it seemed that George W. Bush had carried Florida by an even thinner margin and had won the election. Gore conceded the election and then rescinded his concession. Questions emerged about questionable vote returns in a number of Florida counties. Litigation and hand counts of the ballots took place. Though she was worried about the outcome and had questions about the vote, Barbara Bush made no public comment about the recount. She wrote, "The rest of us [the Bush family] could not yell or shout, but felt like it."[39] Finally, the Supreme Court of the United States declared that the hand count had to be halted, and George W. Bush, who still held a slim lead, was declared the winner on 13 December 2000. Eight years and a month after his father's defeat at the hands of Bill Clinton, George W. Bush was elected president following one of the most rancorous elections in American electoral history. If Donaldson's assessment is accurate, the sons truly avenged their parents' loss.

On 20 January 2001, Barbara Pierce Bush became only the second woman since 1825 to have been both first lady and the mother of a president. She wrote at the beginning of *Reflections* that there is a myth that all American mothers harbored the hope that their child would grow up to be president. Mrs. Bush said this was certainly a myth as far as she was concerned: "I never dreamed that any of ours would [become president]; there were days when I hoped that they'd just grow up!"[40] Though she was overwhelmed by feelings of pride on Inauguration Day, Mrs. Bush's thoughts drifted to Al Gore: how must he be feeling? She concluded, "He is gracious, and . . . came over to shake our hands and to meet Jenna and Barbara, George and Laura's twin daughters. We've lost and losing is not easy."[41] For Barbara Bush, the day had to be especially satisfying. The loss to Bill Clinton was finally avenged.

On 11 September 2001, George and Barbara Bush were on an airplane, flying to give speeches in St. Paul, Minnesota, when they received the news that a plane had flown into the World Trade Center. A few minutes later, their plane was diverted to Milwaukee, Wisconsin, and once on the ground the former president and first lady were driven to a motel by the Secret Service. They were relieved to learn that all their children and grandchildren were safe. The Bushes, along with the president and first lady and the Carters, Clintons, and Fords, took part in a prayer service at the National Cathedral in Washington on 14 September. Mrs. Bush wrote that she was especially proud of her son as he addressed emergency workers, firefighters, and police officers at Ground Zero in New York City.[42] Mrs. Bush's words reflect the same questions that troubled many Americans: "The days after 9/11 were confusing for us all. How could people accept our hospitality for years, be educated at our universities, and live among us while planning to kill us?"[43]

As she approached her eightieth birthday, Mrs. Bush was still active with various organizations and continued as a strong advocate for literacy. In 2003, she published *Reflections: Life after the White House,* which provided details about her busy years after leaving Washington. Frothy and bursting with bonhomie, the book recounted the Bushes' visits with a never-ending parade of foreign diplomats and American politicians and friends. The book enjoyed commercial success, but similar to *A Memoir,* critical reaction was mixed. A review in the *New York Times* neither praised nor criticized the book. Writer Michiko Kakutani focused on some of the things that Mrs. Bush did not say: she had fond memories of Secretary of State Colin Powell, but said nothing about Secretary of Defense

Donald Rumsfeld. She was proud of her son George W. Bush but offered "several spirited defenses in these pages of her husband's conduct of the first Gulf War and his multilateral approach to foreign
policy, which her son's administration has repudiated."[44] A review
that appeared in *White House Studies* was less generous; it noted that
Barbara Bush was a product of an earlier generation, a fact that was
especially evident in her new book. "What will stick out to most
twenty-first century readers," wrote the reviewers, "is Mrs. Bush's
frustrating acceptance of her accommodating status as wife and
mother of two presidents." Amid the political observations, there
were recipes and lists of guests who had visited with the family. The
critique continued that most twenty- and thirty-year-old women
would not find much in common with Mrs. Bush. Finally, the reviewers concluded, "It may not be ludicrous to suggest that Mrs.
Bush's granddaughters might find more of a kinship with Hillary
Clinton's *Living History* than their own matriarch's musings."[45]

Throughout 2002 and early 2003, President Bush spoke frequently about weapons of mass destruction that President Saddam
Hussein had hidden at various locations in Iraq. Hussein refused to
permit United Nations personnel to conduct inspections to confirm
the existence of these weapons. All indicators seemed to point to the
distinct possibility of a war if Hussein continued to prohibit inspections. Reporter Bob Woodward recalls that Barbara Bush confronted her old friend David Boren, former chair of the Senate Se-
lect Committee on Intelligence, and asked him, "Are we right to be
worried about this Iraq thing?" Yes, responded Boren, he was very
worried. "Do you think it's a mistake?" Yes, said Boren, "I think it's a
huge mistake if we go in right now, this way." Mrs. Bush went on to
say that George H. W. Bush was losing sleep over the possibility of a
war. When Boren asked her why Bush, an expert in the area, and
someone who had fought a war against Iraq did not speak to his son,
she said, "He doesn't think he should unless he's asked," then she
"shook her head solemnly, almost woefully."[46]

Her conversation with Boren is in broad contrast to comments
Mrs. Bush made to reporter Diane Sawyer a few weeks later. Her observations were made during an interview on 18 March 2003, the
morning before the war in Iraq commenced, and addressed television news in general and Mrs. Bush's attitudes toward war news.

Sawyer asked Mrs. Bush if she watched much television. Mrs. Bush responded that her husband watched, but "I watch none. He sits and listens and I read books, because I know perfectly well that . . . 90 percent of what I hear on television is supposition when we're talking about the news." Mrs. Bush went on to say, "Why should we hear about body bags and deaths and how many, what day it's gonna happen. I mean, it's not relevant. So why should I waste my beautiful mind on something like that?"[47] Her supporters offered a weak defense and said that Mrs. Bush was dismissing conjecture about the number of probable war casualties. The charges of insensitivity that had been leveled at her husband were now directed at the former first lady.

In spite of the war and mounting American deaths, George W. Bush ran for reelection in 2004, and Mrs. Bush found herself on the campaign trail once again. She traveled across the country, giving speeches and trying to ignite voters' enthusiasm for her son. She was especially incensed by John Kerry's attacks on her son. George H. W. Bush told a dinner audience that if "Barbara gets her hands on Senator Kerry, he's going to need another Purple Heart."[48] A few days before the election, she told an audience that "the closing days of the race were going to be terrible for her. 'I plan to have a nervous breakdown.'"[49] Sparing his mother a nervous breakdown, Bush was reelected. After her husband's second inauguration, Laura Bush revealed that whenever she and her mother-in-law were together on the campaign trail, they loved to complain about the news media. "Asked if the complaints were about institutions or individuals, she answered, 'All.'"[50]

In a strange twist, George H. W. Bush and his old nemesis Bill Clinton found themselves working together. On 26 December 2004, an earthquake measuring 9.1 on the Richter scale originated on the floor of the Indian Ocean and triggered a tsunami that devastated parts of Indonesia, India, Thailand, and Sri Lanka. Hundreds of thousands of people were dead or missing. President George W. Bush asked his father and Clinton to organize the American response to the tsunami. The duo raised hundreds of millions of dollars to rebuild the homes and lives of the people affected by the disaster. The former presidents discovered that they liked and respected each other. This caused Barbara Bush to nickname them "The Odd Couple."[51]

The former first lady spoke in support of her son's plans to revise Social Security. She joined him for a swing through Florida on 18 March 2005, and introducing him to an audience in Pensacola, told listeners that she was concerned about the future of Social Security for her seventeen grandchildren: "We want to know, is someone going to do something about it?" she asked.[52]

Five months later, in August 2005, Hurricane Katrina decimated the Gulf Coast. Hundreds of survivors from New Orleans were evacuated to the Astrodome in the Bushes' hometown of Houston, Texas, where they would receive temporary housing, food, clothing, and medical attention. George H. W. Bush, Barbara Bush, Bill Clinton, Senator Hillary Clinton, and Senator Barack Obama toured the Astrodome to investigate conditions and provide support to the survivors. After the visit, Mrs. Bush told National Market Radio, "Almost everyone I've talked to says we're going to move to Houston." Then she added, "And so many people in the arena here, you know, were underprivileged anyway, so this—this is working very well for them."[53]

There was an uproar in the press as critics argued that the comment was further proof that the Bush family had no sensitivity to the plight of the common man. One popular spoof that reached millions by e-mail acknowledged that Mrs. Bush's comments had become a liability to her son's administration. The e-mail, titled "Barbara Bush Relocated. Former First Lady Moved to New Location away from Cameras, Microphones," said that the former first lady had been taken to a location where she would not make media appearances. Playing on the wording of her statement, White House press secretary Scott McClellan was purported to have said, "She will be much more comfortable in this new location, surrounded by armed guards on a 24 hour basis. . . . This is working very well for her." Another Web site, "Role Models on the Web," which had a photo and biographical information about Mrs. Bush, announced, "In light of recent statements made by Barbara Bush concerning the New Orleans evacuees, we have decided to temporarily remove Barbara Bush from our list of role models. We will cut her some slack if she makes an apology and explains what she meant in a way that really makes sense."[54] The story generated a huge and generally critical press response. Apparently the public forgave "Everyone's

Grandmother"; in Gallup's Most Admired Woman poll for 2006, Barbara Bush ranked ninth (daughter-in-law Laura Bush ranked fourth, and Hillary Rodham Clinton was first).

Barbara Bush continues to speak at literacy events, to introduce new readers to her audiences, to visit literacy programs, and to work at raising funds for her foundation. She maintained a correspondence with Paul Simon after he retired from the U.S. Senate and became the head of the Public Policy Institute at Southern Illinois University. In April 1999, she joined Simon in unveiling an eighteen-point action plan to integrate libraries into the fight against illiteracy in the United States.[55] A few months later she wrote to him: "By the most conservative estimate, 23 million Americans cannot read a newspaper. . . . We still are working—last week we awarded our Maine literacy grants. It is so moving to talk to the students."[56] An article in the 1 May 2006 online edition of the *Houston Chronicle* reported that the annual Celebration of Reading hosted by former president and Mrs. Bush had raised almost $2 million for Mrs. Bush's foundation and the Barbara Bush Texas Fund for Family Literacy.[57]

The Bushes live six months of the year in Houston and six months in Kennebunkport, although they still travel extensively. Mrs. Bush continues to serve on the boards of AmeriCares and the Mayo Clinic and is still involved in the Barbara Bush Foundation for Family Literacy. At the age of eighty-two, Mrs. Bush can look back on an active life filled with challenges, achievements, and some disappointments. Her son's presidency did not turn out to be the triumph his parents had hoped for, and questions about the future of the Bush "dynasty" have been raised. Historians will eventually weigh in on Mrs. Bush as both first lady and mother of a president. Still, Barbara Bush occupies a unique place in this fascinating and complex American institution.

CHAPTER 8

CONCLUSIONS

Shortly after her wedding to George Bush, Barbara was asked if she would like her husband to be president. "'I'd like it,' she answered without hesitation. 'Because you know, I'm going to be the first lady sometime.'"[1] Though she asserted in a 2005 interview that politics did not seem to be in George Bush's plans, perhaps they always were, and the White House was forever the goal.[2]

Raised with values, manners, and discipline, Barbara Bush fit the mold of a traditional wife and mother. Every action was aimed at helping George Bush's career. She took care of their large, growing family, which would contribute to an image of a happy home life. During her husband's many absences, she watched over the brood. If she was bitter or jealous, she would live with those feelings and move on. Still, she had an edge that her husband did not possess. He was extroverted, friendly, and trusting. She was tougher, more discriminating, and always on the lookout for someone else's less than pure motives. A reporter who covered the White House and had regular contact with Mrs. Bush said, "That's one tough Yankee housewife."[3]

She was the perfect political wife in that she was accepting of her lot, was a good campaigner when needed, and would not publicly meddle in George H. W. Bush's business. The Bushes did not always agree on issues, but Barbara kept her dissent to herself. She loved China, she was not happy about her husband's job as chairman of the Republican National Committee, and she strongly opposed his becoming director of the CIA. She counseled him not to accept the latter two positions, but he did not heed her warnings.

The ultimate prize, the White House, became theirs in January 1989. Barbara was more than "not Nancy"; she was grace and gentility returned to the Executive Mansion. She seemed real, concerned, and engaging—normal, after Nancy Reagan. She was multifaceted, interested in politics and issues of the day. In the words of one historian, as first lady she took advantage of Americans' complicated attitudes toward women, power, aging and beauty."[4]

The title of the *New York Times* book review of *Barbara Bush: A Memoir* is "Qualities Americans Like: She Was Dignified, She Was Loyal and She Wore $29 Shoes."[5] This might well be a concise summation of the public Barbara Bush. An oasis of calm, she was popular and well liked; she was everyone's good-sport grandmother, and she used her celebrity to win Americans' affection. Her image was managed so deftly that she never had to deal with charges of being involved in George Bush's presidency. Privately, she was an influential force in her husband's administration.

According to an old Bush friend, Barbara was crucial to her husband's political success because she knew how to hate; George Bush did not. Barbara watched her husband's back, never forgot a slight or rude behavior, and was not shy about giving back in kind.[6] She became skilled at the one-liner that hurt and was remembered by the victim and others who witnessed it. She was a strong, competitive woman who worked hard to seem submissive and therefore avoid dwarfing her husband. She was a keen judge of people, and her husband came to rely on her assessments gleaned from extensive travel and talking with varied and diverse groups of people. As with many presidents, the first lady's was one of the few voices he heard that was honest and without an agenda; she wanted him to succeed and be admired. She was a cheerleader, motivator, and confidante, but she was not a copresident.[7]

Like her husband, Mrs. Bush seemed to have issues with a free and uncensored press, and she would rise up in anger if George H. W. Bush or her children were the targets of criticism. She could be stern: on one occasion she told an interviewer who had written a previous piece about her that she was in error when she wrote that

Mrs. Bush had screamed at her children when they were growing up. "I never screamed at my children," she declared.[8]

A reporter who requested anonymity recalled that on one occasion she was part of a press pool assigned to cover an event at the Bushes' Kennebunkport home. The morning of the event was rainy and dreary. The members of the press pool walked up to the Bushes' front door and knocked. Mrs. Bush answered the door and invited the reporters in, but not without reminding them to "be sure to wipe your feet."[9] Another reporter said that if a journalist wrote a negative story about one of the Clintons, he or she might be given one more chance to have access to the president and first lady. Not so with the Bushes, said the reporter. One negative story and you might as well wait until the next administration begins because your access was gone.[10]

Even though she played an important role in her husband's presidential campaign and his reelection effort, and as first lady in general, Barbara Bush's contributions seemed to have limited value in the view of George H. W. Bush and the males who ran the White House. Professor Stephen Lee of the University of Virginia's Miller Center, the organization charged with executing the George Bush Oral History Project, confirmed this when he said that Barbara Bush was *not* one of the people selected by former president Bush to share memories and impressions of his administration. According to Professor Lee, no women were included in the oral history interviews. One wonders if the former president wanted to protect Mrs. Bush's privacy, if she was asked to participate and refused, or if, in the president's estimation, she was not worthy of inclusion in the program. Maybe the decision not to interview Barbara Bush was a continuation of the lifelong division of labor in the George H. W. Bush household. The exclusion of her oral testimony is a loss: Barbara Bush was an eyewitness to history and could offer her own unique evaluations of her husband's presidency.[11]

By almost any measure, Barbara Bush was more of a success as first lady than George H. W. Bush was as president. The first lady believed that she was popular and well liked because she was seen as benign and well intentioned, with no desire to influence public policy. In 1993 a Siena Research Institute First Lady Survey ranked her eighth out of thirty-seven presidential spouses, just barely trailing

Jacqueline Kennedy. The first ladies were rated by scholars who considered background, value to country, integrity, leadership, intelligence, being her own woman, accomplishments, courage, public image, and value to the president. Mrs. Bush did not fare as well in the 2003 survey, falling to fifteenth, trailing Lucy Hayes (first lady, 1877–1881). Mrs. Bush ranked fifth in the category of public image, but this was not enough to sustain her earlier ranking. The passing of time and changing historical evaluations may well have contributed to her decline on the first lady exchange. In the 2002 Siena Research Institute Presidential Ranking Survey, George H. W. Bush was ranked twenty-second of forty-three chief executives.[12] At the same time, Mrs. Bush became a virtual fixture in Gallup's Most Admired Woman poll. In 2004, after being gone from the White House for more than ten years, she ranked sixth in the poll, behind Hillary Clinton, Oprah Winfrey, and her daughter-in-law, Laura.[13]

Mrs. Bush did not redefine the position and made no institutional changes to the Office of First Lady. One historian offered the opinion that although George Bush was "an unsuccessful, one term President, he and Barbara were a popular couple."[14] Another historian wrote that Mrs. Bush was a disappointment to feminists, who suspected that she supported their views but would not articulate her own feelings even though it seemed that she was sympathetic to their cause.[15] The same could probably be said of moderate Republicans, especially after the right wing of the party took more extreme stances at the 1992 party convention. After leaving the White House, Mrs. Bush explained why she never spoke out about abortion, one of the hot-button issues of her husband's White House tenure. She said, "I had priorities. I really wanted you [the American people] to be interested in fighting the battle against illiteracy, and I knew the minute I veered off and got into something else, the whole world would fall down and no one would care about illiteracy."[16]

In a 2005 interview, Mrs. Bush was asked about her legacy. She said it was the literacy project that she advocated and the foundation that she helped launch. She was proud of the fact that the Barbara Bush Foundation for Family Literacy is thriving, providing grants to literacy programs around the country many years after she left the White House. She mentioned that whenever she travels, she tries to highlight the work of the foundation by introducing a new reader to her audience. She told an interviewer about a man she had known for years. When his wife was disabled by a stroke, it became evident that the man was unable to read and that his wife had covered his deficiencies throughout their married life. The man had made the decision to learn to read and took advantage of a local literacy program. He was currently reading "at a children's book level," said Mrs. Bush, and while progress was slow and the work tedious, he was succeeding. She was very impressed with his tenacity and the support he was receiving from literacy volunteers. She felt that triumphs such as this gave legitimacy to her work.[17]

In the same interview, she was asked to identify specific pieces of legislation passed by the Bush administration for which she had advocated. She refused to do this but admitted that she had influenced the National Literacy Act of 1991.[18] As always, the disconnect between the public and private Barbara Bush is evident. Because her main White House project had been literacy, it was safe, even appropriate, for the former first lady to admit that she lobbied the president on behalf of the Literacy Act. Unless she reverses years of silence on the topic, it will never be known if she argued for or against the Civil Rights Bill, the Americans with Disabilities Act, or the Clean Air Act. It will be almost impossible to learn the exact extent to which she influenced presidential decision making. The most informed guess on both is that she wielded significant power.

First ladies are rarely representative of the time they serve in the White House; most are typical of the era of their upbringing. This was the case with Barbara Bush, who seemed to have more in common with Bess Truman (who served as first lady from 1945 to 1953) than with any other first lady of the twentieth century. Both women were devoted to their families and their husbands. Both were traditional first ladies who discharged the ceremonial responsibilities of their position and swore they had no influence with the president. Both exercised significant influence in private.

Barbara Pierce Bush remains an enigma, but few would argue with her celebrity, popularity, or influence. That she used her considerable energies to improve the lot of Americans in the area of literacy is a testament to her White House tenure, and she has surely earned the title "First Lady of Literacy." She became the public face of the

George H. W. Bush administration with constant travel, participation in ceremonial events, and speeches. She used the White House podium effectively to articulate her views and concerns. She was a perceptive politician who knew how to work a crowd or bend an arm, if necessary. During her busy public life, she made a number of comments that may have tarnished her image, but her good works have more than restored the sheen. Barbara Bush has lived a busy life in service to George Bush and her family, friends, and country. While there has been an ebb and flow to events, hers has been a life well lived, benefiting many.

NOTES

PREFACE

1. Mrs. Bush's Remarks at Smith College Convocation, Northampton, Massachusetts, 6 September 1989, Kathy Steffy Files, Barbara Bush's Speeches, 9/89–12/89, IA/OA 08384, George Bush Library (hereafter GBL). Mrs. Bush was very impressed with Mrs. Johnson's comments and repeated them to the author during her interview. Author interview with Barbara Bush, 25 April 2005.

2. Author interview with Sheila Weidenfeld, 9 July 1982.

CHAPTER 1: "NO MAN, WOMAN, OR CHILD EVER HAD A BETTER LIFE"

1. "$134,553 Paid Head of Publishing Firm," *New York Times,* 25 April, 1935, p. 33.

2. Herbert S. Parmet, *George Bush: The Life of a Lone Star Yankee* (New York: Scribner's, 1997), p. 45.

3. Margaret Truman, *First Ladies* (New York: Random House, 1995), p. 314.

4. Barbara Bush, *Barbara Bush: A Memoir* (New York: Scribner's, 1994), p. 7.

5. Joseph P. Lash, *Eleanor and Franklin* (New York: Norton, 1971), p. 33.

6. Marjorie Williams, "Barbara's Backlash," *Vanity Fair,* August 1992, p. 124.

7. June Biedler interviewed on "Barbara Bush: First Mom," Arts and Entertainment Television Network; first broadcast in 1996.

8. Bush, *Barbara Bush,* p. 7.

9. Ibid., p. 9.

10. Barbara Bush quoted in Jean Becker, "Barbara Bush," in *The Report to the First Lady, Laura Bush, 2005,* ed. Robert P. Watson (New York: Nova History Publications, 2005), p. 156.

11. Bush, *Barbara Bush,* p. 12.

12. Ann Grimes, *Running Mates: The Making of a First Lady* (New York: Morrow, 1990), p. 55.

13. Claudia Brinson, "At Ashley Hall, Girls Learn to Ask Questions," *The State,* www.thestate.com/mid/thestate/living/11474919.htm. Ashley Hall became a day school in 1950 and currently has a student body of more than 600 female

students (classes are coeducational until first grade), from two-year preschool through twelfth grade. Barbara Pierce Bush, class of 1943, is listed as one of the outstanding alumnae of Ashley Hall. Other distinguished alumnae include the authors Madeleine L'Engle, class of 1936; Alexandra Ripley, class of 1951; and Josephine Humphreys, class of 1963. Ashley Hall awards a Barbara P. Bush Scholarship for academic achievement in the rising ninth-grade class or for students new to the upper school. Additional information about Ashley Hall can found on the school's Web site, www.ashleyhall.org.

14. Patricia Leigh Brown, "The First Lady-Elect: What She Is and Isn't," *New York Times*, 11 December 1988, p. 1.

15. Bush, *Barbara Bush*, p. 15.

16. Mrs. Bush explained the name "Poppy": "George was named after his maternal grandfather, George Herbert Walker. He had four young uncles who called their father 'Pops,' So they called their nephew 'Little Pops,' which soon became 'Poppy.'" Bush, *Barbara Bush*, p. 17n.

17. Ibid., pp. 16–17; Joe Hyams, *Flight of the Avenger: George Bush at War* (New York: Harcourt, 1991), p. 25.

18. Parmet, *George Bush*, p. 45.

19. Hyams, *Flight of the Avenger*, p. 25.

20. Marvin Bush interviewed on "Barbara Bush: First Mom," Arts and Entertainment Television Network.

21. Brown, "The First Lady-Elect," p. 42.

22. Margaret Garrard Warner, "Bush Battles the 'Wimp Factor,'" *Newsweek*, 19 October 1987, p. 29. Former president Bush told a similar story during a lecture in College Station, Texas, on 25 April 2005.

23. Kati Marton, *Hidden Power: Presidential Marriages That Shaped Our Recent History* (New York: Pantheon, 2001), pp. 279–280.

24. John Meachem interviewed on "Barbara Bush: First Mom," Arts and Entertainment Television Network.

25. Archivists at the George Bush Library, College Station, Texas, told the author that Mrs. Bush had reported that her letters to Mr. Bush had probably been lost during one of the family's many moves. Author conversation with Bush Library archivists, 28 July 2004.

26. George Bush Personal Papers, World War II Correspondence, Chapel Hill, August–10 September 1942, GBL. Many of Bush's letters to his parents were undated but have been placed in dated folders by the Bush Library. I have cited the relevant folders where the letters can be located.

27. George Bush Personal Papers, World War II Correspondence, Chapel Hill, August–10 September 1942, GBL.

28. George Bush Personal Papers, World War II Correspondence, Minneapolis, November 1942–February 1943, GBL.

29. George Bush Personal Papers, World War II Correspondence, 28 June 1943, GBL.

30. George Bush Personal Papers, World War II Correspondence, 11 July 1943, GBL.

31. Ibid.

32. Bush, *Barbara Bush*, p. 19.

33. Ibid.

34. Ibid.

35. Bonnie Angelo, *First Mothers: The Women Who Shaped the Presidents* (New York: Perennial, 2001), p. 343.

36. George Bush quoted Parmet, *George Bush*, p. 48.

37. Kitty Kelley, *The Family: The Real Story of the Bush Dynasty* (New York: Doubleday, 2004), p. 87.

38. Williams, "Barbara's Backlash," p. 176.

39. Marton, *Hidden Power*, p. 279.

40. George Bush Personal Papers, World War II Correspondence, 13 November 1943, GBL.

41. "Barbara Pierce Engaged to Wed," *New York Times*, 12 December 1943, p. 66.

42. George Bush quoted in Jean Becker, "Barbara Bush," in *The Report to the First Lady, Laura Bush, 2005*, ed. Robert P. Watson (New York: Nova, 2005), p. 156.

43. Hyams, *Flight of the Avenger*, p. 68.

44. Doro Bush Koch, *My Father, My President: A Personal Account of the Life of George H. Bush* (New York: Warner, 2006), p. 17.

45. Frank Bruni, *Ambling into History: The Unlikely Odyssey of George W. Bush* (New York: HarperCollins, 2002), pp. 177–178.

46. Williams, "Barbara's Backlash," p. 176.

47. Fitzhugh Green, *George Bush: An Intimate Portrait* (New York: Hippocrene, 1989), p. 44.

48. "Barbara Bush and the Norms of '47," *New York Times*, 1 June 1990, p. A28.

49. George Bush Personal Papers, World War II Correspondence, 26 September 1943, GBL.

50. George Bush Personal Papers, World War II Correspondence, 5 March 1944, GBL.

51. Hyams, *Flight of the Avenger*, p. 111.

52. Parmet, *George Bush*, p. 58. The most comprehensive account of Bush's wartime service can be found in Hyams, *Flight of the Avenger*. Another description of his naval service can be found in "Lieutenant Junior Grade George Bush, USNR," Department of the Navy—Naval Historical Center. This information may be accessed at the Naval Historical Center's Web site: www.history.navy.mil/faqs/faq10–1.htm.

53. George Bush Personal Papers, World War II Correspondence, 3 September 1944, GBL.

54. George Bush Personal Papers, World War II Correspondence, 23 November 1944, GBL.

55. Bush, *Barbara Bush*, pp. 22–23. Mrs. Bush writes that her father was well aware that Pauline Pierce was a spendthrift who kept her unpaid bills in a bedside drawer. When her mother died in 1949, vendors from around the country contacted Marvin Pierce for payment of her purchases.

56. Parmet, *George Bush*, p. 60.

57. "Miss Pierce Is Wed to Lieut. G. H. Bush," *New York Times*, 7 January, 1945, p. 36.

58. Parmet, *George Bush*, p. 61.

59. Ibid.

60. Williams, "Barbara's Backlash," p. 176.

61. Hyams, *Flight of the Avenger*, p. 54.

62. Bush, *Barbara Bush*, pp. 26–28.

63. Some information in this section was drawn from the Yale University yearbook for 1948, GBL.

64. Author interview with Barbara Bush, 25 April 2005.

65. George H. W. Bush, *All the Best: My Life in Letters and Other Writings* (New York: Scribner's, 1999), p. 62.

66. Peggy Noonan, *What I Saw at the Revolution: A Political Life in the Reagan Era* (New York: Random House, 1990), p. 303.

67. Angelo, *First Mothers*, p. 413.

68. Helen Thomas, *Front Row at the White House: My Life and Times* (New York: Touchstone, 1999), p. 280.

69. "Auto Crash Kills Publisher's Wife as He Reaches for Spilling Cup," *New York Times*, 24 September 1949, p. 1.

70. Bush, *Barbara Bush*, p. 36.

71. Koch, *My Father*, p. 30.

72. Pamela Kilian, *Barbara Bush: A Biography* (New York: St. Martin's, 1992), p. 54.

73. Bush, *Barbara Bush*, p. 39.

74. George H. W. Bush interviewed on "Barbara Bush: First Mom," Arts and Entertainment Television Network.

75. Bush, *Barbara Bush*, p. 40.

76. Ibid., p. 44.

77. Marton, *Hidden Power*, p. 284; John B. Roberts II, *Rating the First Ladies: The Women Who Influenced the Presidency* (New York: Citadel, 2003), p. 333.

78. Bush, *Barbara Bush*, p. 25.

79. Koch, *My Father*, p. 34.

80. Ibid., p. 36.

81. Bush, *Barbara Bush*, p. 45.

82. Angelo, *First Mothers*, p. 415.

83. Bush, *Barbara Bush*, p. 47.

84. George W. Bush interviewed on "Barbara Bush: First Mom," Arts and Entertainment Television Network.

85. Barbara Bush interviewed by Rexalla Van Impe for "Rexalla: One on One," broadcast approximately 1982, Van Impe Video.

86. President Meets with Displaced Workers in Town Hall Meeting, www.whitehouse.gov/news/releases/2001/12/20011204-17.html.

87. "Looking Back with Barbara Bush," Barbara Bush interviewed by Jamie Gangel for MSNBC, 19 October 2003, www.msnbc.com/news/981674. asp?cp1=1.

88. Williams, "Barbara's Backlash," p. 177.

89. Author interview with Barbara Bush, 25 April 2005.

90. Kilian, *Barbara Bush*, p. 85.

91. Barbara Bush interviewed by Carl Sferrazza Anthony for "The Role of the First Lady" program at George Washington University, broadcast by C-SPAN, 9 October 1994.

92. John Robert Greene, *The Presidency of George Bush* (Lawrence: University Press of Kansas, 2000), p. 17.

93. Bill Minutaglio interviewed on "Barbara Bush: First Mom," Arts and Entertainment Television Network.

94. Parmet, *George Bush*, pp. 128–135.

95. Margaret Truman, *First Ladies* (New York: Random House, 1995), p. 316.

96. Bush, *Barbara Bush,* p. 98.

97. Ibid., p. 108; Gil Troy, *Affairs of State: The Rise and Rejection of the Presidential Couple since World War II* (New York: Free Press, 1997), p. 319.

98. Parmet, *George Bush,* p. 188.

99. George H. W. Bush quoted in Kati Marton, *Hidden Power,* p. 289.

100. Parmet, *George Bush,* p. 189.

101. Ibid., p. 190.

102. Bush, *Barbara Bush,* p. 133.

103. Ibid., p. 135.

104. Ibid.

105. Ibid.

106. Barbara Bush interviewed on "Barbara Bush: First Mom," Arts and Entertainment Television Network.

107. Ann Gerhart, *The Perfect Wife: The Life and Choices of Laura Bush* (New York: Simon and Schuster, 2004), pp. 74–77.

108. Parmet, *George Bush,* p. 207.

109. Hyams, *Flight of the Avenger,* p. 55.

110. Bush, *Barbara Bush,* p. 149.

111. Parmet, *George Bush,* p. 210.

112. Grimes, *Running Mates,* p. 187.

113. Bush, *Barbara Bush,* p. 149.

114. Vivian Castleberry, " 'My Choice Is to Enjoy' Says Barbara Bush," *Dallas Times Herald,* 30 October 1979, p. B2.

115. Bush, *Barbara Bush,* p. 153.

116. In her autobiography, Nancy Reagan wrote, "At the time, I didn't like George Bush. The bitter campaigns of Iowa and New Hampshire were still fresh in my memory, and George's use of the phrase 'voodoo economics' to describe Ronnie's proposed tax cuts still rankled. That's why I've always hated primaries—you're forced to go on the attack against candidates from your own party." Nancy Reagan with William Novak, *My Turn: The Memoirs of Nancy Reagan* (New York: Random House, 1989), pp. 21–213.

117. Parmet, *George Bush,* p. 257.

118. Bush, *Barbara Bush,* p. 152. Mrs. Bush reiterated her feelings about abortion in her interview with Carl Anthony at George Washington University in 1994.

119. Bob Colacello, *Ronnie and Nancy: Their Path to the White House—1911–1980* (New York: Warner, 2004), p. 495.

120. Ibid. pp. 495–496.

121. Parmet, *George Bush,* p. 259. Doro Bush Koch confirms that her mother and Mrs. Reagan were friends but "not fast friends." Koch, *My Father,* p. 170.

122. Marton, *Hidden Power,* pp. 295–296.

123. Parmet, *George Bush,* p. 257.

124. Enid Nemy, "The Active Life of Barbara Bush," *New York Times,* 8 April 1984, p. 68.

125. Bush, *Barbara Bush,* p. 194.

126. Ibid., p. 195.

127. Geraldine A. Ferraro with Linda Bird Francke, *Ferraro: My Story* (Evanston, IL: Northwestern University Press, 1985), pp. 249–250.

128. Bush, *Barbara Bush,* p. 196.

129. Ibid.

130. Ferraro, *Ferraro,* p. 267.

131. Bush, *Barbara Bush,* p. 167.

132. Author interview with Barbara Bush.

133. Grimes, *Running Mates,* p. 60.

134. Bush, *Barbara Bush,* p. 148.

135. Barbara Bush quoted in Grimes, *Running Mates,* p. 200. The first cases of AIDS were reported in the *Morbidity and Mortality Weekly Report (MMWR),* issued by the Centers for Disease Control, on 5 June 1981.

136. Comments by Mrs. George H. W. Bush, *Official Report of the Proceedings of the Thirty-fourth Republican National Convention, 15–18 August 1988,* reported by Asher and Associates, Inc.

137. Grimes, *Running Mates,* p. 144.

138. Barbara Bush's 1988 campaign speeches are not currently available for research.

139. Marton, *Hidden Power,* p. 292.

140. Williams, "Barbara's Backlash," p. 122.

141. Grimes, *Running Mates,* p. 199.

142. Roberts, *Rating the First Ladies,* pp. 330–331.

143. Ibid.

144. Jean-Philippe Faletta, "Presidential Campaign Rhetoric in 1988: Its Consequences for the Bush Administration's Performance in Office and the Election of 1992," in *Honor and Loyalty: Inside the Politics of the George H. W. Bush White House,* ed. Leslie D. Feldman and Rosanna Perotti (Westport, CT: Greenwood Press, 2002), p. 335. See, too, Joe Klein, *Politics Lost: How American Democracy Was Trivialized by People Who Think You're Stupid* (New York: Doubleday, 2006), pp. 103–106.

145. Kelley, *The Family,* p. 463.

146. Bush, *Barbara Bush,* p. 243. Roberts suggests that an outside political group, Americans for Bush, which had strong ties to the campaign, was responsible for the ad. He also writes that Republicans were so embarrassed by the ad that later they tried to dissociate themselves from it by arguing that Senator Al Gore had referred to the prison furlough program during the 1988 New York primary. While this is true, Gore referred only to the furlough program, not to Willie Horton. Roberts, *Rating the First Ladies,* p. 331.

147. Klein, *Politics Lost,* p. 107.

148. Grimes, *Running Mates,* p. 201.

149. Noonan, *What I Saw at the Revolution,* p. 303.

150. "George Bush, Lover Boy," *LA Weekly,* 14 October 1988.

151. Kilian, *Matriarch of a Dynasty,* p. 197.

152. Kelley, *The Family,* pp. 138, 327–328, 341, 354, 375–377, 434–436, 479, 523–528. A source who requested anonymity told the author that George Bush was a regular visitor to Jennifer Fitzgerald's townhouse for many years and the affair was an open secret. People in the neighborhood grew familiar with the black government sedan that parked on their street and was guarded by Secret Service agents.

153. Marton, *Hidden Power,* p. 288.

154. Ibid., p. 289.

155. Parmet, *George Bush,* p. 179. Other writers who have commented on the rumors surrounding Bush and Fitzgerald include Koch, *My Father,* p. 224; Roberts, *Rating the First Ladies,* p. 334; and Troy, *Affairs of State,* 325. Even Barbara Bush comments about a possible series of articles about the rumor that was going to be printed by the *Washington Post,* Bush, *Barbara Bush,* p. 240.

156. Parmet, *George Bush,* p. 179.

157. Harold Meyerson, "Polls, Pols and Propositions: Twenty Years of Political Coverage," *LA Weekly* online, 18 November 1998, http://www.laweekly.com/index3.php?option=com_content&task=v.

158. Marton, *Hidden Power,* p. 293.

159. Ibid., p. 294.

160. Brown, "The First Lady-Elect," p. 1.

161. Author interview with Jean Becker, 25 April 2005.

CHAPTER 2: "IF I SAID IT, I SAID IT"

1. James G. Benze Jr., *Nancy Reagan: On the White House Stage* (Lawrence: University Press of Kansas, 2005), p. 77.

2. The Iran-Contra affair was a mid-1980s political scandal of the Ronald Reagan administration. In direct violation of American law, the administration sold arms to Iran (engaged in the Iran-Iraq War) in the hope that it would use its influence to help free Americans being held in Lebanon. Funds were then provided to Contra rebels in Nicaragua to fight the ruling Sandinista government. The resulting congressional investigation reflected poorly on the Reagan administration.

3. Barrett Seaman, "Good Heavens! An Astrologer Dictating the President's Schedule? So Says Former White House Chief of Staff Donald Reagan in an Explosive Book," *Time*, Archives Online, 16 May 1988, http://www.highbeam.com.

4. John Robert Greene, *The Presidency of George Bush* (Lawrence: University Press of Kansas, 2000), p. 47.

5. Herbert S. Parmet, *George Bush: The Life of a Lonestar Yankee* (New York: Scribner's, 1997), pp. 360–361.

6. "Barbara Bush: First Mom," Arts and Entertainment Television Network.

7. Arnold Scaasi interviewed for "Barbara Bush: First Mom," Arts and Entertainment Television Network; "Custom Made Dress for Next First Lady," *New York Times*, 14 January 1989, p. 7.

8. Pamela Kilian, *Barbara Bush: Matriarch of a Dynasty* (New York: St. Martin's, 2002), p. 9.

9. Paul Costello comments in Leslie D. Feldman and Rosanna Perotti, eds., *Honor and Loyalty: Inside the Politics of the George H. W. Bush White House* (Westport, CT: Greenwood Press, 2002), p. 471.

10. Pamela Kilian interviewed on "Barbara Bush: First Mom," Arts and Entertainment Television Network.

11. Maureen Dowd, "Qualities Americans Like: She Was Dignified, She Was Loyal and She Wore $29 Shoes," *New York Times Book Review*, 27 November 1994, p. 1.

12. Barbara Bush, *Barbara Bush: A Memoir* (New York: Scribner's, 1994), p. 284.

13. "Barbara Bush Goes Red," www.museumofhoaxes.com/af_1989.html.

14. *Prime Time* tour of the White House, ABC, televised 21 September 1989.

15. Ibid.

16. Ibid.

17. Author interview with Anna Perez, 10 July 1994.

18. Ibid.

19. www.pbs.org/newshour/vote2004/first_ladies3.html.

20. Maureen Santani quoted in Maurine H. Beasley, *First Ladies and the Press: The Unfinished Partnership of the Media Age* (Evanston, IL: Northwestern University Press, 2005), p. 197.

21. "First Lady Says Law Should Ban Assault Weapons," Associated Press story, 4 February 1989.

22. Donnie Radcliffe, "Barbara Bush's Vow of Silence: Decision to Be Mum on Controversial Issues Announced in Tokyo," *Washington Post*, 24 February 1989, p. C1; Gil Troy, *Affairs of State: The Rise and Rejection of the Presidential Couple since World War II* (New York: Free Press, 1997), p. 456.

23. Frank Murray comments in Feldman and Perotti, *Honor and Loyalty*, p. 473.

24. Author interview with Barbara Bush, 25 April 2005.

25. Bush, *Barbara Bush*, p. 442.

26. Author interview with Jean Becker, 25 April 2005. An account of Doro Bush Koch's wedding can be found in Doro Bush Koch, *My Father, My President: A Personal Account of the Life of George H. W. Bush* (New York: Warner, 2006), pp. 396–399.

27. Bush, *Barbara Bush*, pp. 316–317; author interview with Jean Becker; Susan Porter Rose comments in Feldman and Perotti, *Honor and Loyalty*, p. 468.

28. Bush, *Barbara Bush*, p. 370.

29. Author interview with Barbara Bush.

30. The finding aid at the George Bush Library lists 265 speeches. The number might be higher. Currently, only a handful of Mrs. Bush's vice presidential speeches are open to research.

31. The breakdown of Mrs. Bush's speeches is 55 speeches in 1989, 111 in 1990, 90 in 1991, and 193 in 1992.

32. Molly Meijer Wertheimer, "Barbara Bush: Her Rhetorical Development and Appeal," in *Inventing a Voice: The Rhetoric of American First Ladies in the Twentieth Century*, ed. Molly Meijer Wertheimer (Lanham, MD: Rowman and Littlefield, 2004), p. 388.

33. Ibid., p. 393.

34. Author interview with Susan Porter Rose, 7 June 1994.

35. Author interview with Barbara Bush.

36. Elizabeth Bumiller, "First Lady Yuks It Up with Correspondents: Laura Bush Steals Show from President—and Uses Humor to Humanize Her Husband," *San Francisco Chronicle Online*, 2 May 2005, *New York Times* Syndicate.

37. For example, see Mrs. Bush's Remarks for the American Newspaper Publishers Association Annual Conference, 26 April 1989, Chicago, Illinois, Kathy Steffy Files, Barbara Bush Speeches, January–April 1989, OA/IA 08382, GBL;

this speech contains a reference to Yogi Berra. Mrs. Bush's Suggested Remarks at a Tea for Barbara Bush Foundation Symposium Participants, The White House, 23 January 1990, Kathy Steffy Files, Barbara Bush Speeches, January–April 1990, OA/IA 08382, GBL; this speech contains a reference to Theodore Roosevelt. Mrs. Bush's Remarks for the Houston Read Commission Literacy Symposium, Houston, Texas, 31 October 1991, Kathy Steffy Files, Mrs. Bush's Speeches, September–December 1991, OA/IA 08382, GBL; this speech contains a reference to Winston Churchill.

38. Author interview with Anna Perez.

39. Mrs. Bush's Remarks at the McKernan for Governor Fundraiser, 5 October 1990, Kennebunkport, Maine, First Lady's Press Office, Family/Background, 1990 Speeches, September–December, OA/ID 07478, GBL.

40. Mrs. Bush's Remarks at the Mammography Conference Reception, 23 January 1991, Kathy Steffy Files, Barbara Bush Speeches, January–February 1991, OA/ID 08382, GBL.

41. Mrs. Bush's Remarks for the American Magazine Conference, 23 October 1989, Naples, Florida, First Lady's Press Office/Background, 1989 Speeches, IA/OA 07478, GBL.

42. Suggested Remarks for Mrs. Bush for St. Louis University Commencement, 19 May 1990, St. Louis, Missouri, Kathy Steffy Files, Barbara Bush Speeches, May–August 1990, OA/ID 08382, GBL.

43. Mrs. Bush's Remarks at the Reception for the Year of the Young Reader, 15 November 1989, Kathy Steffy Files, Mrs. Bush's Speeches, September–December 1989, OA/ID 08382, GBL.

44. Mrs. Bush's Remarks on receiving the Harry S. Truman Award, 30 March 1989, Washington, D.C., Kathy Steffy Files, Barbara Bush Speeches, January–April 1989, GBL.

45. Author interview with Barbara Bush.

46. For example, see Mrs. Bush's Remarks at the Pete Wilson for Governor Dinner, 1 October 1990, Los Angeles, California, First Lady's Press Office/Family-Background, 1990 Speeches, September–December, OA/ID 07478, GBL.

47. John Podhoretz, *Hell of a Ride: Backstage at the White House Follies* (New York: Simon and Schuster, 1993), p. 82.

48. Charles Kolb, *White House Daze: The Unmaking of Domestic Policy in the Bush Years* (New York: Free Press, 1994), p. 4.

49. Podhoretz, *Hell of a Ride*, p. 81.

50. Author interview with Barbara Bush.

51. Mrs. Bush's Remarks at Smith College Convocation, 6 September 1989, Northampton, Massachusetts, Barbara Bush Speeches, 1989 Speeches, OA/ID 07478, GBL.

52. Mrs. Bush's Remarks at the New York Public Library's "A Decade of Literary Lions: A Walk through the 1980's" Dinner, New York, New York, 8 November 1990, Barbara Bush Speeches, September–December 1990, OA/ID 08382, GBL.

53. Mrs. Bush's Remarks at the Buster Brown for Texas State Attorney General Fundraiser, 26 October 1990, Houston, Texas, Barbara Bush Speeches, Kathy Steffy Files, 1990 Speeches, September–December, OA/ID 07478, GBL.

54. Mrs. Bush's Remarks at the Ally Milder for Congress Rally, 1 November 1990, Omaha, Nebraska, Barbara Bush Speeches, Kathy Steffy Files, 1990 Speeches, September–December, OA/ID 07478, GBL.

55. Mrs. Bush's Remarks for Gary Franks for Congress Fundraising Breakfast, 25 October 1990, Newtown, Connecticut, First Lady's Press Office, Family/ Background, 1990 Speeches, September–December, OA/ID 07478, GBL.

56. Mrs. Bush's Remarks at the Pete Wilson for Governor Dinner, 1 October 1990.

57. Bush, *Barbara Bush*, p. 369.

58. Ibid.

59. Mrs. Bush's Remarks at the Pennsylvania Republican Party Fundraising Luncheon, 19 June 1991, Pittsburgh, Pennsylvania, Barbara Bush Speeches, Kathy Steffy Files, February–July 1991, OA/ID 08383, GBL.

60. Letter, Nannerl Keohane to Barbara Bush, 22 December 1989, First Lady's Press Office/Background, 1989 Speeches, OA/ID 07478, GBL.

61. Julie Cooke's written answers to the author's questions, 8 October 2006.

62. Bush, *Barbara Bush*, p. 335.

63. Elizabeth Drew, "Barbara Bush at Wellesley: A Lesson . . . ," *Washington Post* (Weekly Edition), 14–20 May 1990.

64. Peggy Reid, "We Didn't Criticize Mrs. Bush," *New York Times*, 16 May 1990, p. A27.

65. Michele N-K Collison, "Amid Hype and Hoopla, Barbara Bush Greeted Warmly at Wellesley," *Chronicle of Higher Education*, 13 June 1990, p. A28.

66. Megan Rosenfeld, "Protest and Learning at Wellesley College," *Washington Post*, 28 May 1990, p. B6.

67. Barbara Bush quoted in Carl Sferrazza Anthony, *First Ladies: The Saga of the Presidents' Wives and Their Power, 1961–1990* (New York: Morrow, 1991), p. 434.

68. Fox Butterfield, "At Wellesley, a Furor over Barbara Bush," *New York Times*, 4 May 1990, p. 1.

69. Bush, *Barbara Bush*, p. 338. Mrs. Bush has reiterated this sentiment to interviewers; author interview with Barbara Bush. Barbara Bush interviewed by Carl Sferrazza Anthony for "The Role of the First Lady," 4 October 1994, C-SPAN Network.

70. Mrs. Bush's Remarks at the University of Pennsylvania Commencement, 14 May 1990, Philadelphia, Pennsylvania, and Suggested Remarks for Mrs. Bush for St. Louis University Commencement, 19 May 1990, St. Louis, Missouri, Kathy Steffy Files, Barbara Bush Speeches, May–August 1990, OA/ID 08382, GBL.

71. Bush, *Barbara Bush*, p. 337.

72. *Public Paper of the Presidents of the United States: George H. W. Bush, 1990*, vol. 1 (Washington, DC: U.S. Government Printing Office, 1991), pp. 615–616.

73. Erma Bombeck, "In Defense of Barbara," 17 May 1990, syndicated column.

74. Letter, Melinda Snider to Barbara Bush, 23 April 1990, Events File—Wellesley, OA/ID 06944, GBL.

75. Drew, "Barbara Bush at Wellesley."

76. Transcript, *MacNeil/Lehrer NewsHour*, 17 May 1990, WNET, New York.

77. Ibid.

78. Angie Hickman quoted in Pamela Kilian, *Barbara Bush: A Biography* (New York: St. Martin's, 1992), p. 11.

79. "The End of Another Cold War," *Time*, 11 June 1990, p. 21.

80. Felicity Barringer, "Raisa Gorbachev's Thaw in Relations," *New York Times*, 1 June 1990, p. A4.

81. All quotations from Mrs. Bush's speech at Wellesley College can be found in "Choices and Change," *Vital Speeches*, 1 July 1990, p. 549.

82. Susan Baer, "First Ladies Charm Crowd at Wellesley," *Austin American-Statesman*, 2 June 1990, p. A10.

83. Butterfield, "At Wellesley, a Furor over Barbara Bush," p. 1.

84. Margery Eagan, "Bush Speech All Style and No Substance," *Boston Herald*, 2 June 1990, Commencement Address—Wellesley College/Boston Garden Visit—Mrs. Gorbachev, 1 June 1990, OA/ID 06944, GBL.

85. Marianne Means, "Barbara to Wellesley: Just Stay Home, Ladies," *Austin American-Statesman*, 11 June 1990.

86. Shirley M. Green to Susan Porter Rose, 1 June 1990, Events File/Wellesley IA/OA 06944, GBL.

87. Many similarities and identical passages can be found in Mrs. Bush's commencement address at Wake Forest University, 21 May 2001, Wake Forest News Service, 23 May 2001.

88. Author interview with Barbara Bush.

89. Ibid. The cover story and a number of articles in *Wellesley,* the alumni magazine of Wellesley College, dealt with the controversy over the first lady's speech. See *Wellesley* 74, no. 4 (Summer 1990). Also, Mrs. Bush commented on the Wellesley controversy in her interview with Carl Sferrazza Anthony.

90. "First Lady Declines UCLA Commencement Invitation," *American Libraries Online,* 4 March 2002, www.ala.org/alomline/currentnews/newsarchive /2002/March2002/first lady declines. See, too, Ellen Sorokin, "First Lady Objected to as Speaker at UCLA: Students, Faculty at Grad School Protest," *Washington Times* Online, www.ecnext.com/premium/0199/0199–1571363.html.

CHAPTER 3: "IF YOU COULDN'T BE HAPPY IN THE WHITE HOUSE, YOU COULDN'T BE HAPPY ANYWHERE"

1. Liz Carpenter, *Ruffles and Flourishes* (New York: Pocket, 1971), p. 4.

2. Barbara Bush, *Barbara Bush: A Memoir* (New York: Scribner's, 1994), p. 27.

3. Ibid., p. 279.

4. Gil Troy, "'Half-Eleanor, Half-Bess': Barbara Bush as 'Co-President,'" in *Honor and Loyalty: Inside the Politics of the Bush White House,* ed. Leslie D. Feldman and Rosanna Perotti (Westport, CT: Greenwood Press, 2002), p. 457.

5. Author interview with Betty Ford, 17 July 1979.

6. Barbara Bush quoted in Troy, "'Half-Eleanor, Half-Bess,'" p. 457.

7. Mrs. Bush's handwritten notes on President Bush's Remarks on the Occasion of Volunteer Awards, 11 April 1989, Kathy Steffy Files, Speech Facts, IA/OA 08384, GBL. Undated handwritten memo, Barbara Bush to Anna Perez, Files of the First Lady's Press Office/Family Background/Commencement Speeches, IA/OA 07478, GBL.

8. See the President's Remarks at the University of Michigan Commencement, Ann Arbor, Michigan, 4 May 1991, Kathy Steffy Files, Commencement Speeches, OA/IA 08034, GBL.

9. Bush, *Barbara Bush,* p. 279.

10. Ibid., p. 289.

11. Ibid., pp. 278–279.

12. Anna Perez quoted during the First Ladies' Press Secretaries Forum, 30 April 2004, GBL.

13. Author interview with Susan Porter Rose, 7 June 1994.

14. Ibid.

15. Donnie Radcliffe, "Watchdog at the East Gate: Susan Porter Rose, Guard of the First Lady's Realm," *Washington Post,* 19 November 1991, p. C8.

16. Bush, *Barbara Bush,* p. 159.

17. Ibid., p. 253.

18. Author interview with Barbara Bush, 25 April 2006.

19. Bush, *Barbara Bush,* p. 254.

20. Anna Perez quoted during the First Ladies' Press Secretaries Forum, 30 April 2004, GBL.

21. Susan Porter Rose, Anna Perez, and Jean Becker told the author in separate interviews that they enjoyed working for Mrs. Bush. Author interview with Susan Porter Rose; author interview with Anna Perez, 10 July 1994; author interview with Jean Becker, 25 April 2006.

22. Jean Becker's written answers to author's questions, 8 October 2006.

23. Julie Cooke's written answers to author's questions, 8 October 2006.

24. Helen Thomas, *Front Row at the White House: My Life and Times* (New York: Touchstone, 1999), p. 281.

25. Author interview with Catherine Fenton, 17 July 2007.

26. Gil Troy, *Affairs of State: The Rise and Rejection of the Presidential Couple since World War II* (New York: Simon and Schuster, 1997), p. 330.

27. Kati Marton, *Hidden Power: Presidential Marriages That Shaped Our Recent History* (New York: Pantheon, 2001), p. 288.

28. Marjorie Williams, "Barbara's Backlash," *Vanity Fair,* August 1992, p. 123.

29. Author interview with Catherine Fenton.

30. Barbara Matusow quoted in Maurine H. Beasley, *First Ladies and the Press: The Unfinished Partnership of the Media Age* (Evanston, IL: Northwestern University Press, 2005), p. 198.

31. Bush, *Barbara Bush,* p. 273; "Barbara Bush Hugs for AIDS," *Newsmakers,* 23 March 1989.

32. Author interview with Catherine Fenton.

33. Laurie Firestone, *An Affair to Remember,* privately published, 2007, p. 2.

34. Author interview with Catherine Fenton.

35. Ibid.

36. Firestone, *An Affair to Remember,* p. 2.

37. Ibid., p. 11; author interview with Catherine Fenton.

38. Author interview with Catherine Fenton.

39. Doro Bush Koch, *My Father, My President: A Personal Account of the Life of George H. W. Bush* (New York: Warner, 2006), p. 396.

40. Herbert S. Parmet, *George Bush: The Life of a Lone Star Yankee* (New York: Scribner's, 1997), p. 395.

41. Louis DeBose, "O, Brother! Where Art Thou?" *Austin Chronicle.com,* 16 March 2001, www.austinchronicle.com/gyrobase/issue/story?oid=oid%3A81085.

42. There are varying estimates of the cost to taxpayers of the savings and loan crisis. Parmet puts it from $98 to 132 billion; Parmet, *George Bush,* p. 395. The *CPA Journal* has a more conservative estimate, $183 million. Ahmed W. Salam, "Congress, Regulators, RAP, and the Savings and Loan Debacle (Regulatory Accounting Principles)," *CPA Journal Online,* January 1994. Another source, Rational Revolution, suggested a high-end figure of $1.4 trillion. "The Bush Family and the S & L Scandal," March and April 2003, www.rationalrevolution.net/war/bush_family_andthe_shtmd.

43. Nathaniel C. Nash, "U.S. Regulators Accuse Bush Son in Savings Case," *New York Times,* 27 January 1990, p. 1.

44. Bush, *Barbara Bush,* p. 325.

45. Kathy Lewis, "Straight Talk," *Dallas Morning News,* 16 April 1991, p. 6A.

46. Ibid.

47. Edward Wong, "The Clinton Pardons: A Closer Look: Politics and Families, Mixed: Presidential Relatives and Headaches They Caused," *New York Times,* 23 February 2001, p. 16A.

48. Dubose, "O Brother! Where Art Thou?" On 13 December 1989, President Bush wrote to his good friend and Yale classmate Congressman Thomas Ludlow "Lud" Ashley about Neil's problems and the possibility that Ashley might be able to help: "I would appreciate any help you could give Neil. He tells me he never had any insider dealings. . . . I know the guy is totally honest. . . . I think he is worried about the publicity and the 'shame.' I tell him not to worry about that but any advice you can give as this matter unfolds would be greatly appreciated." Letter, George H. W. Bush to Thomas Ludlow Ashley, reproduced in George Bush, *All the Best, George Bush: My Life in Letters and Other Writings* (New York: Scribner's, 1999), p. 449. Ashley, who was Neil Bush's godfather, set up the defense fund that paid legal expenses in the case.

49. Susan Heller Anderson, "Chronicle," *New York Times,* 4 April 1990.

50. Lawrence K. Altman "First Lady Has Radiation Therapy for Relieving Her Eye Discomforts," *New York Times,* 4 January 1990, p. 1. John Robert Greene writes that both Bushes came down with Graves' disease, and Millie came down with lupus, all within a year of moving into the White House. This set off much speculation regarding whether the White House environment posed serious health hazards. John Robert Greene, *The Presidency of George Bush* (Lawrence: University Press of Kansas, 2000), p. 153n.

51. Lawrence K. Altman, "A White House Puzzle: Immunity Ailments," *New York Times,* 28 May 1991, p. A1; Lawrence K. Altman, "Clues to Bushes' Disease

Sought in Water," *New York Times,* 29 May 1991, p. A16; Greene, *The Presidency of George Bush,* p. 153n.

52. Mrs. Bush's Remarks, "Victory '92," New Orleans, Louisiana, 30 September 1992, Kathy Steffy Files, September–October 1992, OA/IA 08383, GBL.

53. Donnie Radcliffe, *Simply Barbara Bush: A Portrait of America's Candid First Lady* (New York: Warner, 1989), p. 33.

CHAPTER 4: "IF EVERYONE COULD READ . . . "

1. George W. Bush quoted in Pamela Kilian, *Barbara Bush: A Biography* (New York: St. Martin's, 1992), p. 74.

2. Neil Bush quoted in Kilian, *Barbara Bush,* p. 74.

3. Barbara Bush, *Barbara Bush: A Memoir* (New York: Scribner's, 1994), p. 145.

4. Author interview with Barbara Bush, 25 April 2005.

5. Betty Boyd Caroli, *First Ladies* (New York: Oxford University Press, 1995), p. 283.

6. Author interview with Barbara Bush. The same anecdote can also be found in Bush, *Barbara Bush,* pp. 145–146.

7. Jonathan Kozol, *Prisoners of Silence: Breaking the Bonds of Adult Illiteracy in the United States* (New York: Continuum, 1980), p. 2.

8. Ibid., p. 101.

9. Barbara Bush's answer to author's question; e-mail, Jean Becker to Myra Gutin, 27 July 2007.

10. *Literacy Newsletter,* 1 March 2002, www.nifl.gov/nifl/eliteracy/02_03_01 .html.

11. Ibid.

12. Benita Somerfield's written answers to author's questions, 23 August and 5 October 2005.

13. "Tribute to Susan Green, 1944–2002," in *e Literacy,* 1 March 2002.

14. Author interview with Marie M. Adair, 4 January 2006. Jonathan Kozol's *Prisoners of Silence: Breaking the Bonds of Adult Illiteracy in the United States* was one of the most influential books about literacy during the 1980s. Other researchers and scholars who were working in the area of literacy included Richard Allington, David Cooper, Susan Mandel Glazer, Regie Routman, and Dorothy Strickland.

15. Benita Somerfield's comments in Leslie D. Feldman and Rosanna Perotti, *Honor and Loyalty: Inside the Politics of the George H. W. Bush White House*

(Westport, CT: Greenwood Press, 2002), p. 475. See, too, Molly Meijer Wertheimer, "Barbara Bush: Her Rhetorical Development and Appeal," in *Inventing a Voice: The Rhetoric of American First Ladies of the Twentieth Century,* ed. Molly Meijer Wertheimer (Lanham, MD: Rowan and Littlefield, 2004), p. 399.

16. Benita Somerfield's answers to author's questions, 23 August 2005.

17. Letter, Barbara Bush to Mr. Duncan, 21 June 1988. This letter was offered for sale on eBay during July 2005.

18. Barbara Bush, *C. Fred's Story* (Garden City, NY: Doubleday, 1984), p. 2.

19. Ibid., p. 83.

20. Bush, *Barbara Bush,* p. 189.

21. Mrs. Bush's Remarks to the Texas Library Association Convention, Corpus Christi, Texas, 6 April 1984, Kathy Steffy Files, Library Speeches, IA/OA 08384, GBL.

22. Ibid.

23. Mrs. Bush's Remarks at Evansville Public Library Friends Luncheon, Evansville, Indiana, 20 November 1986, Kathy Steffy Files, Library Speeches, IA/OA 08384, GBL.

24. Ibid.

25. Bush, *Barbara Bush,* p. 218.

26. This is due to the constraints of the Presidential Records Act and the priority assigned to the material. Future researchers could file Freedom of Information Act (FOIA) requests, which would formally ask that the material be opened, but a FOIA can take years to process. Given these circumstances and comments made by Mrs. Bush in her *Memoir,* the author is certain, though she cannot confirm, that Mrs. Bush gave many more than forty-eight literacy speeches from 1981 to 1989.

27. Benita Somerfield's written answers to the author's questions, 25 August 2006.

28. Eden Ross Lipson, "Reading Along with Barbara Bush: The Endings Are Mostly Happy," *New York Times Book Review,* 21 May 1989, p. 36.

29. Author interview with Anna Perez, 10 July 1994.

30. Web site of the Barbara Bush Foundation for Family Literacy, www.barbarabushfoundation.com.

31. Barbara Gamarekian, "Barbara Bush Announces Formation of Literacy Foundation," *New York Times,* 7 March 1989, p. 1.

32. William Raspberry, "First Lady Adopts Literacy Foundation," 17 March 1989, *Washington Post* Syndicate.

33. Benita Somerfield's written answers to the author's questions, 23 August 2005, and Web site of the Barbara Bush Foundation for Family Literacy.

34. Mrs. Bush's Remarks to the American Newspaper Publishers Association Annual Conference, Chicago, Illinois, 26 April 1989, Kathy Steffy Files, Barbara Bush Speeches, January–April 1989, IA/OA 08382, GBL. The first lady's relationship with the American Newspaper Publishers Association helped her to advance literacy with articles and special sections devoted to the topic.

35. Betty Debnan, "The Mini Page," *Washington Post,* 3 September 1989.

36. Lipson, "Reading Along with Barbara Bush," p. 36.

37. Mrs. Bush's Remarks at the University of Pennsylvania Commencement, Philadelphia, Pennsylvania, 14 May 1990, Kathy Steffy Files, Barbara Bush's Speeches, May–August 1990, IA/OA 08382, GBL.

38. Barbara Bush, *Millie's Book: As Dictated to Barbara Bush* (New York: Morrow, 1990), p. 85.

39. Ibid., p. 19.

40. Mrs. Bush's Draft Talking Points for *Millie's Book* Event, Houston, Texas, 27 September 1990, First Lady's Press Office, Barbara Bush Speeches, September–December 1990, IA/OA 07478, GBL.

41. Remarks by the President at a Fundraising Breakfast for Senator Jesse Helms. Raleigh, North Carolina, 10 October 1990, speech online at www.bush library.tamu.edu.

42. Mrs. Bush's Remarks at the Ally Milder for Congress Rally, Omaha, Nebraska, 1 November 1990, First Lady's Press Office, Barbara Bush Speeches, September–December 1990, IA/OA 07478, GBL. Similar additional examples of her endorsement of literacy can be found in campaign speeches for Pete Wilson, 1 October 1990; Gary Franks, 25 October 1990; and Buster Brown, 26 October 1990.

43. Mrs. Bush's Remarks for the 20th Anniversary of the U.S. National Conference of Libraries and Information Science, Washington, D.C., 23 January 1991, Kathy Steffy Files, Barbara Bush's Speeches, January–February 1991, IA/OA 08384, GBL.

44. Mrs. Bush's Remarks at the 1991 Florida Literacy Conference, Jacksonville, Florida, 6 March 1991, Kathy Steffy Files, Barbara Bush's Speeches, February–July 1991, IA/OA 08384, GBL.

45. Mrs. Bush's Remarks at the White House Conference on Libraries and Information Services, Washington, D.C., 10 July 1991, Kathy Steffy Files, Barbara Bush's Speeches, February–July 1991, IA/OA 08384, GBL.

46. Lipson, "Reading Along with Barbara Bush," p. 36.

47. Renee Haines, "First Lady Praises Literacy Programs," *Dallas Morning News,* 20 September 1989, p. 36A.

48. Benita Somerfield's written answers to the author's questions, 23 August 2005.

49. Author interview with Anna Perez.

50. Maureen Santini quoted in Maurine H. Beasley, *First Ladies and the Press: The Unfinished Partnership of the Media Age* (Evanston, IL: Northwestern University Press, 2005), p. 197.

51. Bush, *Barbara Bush*, p. 360.

52. Mrs. Bush's Story Time, 10 October 1990, GBL.

53. Mrs. Bush's Remarks for the Reception for "Mrs. Bush's Story Time," Washington, D.C., 21 November 1991, Kathy Steffy Files, Barbara Bush Speeches, September–December 1991, IA/OA 08383, GBL.

54. Barbara Bush, "Parenting's Best Kept Secret: Reading to Your Children," *Reader's Digest*, October 1990, pp. 67–70.

55. Author interview with Barbara Bush.

56. Grant Pick, "Adult Illiteracy: A Stumbling Block to the American Dream," *Illinois Issues*, October 1990, http://www.lib.niu.edu/ipo/1990/ii901023.html.

57. Paul Simon, *P.S.: The Autobiography of Paul Simon* (Chicago: Bonus, 1999), pp. 169–170.

58. See S. 1310, http://thomas.loc.gov/cgi-bin/bdquery/D?d101:49:./temp/~bdFOBw.

59. Simon, *Paul Simon*, p. 170.

60. "Statement on Signing the National Literacy Act of 1991," *Public Papers of the Presidents of the United States: George Bush*, vol. 2, 1 July 1991–31 December 1991 (Washington, DC: Government Printing Office, 1992), p. 961.

61. Ibid., p. 960.

62. Bush, *Barbara Bush*, p. 425.

63. Ibid., p. 222.

64. Benita Somerfield's comments in Feldman and Perrotti, *Honor and Loyalty*, p. 475.

65. Author interview with Marie M. Adair.

66. Fact Sheet, President and Mrs. Bush: Working for Literacy, 20 July 1992, a publication of the Bush-Quayle '92 Committee, GBL.

67. Mrs. Bush's Remarks at the Barbara Bush Foundation for Family Literacy 1992 Grants Announcement Luncheon, Washington, D.C., 24 November 1992, Kathy Steffy Files, Barbara Bush's Speeches, November 1992–January 1993, 08382, GBL.

68. Charles Kolb, *White House Daze: The Unmaking of Domestic Policy in the Bush Years* (New York: Free Press, 1994), pp. 144–145.

69. Gil Troy, "'Half-Eleanor, Half-Bess': Barbara Bush as 'Co-president,'" in *Honor and Loyalty: Inside the Politics of the George H. W. Bush White House*, ed. Leslie D. Feldman and Rosanna Perotti (Westport, CT: Greenwood Press, 2002), p. 449.

70. Benita Somerfield's comments, in Feldman and Perrotti, *Honor and Loyalty*, pp. 475–476.

71. Frank Murray's comments in *Honor and Loyalty: Inside the Politics of the George H. W. Bush White House*, ed. Leslie D. Feldman and Rosanna Perotti (Westport, CT: Greenwood Press, 2002), p. 474.

72. Author interview with Marie M. Adair.

73. National Center for Education Statistics, National Assessment of Adult Literacy (NAAL), *A First Look at the Literacy of America's Adults in the 21st Century* report issued in December 2005, http://nces.ed.gov/NAAL/PDF/2006470_1.PDF. See, too, M. Cecil Smith, *Literacy for the Twenty-first Century: Research, Policy, Practices, and the National Adult Literacy Survey* (Westport, CT: Greenwood Press, 1998).

74. Benita Somerfield's written answers to the author's questions, 25 August 2006.

CHAPTER 5: "IT IS THE DARNDEST WAR"

1. John Robinson, "Mrs. Bush's Rating Is Found to Exceed Her Husband's," *Boston Globe*, 17 May 1990, p. 18.

2. John Robert Greene, *The Presidency of George Bush* (Lawrence: University Press of Kansas, 2000), pp. 111–113.

3. Barbara Bush, *Barbara Bush: A Memoir* (New York: Scribner's, 1994), p. 354.

4. Paula Chin, "In the Eye of the Storm," *People*, 1 October 1990, p. 84.

5. Doro Bush Koch, *My Father, My President: A Personal Account of the Life of George H. W. Bush* (New York: Warner, 2006), pp. 186–187.

6. Elisabeth Bumiller, "White House Letter; At Parent's Home, Bush Resumes Role of Son," *New York Times*, 8 July 2002.

7. Jim Rutenberg, "Putin Arrives in Kennebunkport for a 2 Day Visit with the Bushes," *New York Times*, 2 July 2007, p. A8.

8. "The Bushes of Kennebunkport," *House and Garden*, June 1989, p. 144.

9. Bush, *Barbara Bush*, p. 355.

10. Ibid.

11. For details on the coalition, see Dilip Hiro, *Desert Shield to Desert Victory: The Second Gulf War* (New York: Routledge, 1992); and Michael J. Mazarr, Don M. Snider, and James A. Blackwell Jr., *Desert Storm: The Gulf War and What We Learned* (Boulder, CO: Westview Press, 1993).

12. Susan Cornwell, "Superpower Wives Drink Tea, Wish Husbands Find Gulf Peace," Reuters Dispatch, 9 September 1990, Speech Materials File IA/OA 08386, GBL.

13. David Hoffman, "Bush, Gorbachev Toughen Stand against Iraq," *Washington Post*, 10 September 1990, p. A1. See, too, Bill Keller, "Confrontation in the Gulf: Bush and Gorbachev Say Iraqis Must Obey U.N. and Quit Kuwait," *New York Times*, 10 September 1990, p. A1.

14. Bush, *Barbara Bush*, p. 359.

15. Christopher Connell, "Mrs. Bush Says Saddam Must Give Up Kuwait," Reuters Dispatch, 10 September 1990, Speech Materials File IA/OA 08386, GBL.

16. Gene Gibbons, "Barbara Bush Says U.S. Is Striving for Peace in Gulf," Reuters Dispatch, 10 September 1990, Speech Materials File IA/OA 08386, GBL.

17. Christopher Connell, "Barbara Bush: Saddam Should Consider Children," Reuters Dispatch, 11 September 1990, Speech Materials File IA/OA 08386, GBL.

18. Christopher Connell, "Mrs. Bush Says Saddam Must Give Up Kuwait," Reuters Dispatch, 10 September 1990.

19. Ellen Warren, "Barbara," Knight-Ridder Dispatch, First Lady's Office/ Events File. *Millie's Book* Event, 29 September 1990, 06940. GBL.

20. Helen Thomas, "Barbara Bush Offers Advice to Female Troops," UPI Dispatch, 11 September 1990, Speech Materials File IA/OA 08386, GBL.

21. Mrs. Bush's Remarks for Publication Launch of *Millie's Book*, 19 September 1990, New York, New York, First Lady's Office/Projects, Events File IA/OA 06940, GBL.

22. Mrs. Bush's Draft Talking Points for *Millie's Book* event, Houston, Texas, 27 September 1990, Kathy Steffy Files, Mrs. Bush's Speeches, September–December 1990, IA/OA 08382, GBL.

23. Mrs. Bush's Remarks at the Pete Wilson for Governor Dinner, Los Angeles, California, 1 October 1990, First Lady Press Office/Family-Background, 1990 Speeches, September–December, IA/OA 07478, GBL.

24. Mrs. Bush's Remarks at the McKernan for Governor Fundraiser, Kennebunkport, Maine, 5 October 1990, First Lady Press Office/Family-Background, 1990 Speeches, September–December, IA/OA 07478, GBL.

25. Mrs. Bush's Remarks at the Buster Brown for Texas State Attorney General Fundraiser, Houston, Texas, 26 October 1990, First Lady Press Office/Family-Background, 1990 Speeches, September–December. IA/OA 07478, GBL.

26. Bush, *Barbara Bush,* p. 379.

27. Exchange with Reporters Near Dhahran, Saudi Arabia, 22 November 1990, http://bushlibrary.tamu.edu/research/papers/1990/90112204.html.

28. Bush, *Barbara Bush,* p. 379.

29. A number of resolutions about Iraqi aggression were passed by the United Nations. The first and most well known was Resolution number 660, which established the pattern for future resolutions. Resolution number 660 was passed on 2 August 1990 and called for the immediate withdrawal of Iraqi forces. It threatened both economic and military sanctions for noncompliance.

30. Bush, *Barbara Bush,* p. 382.

31. Greene, *The Presidency of George Bush,* pp. 126–127.

32. http://www.findarticles.com/p/articles/mi_m1282/is_n8_v43/ai_10709732 #continue.

33. Bush, *Barbara Bush,* p. 385.

34. Greene, *The Presidency of George Bush,* p. 123.

35. Bush, *Barbara Bush,* p. 390.

36. Mrs. Bush's Remarks at "I Have a Dream Gala," Boston, Massachusetts, 28 January 1991, Kathy Steffy Files, Barbara Bush Speeches, January–February 1991, IA/OA 09382, GBL.

37. "Radio Address to the Nation on the Persian Gulf Crisis," 5 January 1991, *Public Papers of the Presidents of the United States: George H. W. Bush, 1991,* vol. 1, 1 January 1991–30 June 1991 (Washington, DC: U.S. Government Printing Office, 1992), pp. 10–11.

38. Bush, *Barbara Bush,* p. 388.

39. Ibid., p. 387.

40. Remarks at the Annual Southern Baptist Convention, Atlanta, Georgia, 6 June 1991, *Public Papers of the Presidents of the United States: George Bush,* vol. 1, January–30 June 1991 (Washington, DC: U.S. Government Printing Office, 1992), p. 614.

41. Bush, *Barbara Bush,* p. 391.

42. Ibid, p. 395

43. Anthony DePalma, "A War Again Stirs Anguish, But of a Quieter Kind," *New York Times,* 20 January 1991, p. 18.

44. Rick Atkinson, *Crusade: The Untold Story of the Persian Gulf War* (Boston: Houghton Mifflin, 1993), pp. 158–159.

45. "Mrs. Bush to the Press: Be Patient," *Washington Post,* 26 January 1991, p. D3.

46. Andrew Rosenthal, "Bush's Tight Control," *New York Times,* 23 January 1991, p. A8.

47. Pamela Kilian, *Barbara Bush: Matriarch of a Dynasty* (New York: St. Martin's, 2002), p. 177.

48. Joseph P. Lash, *Eleanor and Franklin: The Story of Their Relationship Based on Eleanor Roosevelt's Private Papers* (New York: Norton, 1971). See chapters 51, 52, and 54.

49. Lady Bird Johnson interviewed by Barbara Walters for *20/20,* March 1995, ABC Television Network.

50. Julie Nixon Eisenhower, *Pat Nixon: The Untold Story* (New York: Simon and Schuster, 1986), p. 270.

51. George H. W. Bush, *All the Best: My Life in Letters and Other Writings* (New York: Scribner's, 1999), pp. 510–511.

52. All speech quotations are from Mrs. Bush's Remarks at Griffiss Air Force Base, Rome, New York, 12 February 1991, Kathy Steffy Files, Barbara Bush Speeches, January–February 1991, IA/OA 08382, GBL.

53. Mrs. Bush's Remarks at the 101st Airborne Division, Ft. Campbell, Kentucky, 22 February 1991, Kathy Steffy Files, Barbara Bush Speeches, January–February 1991, IA/OA 08382, GBL.

54. Ibid.

55. Bush, *Barbara Bush,* p. 399.

56. Author interview with Barbara Bush, 25 April 2005.

57. Norman Friedman, *Desert Victory: The War for Kuwait* (Annapolis, MD: Naval Institute Press, 1991), p. 214.

58. Herbert S. Parmet, *George Bush: The Life of a Lone Star Yankee* (New York: Simon and Schuster, 1997), p. 480.

59. Ibid.

60. Bush, *Barbara Bush,* p. 402.

61. Ibid.

62. Greene, *The Presidency of George Bush,* pp. 130–131.

63. Mrs. Bush's Remarks at Fort George G. Meade, Fort Meade, Maryland, 28 February 1991, Kathy Steffy Files, Barbara Bush Speeches, January–February 1991, OA/IA 08382.

64. Ibid.

65. Mrs. Bush's Remarks at the *USS Forrestal,* Flight Deck, Mayport Naval Air Station, Florida, 6 March 1991, Kathy Steffy Files, Barbara Bush Speeches, March–April 1991, IA/OA 08382, GBL.

66. Mrs. Bush's Remarks at Mayport Naval Air Station, HSL-40 Hangar, Mayport Naval Air Station, Florida, 6 March 1991, Kathy Steffy Files, Barbara Bush Speeches, March–April 1991, IA/OA 08382, GBL.

67. Mrs. Bush's Remarks at the *USS Forrestal*, Flight Deck, Mayport Naval Air Station, Florida, 6 March 1991.

68. Mrs. Bush's Remarks at Marine Corps Air-Ground Combat Center, Twentynine Palms, California, 27 March, 1991, Kathy Steffy Files, Barbara Bush Speeches, March–April 1991, IA/OA 08382, GBL.

69. Kathy Lewis, "Straight Talk," *Dallas Morning News*, 16 April 1991, p. 6A.

70. Ellen Warren, "First Lady Blames War Stress for Bush's Ills," *Austin American Statesman*, 7 June 1991, p. 5.

71. Mrs. Bush's Remarks at the Pennsylvania Republican Party Fundraising Luncheon, 19 June 1991, Pittsburgh, Pennsylvania, Kathy Steffy Files, Barbara Bush Speeches, May–June 1991, IA/OA 08382, GBL.

72. Bill Clinton, *My Life* (New York: Knopf, 2004), pp. 525–526.

73. Barbara Bush, *Reflectjons: Life after the White House* (New York: Scribner's, 2003), p. 16.

74. Kilian, *Barbara Bush*, p. 180.

75. Ibid., p. 181.

76. John Podhoretz, *Hell of a Ride: Backstage at the White House Follies 1989–1993* (New York: Simon and Schuster, 1993), p. 16.

CHAPTER 6: "THE PRESIDENT IS GOING TO WIN!"

Some information in this chapter may be found in Myra G. Gutin, "Barbara Bush at Wellesley and the Republican National Convention: Defining Moments in the Life of the First Lady," in *Honor and Loyalty: Inside the Politics of the George H. W. Bush White House*, ed. Leslie D. Feldman and Rosanna Perotti (Westport, CT: Greenwood Press, 2002).

1. Peter Goldman, Thomas M. DeFrank, Mark Miller, Andrew Murr, and Tom Matthews, *Quest for the Presidency 1992* (College Station: Texas A&M University Press, 1994), p. 299.

2. Barbara Bush, *Barbara Bush: A Memoir* (New York: Scribner's, 1994), p. 460.

3. Ibid., p. 449; Mrs. Bush's schedule for Japan can be found in Events File, "Japan," First Lady's Press Office, 7 January 1992, OA/ID 06936, GBL.

4. Bush, *Barbara Bush*, p. 449.

5. George H. W. Bush, *All the Best: My Life in Letters and Other Writings* (New York: Scribner's, 1999), p. 545. Also see Michael Wines, "Bush Collapses at State Dinner with the Japanese," *New York Times*, 9 January 1992, p. 1.

6. Pamela Kilian, *Barbara Bush: Matriarch of a Dynasty* (New York: St. Martin's, 2002), p. 193.

7. T. J. Reid, "Barbara Bush Impresses Japanese by Taking Charge," *Philadelphia Inquirer,* 10 January 1992, p. D5.

8. Ibid.

9. Yuri Kageyama, Associated Press dispatch, 9 January 1992, Events File, First Lady's Press Office, Japan, 7 January 1992, OA/ID 06936, GBL.

10. Tom Shales, "On Camera, That Queasy Feeling," *Washington Post,* January 9, 1992, p. D4, Events Files, First Lady's Press Office, Japan, 7 January 1992, OA/ID 06936, GBL.

11. Barbara Bush interviewed by Carl Seferrza Anthony for "The Role of the First Lady" program at George Washington University, broadcast by C-SPAN, 9 October 1994.

12. Samuel Popkin, *The Reasoning Voter,* cited in Joe Klein, *Politics Lost* (New York: Doubleday, 2006), p. 109.

13. Helen Thomas, *Front Row at the White House: My Life and Times* (New York: Touchstone, 1999), p. 354.

14. www.c-span.org/executive/transcript.asp?cat.=current_event&code=bush —admin&year=1992.

15. Marjorie Williams, "Barbara's Backlash," *Vanity Fair,* August 1991, p. 180.

16. Maralee Schwartz, "On Stump, Barbara Bush Decries 'Ugly Scapegoating'" *Washington Post,* 24 January 1992.

17. Bush, *Barbara Bush,* p. 457.

18. Ibid., p. 310.

19. Hillary Rodham Clinton quoted in Anne F. Mattina, "Hillary Rodham Clinton. Using Her Vital Voice," in *Inventing a Voice: The Rhetoric of American First Ladies of the Twentieth Century,* ed. Molly Meijer Wertheimer (New York: Rowan, 2004), p. 423.

20. Alessandra Stanley, "Under the Dome: Barbara Bush; The Un-secret Weapon," *New York Times,* 19 August 1992, p. 15.

21. Gil Troy, *Affairs of State: The Rise and Rejection of the Presidential Couple since World War II* (New York: Free Press, 1997), p. 339.

22. Mrs. Bush's Remarks at Farmington Town Hall, Farmington, New Hampshire, 12 February 1992, Kathy Steffy Files, January–February 1992, IA/OA 08382, GBL.

23. Mrs. Bush's Remarks at Luka's Greenhouse Restaurant, Hampton Falls, New Hampshire, 13 February 1992, Kathy Steffy Files, January–February 1992, IA/OA 08382,GBL.

24. Tom Rosenstiel, *Strange Bedfellows: How Television and the Presidential Candidates Changed American Politics, 1992* (New York: Hyperion, 1993), pp. 88–89.

25. John Robert Greene, *The Presidency of George Bush* (Lawrence: University Press of Kansas, 2000), p. 170.

26. Steven A. Holmes and Doron P. Levin, "The 1992 Campaign: Independent Perot's Quest—A Special Report; A Man Who Says He Wants to Be Savior, If He's Asked," *New York Times,* 13 April 1992, p. 1.

27. Ibid. See, too, Herbert S. Parmet, *George Bush: The Life of a Lone Star Yankee* (New York: Scribner's, 1997), p. 320.

28. Gerald Posner, *Citizen Perot: His Life and Times* (New York: Random House, 1996).

29. Ross Perot, *United We Stand: How We Can Take Back Our Country: A Plan for the Twenty-first Century* (New York: Hyperion, 1992).

30. Goldman et al., *Quest for the Presidency 1992,* p. 358.

31. Bush, *Barbara Bush,* p. 436.

32. Gil Troy, *Hillary Clinton: Polarizing First Lady* (Lawrence: University Press of Kansas, 2006), p. 60; EMILY's List, http://www.emilyslist,org/about.

33. R. W. Apple, "Senate Confirms Thomas 52–48 Ending Week of Bitter Battle; 'Time for Healing' Judge Says," *New York Times,* 16 July 1991, p. A1. See, too, Nina Totenberg and Anita Miller, eds., *The Complete Transcripts of the Clarence Thomas–Anita Hill Hearings: October 11, 12, 13, 1991* (Chicago: Academy, 1994).

34. Mrs. Bush's Remarks for Bush/Quayle Rally, Metairie, Louisiana, 5 March 1992, Kathy Steffy Files, Barbara Bush's Speeches, March 1992, IA/OA 08382, GBL.

35. Mrs. Bush's Remarks at a Bush/Quayle Fundraising Dinner, Des Moines, Iowa, 21 April 1992, Kathy Steffy Files, Barbara Bush's Speeches, April 1992, IA/OA 08383, GBL.

36. Mrs. Bush's Remarks at a John Seymour for U.S. Senate Fundraising Reception, Irvine, California, 24 March 1992, Kathy Steffy Files, Barbara Bush's Speeches, March 1992, IA/OA 08382, GBL.

37. Mrs. Bush's Remarks at a Bush/Quayle Fundraising Luncheon, Omaha, Nebraska, 19 June 1992, Kathy Steffy Files, May–June 1992, IA/OA 08382, GBL.

38. Steven A. Holmes, "Perot Says Democratic Surge Reduced Prospect of Victory," *New York Times,* 17 July 1992, p. 1.

39. Anna Perez, Draft for Core Speech for Political Events, 23 July 1992, GBL.

40. Bush, *Barbara Bush,* p. 475.

41. Hillary Rodham Clinton, *Living History* (New York: Simon and Schuster, 2003), p. 109.

42. Mrs. Bush's Remarks at a Bush/Quayle Fundraising Dinner, Little Rock, Arkansas, April 6, 1992, Kathy Steffy Files, April 1992, IA/OA 08383, GBL.

43. Bush, *Barbara Bush*, pp. 478–479.

44. "Bush Angrily Denies a Report of an Affair," *New York Times*, 12 August 1992, p. A14.

45. Alessandra Stanley, "First Lady on Abortion: Not a Platform Issue," *New York Times*, 14 August 1992, p. 16.

46. Craig Hines, "Queries on Infidelity Infuriate First Lady," *Houston Chronicle*, 13 August 1992, p. 1.

47. "Quayle Rails against Media 'Sleaze,'" *New York Times*, 13 August 1992, p. 20.

48. Barbara Bush quoted in Pamela Kilian, *Barbara Bush: A Biography* (New York: St. Martin's, 1992), p. 138.

49. Stanley, "First Lady on Abortion," p. 1.

50. Bush, *Barbara Bush*, p. 480. In a 1994 television interview with Barbara Walters, the following exchange took place: Walters: "In your book, for the first time, you do give your opinion . . . and you are, you are pro-choice." Barbara Bush: "I think that's right and that comes as no surprise to George Bush." This brief exchange can be found in "Barbara Bush: First Mom," Arts and Entertainment Television Network, 1996.

51. Tamar Lewin, "The 1992 Campaign: Issues: Women and Families; Legal Scholars See Distortion in Attack on Hillary Clinton," *New York Times*, 24 August 1992.

52. Stanley, "First Lady on Abortion," p. 14.

53. Anthony Lewis, "Merchants of Hate," *New York Times*, 21 August, 1992, p. A19.

54. Bush, *Barbara Bush*, p. 457.

55. Patrick J. Buchanan, Speech to the 1992 Republican Convention, http://www.buchanan.org/pa-92-0817-rnc.html.

56. Goldman et al., *Quest for the Presidency 1992*, p. 403.

57. George H.W. Bush, *All the Best: My Life in Letters and Other Writings* (New York: Scribner's, 1999), p. 548.

58. Visit to Texas Children's Hospital, August 19, 1992, Audio Visual Collections, GBL.

59. Marilyn Quayle quoted in Rosenstiel, *Strange Bedfellows*, p. 226.

60. Alessandra Stanley, "The Media and the Message: Marilyn Quayle Says the 1960's Had a Flip Side," *New York Times*, 20 August 1992, p. 20.

61. Bush, *Barbara Bush*, p. 482.

62. Ann Brock's Files: Family Night, Barbara Bush Address, 19 August 1992. GBL.

63. "Draft Remarks for Mrs. Bush for the Republican Convention, Houston, Texas," GOP Convention Speech, OA/ID 07474, GBL.

64. All speech quotes are from Barbara Bush, "Family Values: The Country's Future Is in Your Hands," *Vital Speeches*, 15 September 1992, p. 718.

65. Robin Toner, "Bush Is Sent Forth as Champion of Family Values," *New York Times*, 20 August 1992, p. 1.

66. Mary Matalin and James Carville with Peter Knobler, *All's Fair: Love, War and Running for President* (New York: Random House, 1994), p. 310.

67. Alessandra Stanley, "'Family Values' and Women: Is the GOP a House Divided?" *New York Times*, 21 August 1992, p. 1.

68. Peter Applebome, "Voice of Women in the Family Values Debate: A Sampling of North and South," *New York Times*, 21 August 1992, p. 13.

69. "Barbara Bush's Remarks to the 1988 Republican National Convention," Official Proceedings of the Thirty-fourth Republican National Convention, reported by Court Reporting Services, Inc.

70. Robin Toner, "The 1992 Campaign: Political Memo; Backlash for Hillary Clinton Puts Negative Image to Rout," *New York Times*, 24 September 1992.

71. "Barbara Bush Attacks Democrats in Congress," *New York Times*, 28 August 1992.

72. Jack Germond and Jules Witcover, "The Wife Factor," *Washington Post*, 7 September 1992, p. 19.

73. Troy, *Affairs of State*, p. 339.

74. Mrs. Bush's Remarks at a Victory '92 Reception in Fairview Park, Ohio, 15 October 1992, Kathy Steffy Files, Barbara Bush Speeches, September–October 1992, OA/IA 08383, GBL.

75. Bill Minutagelo interviewed for "Barbara Bush: First Mom," Arts and Entertainment Television Network.

76. Mrs. Bush's Remarks at a Red Cross Fundraising Reception, Ft. Myers, Florida, 2 September 1992, Kathy Steffy Files, September–October 1992, OA/IA 08383, GBL.

77. "Mrs. Bush Stumps at Phone Bank," Associated Press article, 9 September 1972, Kathy Steffy Files, Barbara Bush Speeches, September–October 1992, OA/IA 08383, GBL.

78. Steven A. Holmes, "The 1992 Campaign: Ross Perot: More Perot Hints on Renewed Race," *New York Times*, 23 September 1992, p. 21.

79. Mrs. Bush's Remarks, Victory '92 Luncheon, Raleigh, North Carolina, 2 September 1992, Kathy Steffy Files, September–October 1992, OA/IA 08383, GBL.

80. Mrs. Bush's Remarks, Victory '92 Luncheon, Austin, Texas, 16 October 1992, Kathy Steffy Files, September–October 1992, OA/IA 08383, GBL.

81. Ibid.

82. "Talking Points," "The Daily Line for Republican Newsmakers," and "Clinton Facts" can be found in the files of Anna Perez/Political Speech Research Files, GBL.

83. Memorandum for Will Feltus from Michael Caputo, "Questions for Post-Debate POTUS/FLOTUS Interview, 15 October 1992, Anna Perez's Files, Speech Research File, OA/ID 08737, GBL.

84. Elicia Traylor, "First Lady Seeks Hispanic Vote in Austin," *Daily Texan* (Austin), 19 October 1992, p. 1.

85. Bush, *Barbara Bush,* p. 475.

86. Fox News Interview, 22 October 1992, GBL.

87. Troy, *Affairs of State,* p. 339.

88. Mrs. Bush's Remarks at Leisure Village, Lakewood, New Jersey, 30 October 1992, Kathy Steffy Files, September –October 1992, OA/IA 08383, GBL.

89. Ibid.

90. "Iran-Contra Indictment: New Weinberger Notes Contradict Bush Account on Iran Arms Deal," *New York Times,* 1 November 1992, p. 1; and Goldman et al., *Quest for the Presidency 1992,* p. 608. References to Iran-Contra were found in George Bush's private diaries.

91. Kitty Kelley, *The Family: The Real Story of the Bush Dynasty* (New York: Random House, 2004), p. 530.

92. Goldman et al., *Quest for the Presidency, 1992,* p. 607.

93. Bush, *Barbara Bush,* p. 497.

94. *Public Papers of the Presidents of the United States: George Bush, 1992– 1993,* vol. 2, 1 August 1992–20 January 1993 (Washington, DC: U.S. Government Printing Office, 1993), p. 2153.

95. Troy, *Affairs of State,* p. 342.

96. Bush, *Barbara Bush,* p. 498.

97. Ibid., p. 3.

98. Greene, *The Presidency of George Bush,* p. 175.

CHAPTER 7: "THERE IS LIFE AFTER POLITICS! HURRAH!"

1. *People,* 3 October 1994, p. 145, quoted in Gil Troy, *Affairs of State: The Rise and Rejection of the Presidential Couple since World War II* (New York: Free Press, 1997), p. 342.

2. Author interview with Anna Perez, 10 July 1994.

3. Monica Crowley, *Nixon Off the Record* (New York: Random House, 1996), p. 96.

4. Sam Donaldson quoted on "Barbara Bush: First Mom," Arts and Entertainment Television Network, 1996.

5. Barbara Bush interviewed by Carl Sferrazza Anthony for "The Role of the First Lady" program at George Washington University, broadcast by C-SPAN, 9 October 1994.

6. Barbara Bush, *Barbara Bush: A Memoir* (New York: Scribner's, 1994), p. 516.

7. Barbara Bush, *Reflections: Life after the White House* (New York: Scribner's, 2003), p. 6.

8. John Robert Greene, *Betty Ford: Candor and Courage in the White House* (Lawrence: University Press of Kansas, 2004), p. 123.

9. The staff of the George Bush Library has indicated that the diaries will be opened for historical research thirty-five years after Mrs. Bush's death. E-mail, Laura Spencer to Myra Gutin, 30 August 2005.

10. Bush, *Barbara Bush,* p. ix.

11. Michael Wines, "A First Lady Publishes Mild Memoirs," *New York Times,* 11 September 1994, sec. IV, p. 4.

12. Maureen Dowd, "Qualities Americans Like," *New York Times Book Review,* November 1994, p. 1.

13. Eleanor Clift, "'*Barbara Bush: A Memoir*' Book Review" *Washington Monthly,* 1994 November, http://findarticles.com/p/articles/mi_m1316/is_all _v26 /ai_15875520.

14. Frank Rich, "That Nice Mrs. Bush," *New York Times,* 15 September 1994, p. A23.

15. Bush, *Reflections,* p. 8.

16. Kathy Lewis, "Straight Talk," *Dallas Morning News,* 28 April 1989, p. 18A.

17. Bush, *Reflections,* p. 27.

18. Frank Bruni, *Ambling into History: The Unlikely Odyssey of George W. Bush* (New York: HarperCollins, 2002), p. 68.

19. Bush, *Reflections,* p. 63.

20. Bob Woodward, *State of Denial: Bush at War, Part III* (New York: Simon and Schuster, 2006), pp. 2–3.

21. Bush, *Reflections,* p. 65.

22. Ibid., p. 72.

23. George W. Bush interviewed for Barbara Bush: First Mom, Arts and Entertainment Television Network.

24. George W. Bush quoted in Bonnie Angelo, *First Mothers: The Women Who Shaped the Presidents* (New York: Perennial, 2000), p. 357.

25. Ibid., p. 358.

26. "My Heritage Is Part of Who I Am," George W. Bush quoted in *Time,* 7 August 2000, p. 55.

27. Ibid., p. 56.

28. Alison Mitchell, "The 43rd President: The President-Elect; Bush and Cheney Starting to Enlist the Democrats' Help," *New York Times,* 15 December 2000, p. 1.

29. "Inside the Bush Dynasty," *Time,* 7 August 2000.

30. Frank Bruni, "The Bushes Talk of History and How It Favors Their Son," *New York Times,* 8 July 2000, p. A11.

31. Ibid.

32. Ibid., p. A1.

33. Ibid., p. A11.

34. Todd Purdum, "43+41=84," *Vanity Fair,* September 2006, p. 387.

35. Helen Thomas, "No Wonder Bush Doesn't Connect with the Rest of the Country," 15 October 2003, http://seattlepi.nwnewsource.com/opinion 143851_thomas.5.html.

36. Bruni, "The Bushes Talk of History and How It Favors Their Son," p. A11.

37. Pat Neal, 'W Stands for Women' Tour Kicks Off in Michigan," CNN.com/ allpolitics.com, 18 October 2000, http://archives.cmm.com/2000/ALLPOLITICS /stories/10/18/w.women/.

38. Bruni, *Ambling into History,* p. 178.

39. Bush, *Reflections,* p. 376.

40. Ibid., p. 1.

41. Ibid., p. 3.

42. Ibid., p. 390.

43. Ibid., p. 389.

44. Michiko Kakutani, "Books of the Times: A Bush's Keen Eye on Other Bushes," 20 October 2003, *New York Times* online, http://query.nytimes.com/gst /fullpage.html?res=9F06BODD103EF933A15753CIA9659C8B63.

45. Colleen Shogan and Jerome Short, review of *Reflections: Life after the White House, White House Studies,* Summer 2004.

46. Woodward, *State of Denial,* p. 114.

47. Barbara Bush interviewed by Diane Sawyer on *Good Morning America,* 18 March 2003, ABC transcript. See, too, Frank Rich, *The Greatest Story Ever Sold: The Decline and Fall of the Truth from 9/11 to Katrina* (New York: Penguin, 2006), p. 76.

48. Michael Slackman, "Politics as Usual Does Not Intrude on Dinner," *New York Times,* 22 October 2004, p. B3.

49. Richard W. Stevenson, "The 2004 Campaign: The President; In the Last Lap, Joking, Jockeying and Hiding the Sweat," *New York Times,* 1 November 2004, p. A1.

50. Maurine H. Beasley, *First Ladies and the Press: The Unfinished Partnership of the Media Age* (Evanston, IL: Northwestern University Press, 2005), p. 185.

51. Michael Duffy, "Bill Clinton and George H. W. Bush: Proving the Power of Two," *Time,* 30 April 2006, http://www.time.com/time/magazine/article/ 0.9171.1187350.00.html; "Person of the Week: Bill Clinton and George H. W. Bush," *Time,* 27 December 2005.

52. Michael A. Fletcher, "Act Now on Social Security, Bush Says," *Washington Post,* 19 March 2005, p. A11.

53. "Barbara Bush: Things Working Out 'Very Well' for Poor Evacuees from New Orleans," http://editorandpublisher.com/eandp/news/article_display.jsp ?vnu_content_id=10010547.19. Rich, *The Greatest Story Ever Sold,* p. 200.

54. Role Models on the Web, Barbara Bush, http://www.rolemodel.net/bush /bush.htm.

55. "Barbara Bush, Paul Simon Believe Librarians Should Lead Assault on Illiteracy," American Libraries Online, 5 April 1999, www.ala.org/al_onlineTemplate .cfm?Section=april 1999&Template=/ContentManage.

56. Letter, Barbara Bush to Paul Simon, 12 July 1999; offered for sale on eBay.

57. Shelby Hodge, "1.9 Million Raised," Houston Chronicle.com, 1 May 2006, http://www.chron.com/disp/story.mpl/life/society/3822670.htm.

CHAPTER 8: CONCLUSIONS

1. Kati Marton, *Hidden Power: Presidential Marriages That Shaped Our Recent History* (New York: Pantheon, 2000), p. 281.

2. Author interview with Barbara Bush, 25 April 2005.

3. Author conversation with Helen Thomas, 24 January 1991.

4. Gil Troy quoted in Maurine Beasley, *First Ladies and the Press: The Unfinished Partnership of the Media Age* (Evanston, IL: Northwestern University Press, 2005), p. 186.

5. Maureen Dowd, "Qualities Americans Liked: She Was Dignified, She Was Loyal and She Wore $29 Shoes," *New York Times Book Review,* 27 November 1994, p. 1.

6. Marton, *Hidden Power,* pp. 279–281.

7. Gil Troy, *Affairs of State: The Rise and Rejection of the Presidential Couple since World War II* (New York: Free Press, 1997), p. 340.

8. Author interview with Barbara Bush.

9. Author conversation with reporter, August 2007.

10. Author conversation with reporter, December 2004.

11. Author conversation with Professor Stephen Lee, Miller Center for Public Affairs, University of Virginia, 5 February 2005.

12. www.siena.edu/sri/results/2003/03First Ladies.htm. Laura Bush ranked twenty-fourth in the 2003 survey; http://www.siena.edu/sri/results/2002/02Aug PresidentsSurvey.html.

13. A report about the 2004 Gallup Poll's Most Admired Men and Women can be found at http://www.newsmax/archives/ic/2004/12/29/I24040.shtml.

14. Troy, *Affairs of State,* p. 333.

15. Betty Boyd Caroli, *First Ladies* (New York: Oxford University Press, 1995), pp. 286–287.

16. Barbara Bush interviewed by Carl Sferrazza Anthony for "The Role of the First Lady," 4 October 1994, C-SPAN Network.

17. Author interview with Barbara Bush.

18. Ibid.

BIBLIOGRAPHIC ESSAY

PRIMARY MATERIALS

Manuscripts

Barbara Bush's papers and personal diaries are housed at the George Bush Library, College Station, Texas. A great deal of material is currently unavailable for research as a result of the 1978 Presidential Records Act (PRA). The intent of the PRA is ostensibly to make records available while protecting subjects; in operation, however, the PRA has imposed a twelve-year embargo on opening certain types of records. The PRA was scheduled to expire for materials in the George Bush Library on 20 January 2005. However, in November 2001, Executive Order No. 13233 was signed by President George W. Bush. This superseded the PRA and said that current or past presidents could claim executive privilege and close certain records from their administrations. This new process is without time limits; thus files could be closed to research for years. Information can be accessed through Freedom of Information requests, but the average waiting time for processing is approximately two years.

Mrs. Bush's personal diaries have been deeded to the Bush Library but are closed to research until thirty-five years after her death. Since the diaries served as the basis for *Barbara Bush: A Memoir* and *Reflections,* their inaccessibility is disappointing.

Despite limited primary materials, some series of papers are open to research. The papers of Anna Perez stand out in terms of quality and usefulness. Perez served as Barbara Bush's press secretary, but she was involved in political and public relations decisions, speechwriting, press briefings and press luncheons with the first lady, projects and trips both foreign and domestic. The primary material reflects her many roles in the East Wing. Included in Perez's papers are files on Mrs. Bush's speech at Wellesley College, June 1990, and the controversy that surrounded her comments.

Kathy Steffy's files contain all of Barbara Bush's speeches and statements during her White House tenure. Occasionally, there are speech cards that were used during presentations and contain Mrs. Bush's notations. There is also some press and public reaction to the speeches. The best series within the Kathy Steffy files is the information on the campaign of 1992. In addition to drafts of Mrs. Bush's speech to the Republican National Convention in 1992, there are memos about dealing with the press, advice on countering charges made by Governor Bill Clinton, and material that might be included in campaign speeches.

The files of Susan Porter Rose, Mrs. Bush's chief of staff, also address political and public relations decisions. Porter Rose was involved in all aspects of Mrs. Bush's tenure and was also active in the literacy project. There are files on suggested projects, speaking engagements, speeches, and appearances.

Julie Cooke's files, which are part of the First Ladies Project Office files, span a variety of topics, including Education 2000, AIDS, American Foundation for AIDS Research (AMFAR), invitations and responses, and Victory '92.

One of the most moving and enlightening collections of papers is George Bush's World War II correspondence. Most of the letters are handwritten and were sent to Bush's parents. They follow Bush through his early training as a naval aviation cadet, his engagement to Barbara Pierce, and his commissioning as an ensign in the U.S. Navy and harrowing combat experiences. Bush's affection for his family and his growing love for his fiancée are evident; his description of combat is stark and reflects his anguish at losing crew members when their plane was shot down over the Pacific. Mrs. Bush has said that she maintained a correspondence with her husband during the war, but those letters were lost during one of the family's many moves.

The David Hoffman papers are very helpful in studying the 1988 presidential campaign. Hoffman covered Bush for the *Washington Post* and filed almost daily reports about candidate Bush. The dispatches reflect campaign highs and lows along with analysis of some of Bush's missteps.

The Bush Family papers included Mrs. Prescott Bush's newspaper columns on life in Washington, D.C., while Prescott Bush served in the U.S. Senate.

Autobiographies and Other Writings

Barbara Bush has written four books: *C. Fred's Story* (1984), *Millie's Book* (1990), *Barbara Bush: A Memoir* (1994), and *Reflections: Life after the White House* (2003). The two former works are a lighthearted look at the Bushes' hectic life through the eyes of their dogs. They are sprinkled with amusing anecdotes and the names of prominent and famous people who visited at the vice president's residence or at the White House.

For insight into Barbara Bush, the most helpful book is *Barbara Bush: A Memoir*. Mrs. Bush begins her story with her upbringing in Rye, New York, and meticulously traces her life through 21 January 1993, the day that she and George H. W. Bush left the Executive Mansion after Bush's defeat at the hands of Bill Clinton. Though crowded with names and too many superlatives, there are enlightening and moving moments for a woman who has lived in the public eye for most of her adult life.

Reflections follows the Bushes after they return to "normal" life in Houston, Texas, in 1993. A sense of vindication pervades *Reflections* as Mrs. Bush observes and participates in the campaign that results in the selection of George W. Bush as president in 2000.

Interviews

Barbara Bush spoke with the author on 25 April 2005. The interview took place at the George Bush Library in College Station, Texas. It was tape-recorded to ensure accuracy.

A number of former staff members offered their thoughts on Mrs. Bush as first lady. Former chief of staff Susan Porter Rose was interviewed by telephone on 7 June 1994. Former press secretary Anna Perez was interviewed by telephone on 10 July 1994. Former deputy press secretary and current Bush family chief of staff Jean Becker was interviewed in College Station, Texas, on 25 April 2005. Ms. Becker and former director of projects Julie Cooke responded to written queries in October 2006. Former deputy social secretary Catherine Fenton was interviewed in Princeton, New Jersey, on 17 July 2007.

Benita Somerfield, executive director of the Barbara Bush Foundation of Family Literacy, responded to queries via e-mail on four separate occasions: 23 August and 5 October 2005, 25 August 2006, and 8 October 2006.

Two other interviews provided excellent frameworks for understanding the pressures of being first lady and the demands of the media. Helen Thomas, former chief White House correspondent for United Press International, and Sheila Rabb Weidenfeld, former press secretary to first lady Betty Ford, spoke with the author in July 1982.

Professor Stephen Lee of the Miller Center for Public Affairs at the University of Virginia discussed the George Bush Oral History project in a telephone conversation with the author during January 2005.

Marie M. Adair, executive director of the New Jersey Association for Supervision and Curriculum Development, offered an evaluation of Mrs. Bush's role in the literacy movement in a telephone interview on 4 January 2006.

Visual Archives

The Bush Library retains thousands of photos of Barbara Bush and the Bush family, which were taken from George Bush's entrance into public life through the post–White House period. Many of these photos were taken by White House photographers and are in the public domain.

The library also retains video copies of a few of Mrs. Bush's speeches, including her comments at the Republican National Convention in both 1988 and 1992. Of greatest importance is her 1990 commencement address at Wellesley College. The library also retains footage of a visit that Mrs. Bush made to the Texas Children's Hospital on 19 August 1992.

Mrs. Bush hosted and participated in a program, "First Ladies' Press Secretaries Forum," that took place at the Bush Library on 30 April 2004. Mrs. Bush's obvious affection and respect for her former press secretary, Anna Perez, is evident. Mrs. Bush was interviewed by Carl Seferraza Anthony on 9 October 1994 for a series of lectures at George Washington University titled "The Role of the First Lady." The lectures were broadcast on C-SPAN. Members of the Bush family and Bush family friends were interviewed for "Barbara Bush: First Mom," a program that was broadcast by the Arts and Entertainment Television Network in 1996. A less enlightening interview with Mrs. Bush was conducted by talk show host Rexalla Van Impe in approximately 1982.

SECONDARY MATERIALS

Books

Interesting perspectives on Barbara Bush were offered during the Hofstra University conference on the Bush presidency held from 17 to 19 April 1997. One session, titled "The Role of the First Lady," was devoted entirely to Mrs. Bush and included academic papers written by Gil Troy, " 'Half-Eleanor, Half-Bess': Barbara Bush as 'Co-president,' " and the author, Myra G. Gutin, "Barbara Bush at Wellesley and the Republican National Convention: Defining Moments in the Life of the First Lady." The discussants for the session were Susan Porter Rose, Mrs. Bush's former chief of staff; Benita Somerfield, executive director of the Barbara Bush Foundation for Family Literacy; presidential historian Stephen J. Wayne of Georgetown University; Frank Murray, senior White House correspondent for the *Washington Times,* who covered the Bush family during their White House tenure; and Paul Costello, who served as a spokesman for former first lady Rosalynn Carter. Unexpectedly, Barbara Bush joined the session in its closing minutes to offer some thoughts, but she did this without having heard the presentation of academic papers or the discussion that followed. The text of the papers and the transcript of the discussion that followed can be found in Leslie D. Feldman and Rosanna Perotti, eds., *Honor and Loyalty: Inside the Politics of the George H. W. Bush White House* (Westport, CT: Greenwood Press, 2002), pp. 441–489.

George H. W. Bush has written three books. *Looking Forward: An Autobiography,* written with the help of Victor Gold (New York: Doubleday, 1987), covers Bush's life through the vice presidential years. *A World Transformed* (New York: Knopf, 1998) was written with former national security adviser Brent Scowcroft and addresses the foreign policy issues that Bush confronted as president. *All the Best, George Bush: My Life in Letters and Other Writings* (New York: Scribner's, 1999) is a compilation of letters and notes written by Bush. Mrs. Bush is mentioned in all three books, but she receives the most extensive treatment in the first.

Doro Bush Koch offers interesting perspectives on her mother in *My Father, My President: A Personal Account of the Life of George H. W. Bush* (New York: Warner, 2006).

The best and most analytical discussion of the importance of Barbara Bush appears in Herbert S. Parmet, *George Bush: The Life of a Lone*

Star Yankee (New York: Scribner's, 1997). John Robert Greene, *The Presidency of George Bush* (Lawrence: University Press of Kansas, 2000), and Fitzhugh Green, *George Bush: An Intimate Portrait* (New York: Hippocrene, 1989), have limited references to Mrs. Bush. The most enlightening book about George Bush's wartime service is Joe Hyams, *Flight of the Avenger: George Bush at War* (New York: Harcourt, 1991). It contains references to Barbara Bush.

The state of literacy in 1980 as Barbara Bush began her activity in the field is discussed in Jonathan Kozol's book *Prisoners of Silence: Breaking the Bonds of Adult Literacy in the United States* (New York: Continuum, 1980). Even though she had announced the formation of her foundation two weeks prior, Eden Ross Lipson's article, "Reading Along with Barbara Bush: The Endings Are Mostly Happy," *New York Times Book Review*, 21 May 1989, was the breakthrough piece that brought Mrs. Bush's crusade for literacy to the national stage.

The Persian Gulf War dominated the Bushes' life from August 1990 through the middle of 1991. Good background volumes on the war are Rick Atkinson, *Crusade: The Untold Story of the Persian Gulf War* (Boston: Houghton-Mifflin, 1993), and Norman Friedman, *Desert Victory: The War for Kuwait* (Annapolis, MD: Naval Institute Press, 1991).

Information about Barbara Bush in the 1992 presidential campaign is varied and rich in detail. Hillary Clinton discusses Mrs. Bush briefly in her autobiography, *Living History* (New York: Simon and Schuster, 2003). Books that were helpful included Peter Goldman et al., *Quest for the Presidency 1992* (College Station: Texas A&M University Press, 1994); Joe Klein, *Politics Lost: How American Democracy Was Trivialized by People Who Think You're Stupid* (New York: Doubleday, 2006); and Tom Rosenstiel, *Strange Bedfellows: How Television and the Presidential Candidates Changed American Politics, 1992* (New York: Hyperion, 1993).

Full-length biographies of Mrs. Bush have been written by journalists Donnie Radcliffe, *Simply Barbara Bush: A Portrait of America's Candid New First Lady* (New York: Warner, 1989), and Pamela Kilian, *Barbara Bush: A Biography* (New York: St. Martin's, 1992), and an updated edition, *Barbara Bush: Matriarch of a Dynasty* (New York: St. Martin's, 2002). Mrs. Bush did not participate in the writing of the biographies, but she had been covered by both journalist-authors for a period of years.

Celebrity biographer Kitty Kelley has written a book about the entire Bush clan titled *The Family: The Real Story of the Bush Dynasty* (New

York: Doubleday, 2004). Kelley paints a portrait of Barbara Bush as the ultimate political wife and power behind the throne. Though some of the material is sensational, the book is exhaustively researched and footnoted, and Kelley interviewed scores of people for her work.

Barbara Bush is the subject of separate chapters in general volumes about American first ladies. These include Betty Boyd Caroli, *First Ladies* (New York: Oxford University Press, 1995); Myra G. Gutin, "Barbara Bush," in *American First Ladies: Their Lives and Legacies*, 2nd ed., ed. Lewis L. Gould (New York: Routledge, 2001); Kati Marton, *Hidden Power: Presidential Marriages That Shaped Our Recent History* (New York: Pantheon, 2001); Helen Thomas, *Front Row at the White House* (New York: Touchstone, 1999); Gil Troy, "Perfect Couple, Imperfect President: The Bush Restoration," in Gil Troy, *Affairs of State: The Rise and Rejection of the Presidential Couple since World War II* (New York: Free Press, 1997); Margaret Truman, *First Ladies* (New York: Random House, 1995); and Molly Meijer Wertheimer, "Barbara Bush: Her Rhetorical Development and Appeal," in *Inventing a Voice: The Rhetoric of American First Ladies of the Twentieth Century*, ed. Molly Meijer Wertheimer (Lanham, MD: Rowman and Littlefield, 2004). Of this group, Troy's and Marton's books are the most enlightening. Marton and Truman had access to the first lady for their research.

A fascinating portrait of Mrs. Bush as the wife of the presidential candidate in 1988 emerges in Ann Grimes's *Running Mates: The Making of a First Lady* (New York: Morrow, 1990). Grimes, a reporter, covered both Barbara Bush and Kitty Dukakis during the 1988 presidential campaign and compares and contrasts the two women.

Maurine Beasley provides solid information on Mrs. Bush and the press in her book *First Ladies and the Press: The Unfinished Partnership of the Media Age* (Evanston, IL: Northwestern University Press, 2005). The social side of the White House is explored in former White House social secretary Laurie Firestone's book *An Affair to Remember* (privately published, 2007).

Anecdotal information about Barbara Bush can be found in Bill Adler, ed., *First Mom: The Wit and Wisdom of Barbara Bush* (New York: Rugged Land, 2004).

A different slant on Barbara Bush is offered by former *Time* reporter Bonnie Angelo, who looks at the former first lady as the mother of the president; Bonnie Angelo, *First Mothers: The Women Who Shaped the Presidents* (New York: Perennial, 2001).

George W. Bush enjoys a special relationship with his mother. The relationship and other matters are discussed in Frank Bruni, *Ambling into History: The Unlikely Odyssey of George W. Bush* (New York: HarperCollins, 2002), and Bill Minutaglio, *First Son: George W. Bush and the Bush Family Dynasty* (New York: Three Rivers, 1999). Ann Gerhart provides astute observations about Barbara and George W. Bush in her biography of Laura Bush titled *The Perfect Wife: The Life and Choices of Laura Bush* (New York: Simon and Schuster, 2004).

Two other books offered valuable insights into the Bush White House: Charles Kolb, *White House Daze* (New York: Free Press, 1994), and John Podhoretz, *Hell of a Ride* (New York: Simon and Schuster, 1993).

Article Written by Barbara Bush

Barbara Bush shared her thoughts on literacy in an article written for *Reader's Digest,* which guaranteed significant circulation: Barbara Bush, "Parenting's Best Kept Secret: Reading to Your Children," *Reader's Digest,* October 1990.

Magazine and Newspaper Articles
Written about Barbara Bush

Perhaps the most intriguing episode in Barbara Bush's White House tenure was her speech at Wellesley College in June 1990. Dozens of newspaper and magazine articles were written about the controversy. The *New York Times, Washington Post,* and *Boston Globe* covered the story that began with a petition signed by 150 Wellesley seniors protesting Mrs. Bush's selection as commencement speaker and concluded with the first lady's triumphant speech on 1 June 1990. Peggy Reid's op-ed piece, "We Didn't Criticize Mrs. Bush," *New York Times,* 16 May 1990, attempted to explain the protesters' point of view. Part of the Summer 1990 edition of *Wellesley,* the Wellesley College alumni magazine, was devoted to Mrs. Bush's speech and contains President Keohane's charge to the graduates, which sought to bring closure to the controversy.

Alessandra Stanley looks at reports that Mrs. Bush was pro-choice that emerged during the 1992 presidential campaign in "First Lady on Abortion: Not a Platform Issue," *New York Times,* 12 August 1992. Reactions to Mrs. Bush's speech at the Republican National Convention can be found in Peter Applebome, "Voice of Women in the Family Values Debate," *New York Times,* 21 August 1992. Jack Germond and Jules Witcover consider the influence of both Mrs. Bush and Hillary Rodham Clinton in "The Wife Factor," *Washington Post,* 7 September 1992.

Hundred of articles have been written about Mrs. Bush. The following is a list and description of those that were helpful in writing this book. An article about Barbara Bush that appeared before George Bush made his first run for the presidency provides insight into her opinions and life philosophy: Vivian Castleberry, "'My Choice Is to Enjoy,' Says Barbara Bush," *Dallas Times Herald,* 30 October 1979. An interesting article about Mrs. Bush written a month before she entered the White House is Patricia Leigh Brown's "The First Lady Elect: What She Is and Isn't," *New York Times,* 11 December 1988, p. 1. Mrs. Bush's reactions to the Persian Gulf War and her reaction to criticism of family members is discussed in Paula Chin's article "In the Eye of the Storm," *People,* October 1990. Mrs. Bush blames the war for George Bush's poor health in Ellen Warren, "First Lady Blames War Stress for Bush's Ills," *Austin American Statesman,* 7 June 1991.

A less positive but astute portrait of Barbara Bush is presented in Marjorie Williams's piece "Barbara's Backlash," *Vanity Fair,* August 1992. Another article written during the 1992 campaign agrees with some of the positions taken by Williams in *Vanity Fair:* Marlyn Schwartz, "So That's Why She's Called BARBara: First Lady's Sarcasm, 'Look' Are Formidable Says One Republican," *Dallas Morning News,* 21 August 1992. George and Barbara Bush spoke to the *New York Times* about George W. Bush just prior to the 2000 Republican National Convention: Frank Bruni, "The Bushes Talk of History and How It Favors Their Son," *New York Times,* 8 July 2000. General background about the relationship between George H. W. Bush and George W. Bush and a few references to Barbara can be found in Todd Purdum, "43+41=84," *Vanity Fair,* September 2006.

Another interesting and useful article about the Bushes and their attachment to their home at Walker's Point, Kennebunkport, Maine, is "The Bushes of Kennebunkport," *House and Garden,* June 1989.

miscellaneous materials

The transcript of interviews with Wellesley student Christine Bicknell and Wellesley president Nannerl Keohane on the *MacNeil/Lehrer*

NewsHour, 17 May 1990, explored the reaction to Barbara Bush's selection as commencement speaker.

Barbara Bush's pronouncements about the Persian Gulf War can be found in Susan Cornwell, "Superpower Wives Drink Tea, Wish Husbands Find Gulf Peace," Reuters Dispatch, 9 September 1990; and Chris Connell, "Mrs. Bush Says Saddam Must Give Up Kuwait," Reuters Dispatch, 10 September 1990.

INDEX